Flares of Memory

Flares of Memory

Stories of Childhood
during the Holocaust

Edited by
Anita Brostoff

Conceived and Developed by
Sheila Chamovitz

OXFORD
UNIVERSITY PRESS

OXFORD

UNIVERSITY PRESS

Oxford New York

Auckland Bangkok Buenos Aires
Cape Town Chennai Dar es Salaam Delhi Hong Kong Istanbul
Karachi Kolkata Kuala Lumpur Madrid Melbourne Mexico City Mumbai
Nairobi São Paulo Shanghai Singapore Taipei Tokyo Toronto

and an associated company in Berlin

Copyright © 1998 by the Holocaust Center of the United Jewish Federation of Greater Pittsburgh

First published by Oxford University Press, Inc., 2001
First issued as an Oxford University Press paperback, 2002
198 Madison Avenue, New York, New York 10016

Oxford is a registered trademark of Oxford University Press

Library of Congress Cataloging-in-Publication Data
Flares of memory : stories of childhood during the Holocaust / edited by Anita Brostoff
  with Sheila Chamovitz.
    p. cm.
Includes index.
ISBN 978-0-19-513871-9 (cloth) ISBN 978-0-19-515627-0 (pbk.)
1. Holocaust, Jewish (1939–1945)—Personal narratives. 2. Jewish children in the Holocaust—Biography.
I. Brostoff, Anita. II. Chamovitz, Sheila.
    D804.195 .F53 2001
940.53'18—dc21

                                                              00-044583

The publisher is grateful for permission to quote the epigraphs on the following page from:
Elie Wiesel, *Memoirs: All Rivers Run to the Sea* (New York: Alfred A. Knopf, Inc., 1995), p. 339;
and Lawrence L. Langer, *Holocaust Testimonies: The Ruins of Memory* (New Haven: Yale University Press, 1991), p. 69.

The map on page [xvii] is from: Charles Messenger, *The Chronological Atlas of World War II* (New York: Macmillan
Publishing Co., © 1989 by Bloomsbury Publishing Ltd.), p. 97. Reprinted with permission of Macmillan Publishing
Company.

Copyright of all photographs (except pages 334–35) is retained by the photographer. © 1998 by Joy Berenfield.

9 8 7 6 5 4 3

Printed in the United States of America
on acid-free paper

In truth, my concern has always been the survivors. . . . Did I strive to speak for them, in their name? I strove to make them speak.

For they have lived in isolation for a long time, locked away, remaining aloof so as not to wound those close to them. . . . It was impossible to get them to let go, to touch wounds that would never heal. They had reasons to be suspicious, to think that no one was interested in what they had to say, and that in any case they would not be understood . . . I shared with them my conviction that it is incumbent upon the survivors not only to remember every detail but to record it, even the silence.

—Elie Wiesel, *Memoirs: All Rivers Run to the Sea*

The irony of this revival, however, is the discovery that memory is not only a spring, flowing from the well of the past, but also a tomb, whose contents cling like withered ivy to the mind.

—Lawrence L. Langer, *Holocaust Testimonies: The Ruins of Memory*

Acknowledgments

Our deep gratitude and admiration go first of all to the Holocaust survivors and U.S. Armed Forces liberators who subjected themselves to the work and agonies of writing these stories. Their tireless efforts in writing and re-writing their own stories, as well as in helping each other, have made this book invaluable.

The Holocaust Center of the United Jewish Federation of Pittsburgh provided the funding for this project. The unstinting support of the Holocaust Commission's Director, Linda F. Hurwitz, was critical; we are thankful that her broad knowledge and contacts were always available to us. Our thanks go as well to her staff which provided secretarial and technical help. In addition, we are grateful to Beth Shalom Synagogue and the Jewish Education Institute for providing space for the writing workshops.

We deeply appreciate Professor Lois Rubin's role in inspiring the survivors' writing at the start of the project and her insightful comments on the book's progression. Our thanks go to Isabel Alcoff and Andy Weiss, who helped individual writers to surface and put into words extremely painful memories. Additional supporters for the writers included Eunice Baradon, Chana Brody, Ruth Drescher, Steve Hecht, Edgar Landerman, Ethel Landerman, Toby Levine, Toby Neufeld, Fern Steckel, Mark Stern, Terri Supowitz, Sheila Werner, and Steve Zupcic.

We owe a special debt to friends and colleagues who reviewed early versions of the manuscript. Professor Joel Shatzky made important critical suggestions and educated us about the field of Holocaust publication. Professor David Fowler, by envisioning a more complex view of what we had in the stories, was instrumental in the final form of the book. We are deeply grateful to Professor Russell Brignano, who provided encouragement and advice as well as comments on the stories. Arnold Blum, Laurie Cohen, Professor Lois Fowler, and Beverly Weiss Mann also contributed their expertise to the project. Professor Yaffa Eliach consulted with us and helped us to understand the task we had undertaken.

Bernice Levine typed and re-typed the stories; there is no way to count the hours she volunteered for this project. Joan Rubinstein also typed a great many stories. Joan Dickerson formatted the manuscript, bringing it to printable form.

An advisory committee of survivor-writers helped us finally with tasks ranging from proofreading to research and decision making: Malka Baran, Moshe Baran, Arnold Blum, Fritz Ottenheimer, Goldie Ottenheimer, Marga Randall, and especially Yolanda Avram Willis. Ruth Lieberman Drescher volunteered her expertise in graphic design and her experience in book publishing to design the book. Judy Robinson helped this group to market the book.

The moving photographs taken by Joy Berenfield express the beauty and power of ordinary people who survived extraordinary circumstances.

Our husbands, Dr. Philip Brostoff and Dr. Robert Chamovitz, gave us their loving support, encouragement, and help throughout the creation of this book.

Underwriting for the original, self-published edition of this book was provided by a generous gift from Lester E. and Ruth A. Zittrain.

Contents

Foreword

We crossed an historical bridge from one millennium to another, from the 20th to the 21st century—a century of the most powerful human cruelty, death, and destruction, as well as the human ability of rebuilding new lives. This was the first time in history when Jews were not given a chance of survival. In the past, conversion and expulsion were among the major options. During the Holocaust, Jewish blood was the primitive definition of identity. Even escape was impossible, for the gates in the occupied territories and in most countries around the globe were tightly locked.

This very moving book records the memories of Holocaust survivors, of the most painful human experience. Despite the recollections, hate is not the message, but rather to learn from the most cruel mistakes of European civilization during the Holocaust so that future generations will never be part of such atrocities.

The memories of Holocaust survivors in this book represent the majority of the countries under German occupation. Individuals who experienced the Holocaust—ranging from young children to mature adults—are recalling their past. The book also presents American liberators who opened the gates to hell and brought back to life the ultimate victims.

Future generations will learn countless lessons from this book. They can read about every element of suffering during the Holocaust, death and survival. These experiences are presented in short touching sparks of memory, rather than in long autobiographical accounts. The reader can open the book and focus on any work, sentence, or paragraph, and will immediately be drawn into a close personal relationship with the individual whose touching, heartbreaking, and accurate memories are told. *Flares of Memory* is indeed leading us across the bridge to a creative present and a safe future.

Professor Yaffa Eliach

TIMELINE OF THE HOLOCAUST

This timeline lists major events of the Holocaust and their corresponding dates. Each of the stories in this book is printed in italics under one of these dated events, in order to provide a sense of war events that were happening around the same time as the story. The stories correspond roughly to the date, but not necessarily to the specific event. Stories that occurred over an extended period of time are placed at approximately the date when the story began.

1933

JANUARY 30	Hitler is appointed chancellor of Germany.
MARCH 20	Dachau concentration camp opens; first inmates are 200 communists.
APRIL 26	Gestapo is established.
Herr B.	
MAY 2	Trade union headquarters throughout Germany are occupied, union funds confiscated, the unions dissolved and the leaders arrested.
MAY 10	Books written by Jews, political dissidents and others not approved by the German state are publicly burned.
JULY 14	Law is passed in Germany providing for forced sterilization of handicapped persons, gypsies and blacks.

1934

JANUARY 26	Germany and Poland sign a 10-year nonaggression pact.
AUGUST 2	Hitler proclaims himself *Führer und Reichskanzler* (Leader and Reich Chancellor). Armed forces are required to swear allegiance to him.

1935

SEPTEMBER 15	The Nuremberg Laws, anti-Jewish racial laws, are enacted: Jews are no longer considered German citizens,

Jews cannot marry Aryans, and they cannot fly the German flag.

A German Family

NOVEMBER 15   Germans define a "Jew" as anyone with three Jewish grandparents, or someone with two Jewish grandparents who identifies as a Jew.

1936

MARCH 7   Germans march unopposed into the Rhineland, previously demilitarized by the Versailles Treaty.

JUNE 17   Himmler is appointed Chief of German Police.

JULY   Sachsenhausen concentration camp opens.

OCTOBER 25   Hitler and Mussolini form Rome–Berlin Axis.

1937

JULY 15   Buchenwald concentration camp opens.

Snapshots

NOVEMBER 25   Germany and Japan sign a military and political pact.

1938

MARCH 11–12   The *Anschluss* (incorporation) of Austria into the Reich means that all anti-Semitic decrees are immediately applied in Austria.

A Mother's Courage

MAY 29   The first anti-Jewish law is passed in Hungary, restricting the overall Jewish role in the economy to 20 percent.

The Best-Laid Plans

JULY 6–15   A conference is held at Evian-les-Bains, France, during which representatives from 32 nations discuss the Jewish refugee problem but take little action toward solving it.

JULY 8   On Nazi orders, the Great Synagogue in Munich is torn down.

AUGUST 1   Adolf Eichmann establishes the Office of Jewish Emigration in Vienna to increase the pace of forced emigration.

AUGUST 3   Italy enacts sweeping anti-Semitic laws.

SEPTEMBER 30   At the Munich Conference, Great Britain and France
                agree to German occupation of the Sudetenland,
                previously western Czechoslovakia.

OCTOBER 5   Following a request by Swiss authorities, passports of
                German Jews are marked with the letter "J," for *Jude*, to
                restrict Jewish immigration into Switzerland.

OCTOBER 6   Hungary occupies part of Czechoslovakia.

OCTOBER 28   17,000 Polish Jews living in Germany are expelled; Poles
                refuse to admit them; 8,000 are stranded in the frontier
                village of Zbaszyn.

Leaving Germany, Leaving Home

NOVEMBER 7   Assassination in Paris of German diplomat Ernst von
                Rath by Herschel Grynszpan, son of an expelled Polish
                Jew, is used as excuse for reign of terror.

A Kristallnacht Journey

NOVEMBER 9–10   Kristallnacht (Night of Broken Glass), anti-Jewish
                pogrom in Germany, Austria, and the Sudentenland:
                200 synagogues are destroyed, 7,500 Jewish shops are
                looted, and 30,000 male Jews are sent to concentration
                camps. Jewish applications for immigration visas from
                Germany increase.

An Action against the Jews
Dachau
German Roulette

NOVEMBER 12   All Jews in Germany are forced to transfer retail
                businesses to Aryan hands.

NOVEMBER 15   All Jewish pupils are expelled from German schools.

DECEMBER   Kindertransport. Germany allows emigration of 10,000
                Jewish children to England.

DECEMBER 12   A one billion mark fine is levied against German Jews
                for the destruction of property during Kristallnacht.

1939

JANUARY 30   Hitler in his Reichstag speech says if war erupts, it will
                mean the *Vernichtung* (extermination) of European Jews.

MARCH 15   Germany occupies Bohemia and Moravia.

MAY 5   The second anti-Jewish law is passed in Hungary,
                defining who is a Jew and restricting Jewish participation
                in the economy to six percent.

Escape to England

MAY 17   Publication of the British White Paper on Palestine sharply diminishes the possibility of legal Jewish migration.

AUGUST 23   Molotov–Ribbentrop Pact, nonaggression pact between Russia and Germany, is signed.

   A Life-Defining Impression
   Bar Mitzvah Boy

SEPTEMBER 1   Beginning of World War II: Germany invades Poland.

SEPTEMBER 3   France and Great Britain declare war on Germany.

   The Beginning and the End

SEPTEMBER 17   Parts of eastern Poland are annexed by Russia.

   Unsung Heroes

SEPTEMBER 21   Heydrich issues directives to establish ghettos in German-occupied Poland.

SEPTEMBER 28   Poland is partitioned by Germany and Russia; German forces occupy Warsaw.

OCTOBER 8   The first ghetto established by the Nazis is set up in Piotrkow Trybunalski, Poland.

   The Harbinger of What?

OCTOBER 12   Germany begins deportation of Austrian and Czech Jews to Poland.

   Betrayal

NOVEMBER 23   Jews in German-occupied Poland are forced to wear an arm band or yellow star.

   A Definition of Survival

1940

APRIL 9   Germans occupy Denmark and southern Norway.

MAY 7   Lodz ghetto (*Litzmannstadt*), in Poland, is sealed: 165,000 people occupy 1.6 square miles.

MAY 10   Germany invades the Netherlands, Belgium, and Luxembourg.

MAY 12   Germany crosses French border.

MAY 20   Concentration camp is established at Auschwitz.

JUNE 22–24   France surrenders; Germany occupies the north and Italy occupies the south; Vichy Government controls the center.

JUNE 28   Romania cedes Bessarabia and Bukovina to the U.S.S.R.

JULY 1940–   Thousands of Jews from Bessarabia and Northern
   JUNE 1941   Bukovina are deported to Siberia by the Soviets.

AUGUST 8   Battle of Britain begins.

AUGUST 30   Hungary occupies northern Transylvania.

SEPTEMBER 27   Rome–Berlin–Tokyo Axis is formed.

OCTOBER 22   The German government deports more than 15,000
German Jews from the Rhineland to France, most of
them to Gurs concentration camp, and later from there
to extermination camps in the east.

OCTOBER 28   Italy attacks Greece.

A Hidden Child in Greece

NOVEMBER 16   Warsaw ghetto is sealed: it ultimately contains 500,000
people.

1941

JANUARY 21–31   Hundreds of Jews are butchered in anti-Jewish riots in
Romania.

FEBRUARY 1   German authorities round up Polish Jews from
surrounding areas for transfer to Warsaw Ghetto.

MARCH   Adolf Eichmann is appointed head of the Department
for Jewish Affairs of the Reich Security Main Office.

MARCH   Jews throughout Eastern Europe are forced into ghettos.

MARCH 1   Himmler orders the construction of Auschwitz II
(Birkenau) for the extermination of Jews, gypsies, Poles,
Russians, and others.

MARCH 3–20   A ghetto in Krakow, Poland, is decreed, established, and
sealed.

APRIL 6   Germany invades Greece and Yugoslavia with the help
of Bulgaria. Within weeks Greece is partitioned and
occupied by Germany, Italy, and Bulgaria.

Kaleidoscope: Salonika, Greece, 1945

JUNE 22   Germany invades Russia in "Operation Barbarossa."
Lithuania falls to Germany. Kishinev and Kovno are taken.

War Arrives in Lithuania

JUNE 23   The *Einsatzgruppen*, mobile units of the German
army that carry out mass killing of Jews and other
undesirables, follow the invading army and begin
operations in the U.S.S.R.

The Law in Lithuania

JUNE 24   German forces occupy Vilna, Lithuania.

JUNE 27   Hungary, already allied with Germany, enters the war on
the side of the Axis powers, keeping some autonomy.
Jewish men are forced into Hungarian work battalions
to serve the war effort. Jewish civil liberties and

economic options are suspended, but the Jewish population is not brutalized.

Trying to Go Home

JUNE 29 — Massive pogrom in Jassy, Romania, results in 10,000 victims.

JUNE 30 — German forces occupy Lvov, Poland.

JULY 1 — German forces occupy Riga, Latvia.

JULY 1– AUGUST 31 — *Einsatzgruppe* D, *Wehrmacht* forces, and Echalon Special, a Romanian unit, kill between 150,000 and 160,000 Jews in Bessarabia.

To Bear Witness about the Holocaust

JULY 5–6 — Chernovitz pogrom: Romanian troops kill 5,000 Jews.

JULY 17 — Romanian army enters Kishinev, capital of Bessarabia. Over 10,000 Jews are killed during the first week.

JULY 21 — Heydrich is appointed by Göring to implement the "Final Solution" of the "Jewish question" in Europe.

JULY 24 — A ghetto of approximately 11,500 Jews is established in Kishinev, Bessarabia.

AUGUST — German and Romanian fascists invade Transnistria, which at the time has 330,000 Jews.

AUGUST 2–17 — 70,000 Jews pass through the Drancy transit camp in France, most going to Auschwitz.

The Convent in Marseilles

SEPTEMBER 3 — First experimental gassing at Auschwitz is carried out on Soviet prisoners of war.

SEPTEMBER 15, 1941– OCTOBER 13, 1942 — At least 160,000 Jews from Bessarabia and Bukovina are deported to Transnistria, and some 90,000 die there.

SEPTEMBER 19 — Jews in the Reich are required to wear the yellow badge in public.

SEPTEMBER 29–30 — At Babi Yar, 33,771 Kiev Jews are killed by mobile killing squads of *Einsatzkommando* 4a. It is the single largest massacre of the Holocaust.

What Ever Happened to the Jews of Skudvil?

OCTOBER — Masses of German Jews are deported on a systematic basis; most of these transports go to the Lodz and Warsaw ghettos in Poland, and the ghettos Riga, Kovno, and Minsk in the German-occupied zone of the U.S.S.R.

The Killing Hunger

OCTOBER 1941– MARCH 1942 — 46,067 Prague Jews are deported to the east and to Theresienstadt.

OCTOBER 12 — German forces reach the outskirts of Moscow, and the city is partly evacuated.

Beyond Memory

OCTOBER 16   Germans and Romanians occupy Odessa.

Horrors of War

OCTOBER 23–25   40,000 Jews are killed in Odessa and Dalnik at the
                    hands of German and Romanian fascists.

A Saintly Person

OCTOBER 28   9,000 Jews are killed in an *Aktion* outside Kovno,
                    Lithuania, at the Ninth Fort; 17,412 Jews remain in the
                    Kovno ghetto.

Miracles
The Means to Survive

DECEMBER 7   Japanese attack Pearl Harbor. Hitler issues the *Nacht-
                    und-Nebel-Erlass* (Night and Fog Decree) for the
                    suppression of anti-Nazi resistance in occupied western
                    Europe.

The Promise
Lost Families

DECEMBER 8   Chelmno (Kulmhof) extermination camp begins opera-
                    tions: 340,000 Jews are killed there by the war's end.

DECEMBER 11   Germany and Italy declare war on the United States; the
                    United States reciprocates.

DECEMBER 21–31   54,000 Jews are killed by Romanian fascists in the
                    Bogdanovka Camp in Ukraine; 200 remain alive to burn
                    the corpses, and then 150 of these are executed.

The Skull with the Golden Braid

1942

JANUARY 20   In the Berlin suburb of Wannsee, a conference is held,
                    presided over by Heydrich and attended by top Nazi
                    officials, to coordinate the "Final Solution"—the
                    extermination of all Jews.

The Abandonment of Mielec
The Child

JANUARY–FEBRUARY   18,000 Jews are killed in Domanyevka Camp in
                    Transnistria.

MARCH 17   Killing begins at Belzec; by the end of 1942, 600,000
                    Jews are murdered here.

I Choose Life

MAY   Extermination by gas begins in Sobibor. By October
                    1943, 250,000 Jews are murdered here.

JUNE   Jewish partisan units are established in the forests of Bielorussia and the Baltic states.

Friend or Enemy?

JUNE 11   Adolph Eichmann's office orders the deportation of Jews from the Netherlands, Belgium, and France.

JUNE 26   In the Netherlands, an active schedule of deportations begins, to Westerbork and then to Auschwitz.

My Sister Rieke

JULY   Ghettos are to be emptied. There is armed resistance by Jews in the ghettos of Kletzk, Krements, Lachva, Mir, and Tuchin.

The Kindness of Strangers

JULY 22   The Treblinka extermination camp is completed; by August 1943, 870,000 Jews have been killed here.

In Constant Terror
A Shtetl's Life Is Ended

JULY 22–   Mass deportations from the Warsaw ghetto: 300,000 Jews
SEPTEMBER 12   are deported, 265,000 of them to Treblinka. About 160,000 Jews remain in Warsaw.

Parting
Lithuanian Friends

AUGUST 13–20   The majority of Croatian Jews are deported to Auschwitz.

SEPTEMBER 12   German Sixth Army and Fourth Panzer Army reach the suburbs of Stalingrad; the Battle of Stalingrad begins.

The Farmer Kowarski

NOVEMBER   Ghettos are emptied and Jews are deported from Germany, Greece, and Norway. Jewish partisan movement is organized in forests near Lublin, Poland.

A Narrow Escape
Posing as a Christian

1943

JANUARY 14–24   Roosevelt and Churchill meet in Casablanca and declare the unconditional surrender of Germany to be a central war aim.

Theresienstadt

FEBRUARY 6   Jews in Salonika, Greece, are ordered into two ghettos.

FEBRUARY 26   The first transport of gypsies reaches Auschwitz. They are allowed to stay in family units and are kept in a special section of the camp called "the gypsy camp."

MARCH 14	Krakow ghetto in Poland is liquidated.
MARCH 15	The first transport of Jews from Salonika, Greece, is sent to Auschwitz.
APRIL 19	The Warsaw Ghetto uprising begins as Germans attempt to liquidate 70,000 inhabitants; Jewish underground fights Nazis until early June.
JUNE	Himmler orders the liquidation of all ghettos in Poland and Russia.
JUNE 1	The final liquidation of the Lvov ghetto, Poland, begins. When the Jews resist, 3,000 are killed; 7,000 are sent to Jonowski Camp.
JUNE–AUGUST	Armed resistance by Jews occurs in Bedzin, Bialystok, Chestochowa, Lvov, and Tarnow Ghettos.
JULY 25	Mussolini falls from power in Italy, but is restored with German help.
AUGUST–SEPTEMBER	Large ghettos are liquidated in Minsk, Bielorussia; Vilna, Lithuania; and Riga, Latvia.
SEPTEMBER 8	Italy surrenders, and the country is partitioned: the south is held by the Allies, while central and northern Italy are in German hands and serve as a fascist protectorate called the Italian Socialist Republic, headed by Mussolini. Germany takes control of the Italian sector in Greece and intensifies the persecution.
SEPTEMBER 29	2,000 Amsterdam Jews are sent to Westerbork for deportation, and Holland is declared free of Jews.

The Tenth Woman on Block Ten

OCTOBER 1–2	In Denmark, German police begin rounding up Jews for deportation. The Danish population begins the systematic rescue of 7,200 Danish Jews by ferrying them across the sea to neutral Sweden.
OCTOBER 13	Italy declares war on Germany.
OCTOBER 14	Armed revolt begins in Sobibor extermination camp.
NOVEMBER 6–9	Jews are arrested in Florence, Milan, and Venice.

Among the Righteous

| NOVEMBER 19 | The *Sonderkommando* prisoners in the Jonowski camp revolt. Several dozen escape, and the rest are killed. |

1944

| MARCH 15 | Soviet forces begin the liberation of Transnistria, crossing the Bug River and reaching the Dneister River |

on March 20. Of the 330,000 Jews originally in the region, only about 30,000 are still alive.

Flight to Freedom

The Concentration Camp Lottery

MARCH 19   German forces occupy Hungary after a Hungarian attempt to pull back from the eastern front.

The Last Hiding Place

APRIL 5   Jews in Hungary begin wearing the yellow badge.

An Unforgettable Passover Seder

MAY 15   Nazis begin deporting Hungarian Jews to Auschwitz; by July 9, 437,000 have been sent, and most of these are gassed soon after arrival.

In the Dark

Nazi Murderers

JUNE 6   D-Day: Allied forces land in Normandy with the largest seaborne force in history.

Auschwitz, 1944

JUNE 13   Vilna, Lithuania, is liberated by Soviet forces.

A Son in Deed

JULY 20   An unsuccessful attempt is made on Hitler's life.

JULY 21–25   Children's homes in France, operated by the Union Generale des Israelites de France, are raided: 300 Jewish children, in addition to adult staff, are sent to Drancy and from there to Auschwitz.

JULY 24   Russians liberate the Majdanek killing center.

JULY 28   The first major death march begins with the evacuation of the Gesia Street camp in Warsaw. As the German Army loses ground and Allied armies come nearer to concentration camps, the inmates are forced to march toward the German heartland.

Captain Zimmer

A Surprise Package

The Girl with Wooden Shoes

In Praise of Manual Labor

AUGUST 2   The gypsy camp in Auschwitz is liquidated.

How Many Made It?

The Gypsies

AUGUST 23   Bucharest is liberated by Soviet forces.

AUGUST 24   Kishinev is liberated by Soviet forces.

OCTOBER   Greece is liberated by British and Allied troops.

The Wagon

OCTOBER 6–7   Revolt by inmates at Auschwitz: one crematorium is
                   blown up.

A Family Gone, One by One
Re-Entry

NOVEMBER 8   Death march of approximately 40,000 Jews from
                   Budapest to Austria begins.

DECEMBER 16   German forces launch an offensive, the Battle of the
                   Bulge, in the Ardennes Forest, Belgium.

Mazel

1945

JANUARY 17   Auschwitz is evacuated: 66,000 prisoners are marched on
                   foot toward Wodzislaw, to be sent to other camps, and
                   15,000 die on the way; 48,000 men and 18,000 women
                   prisoners remain in Auschwitz and its satellite camps.

JANUARY 25–   Death march for inmates of Stutthof Camp: 50,000 Jews
    APRIL 25   are evacuated by foot, and 26,000 perish.

The Volunteer Group
One Day War, the Next Day Not

JANUARY 27   Soviet forces enter Auschwitz and find 7,650 prisoners.

A Dream of Milk

FEBRUARY 4–12   Churchill, Roosevelt, and Stalin meet at Yalta.

The Tiny Flame

MARCH 7   American forces cross the Rhine.

Germany, 1945: View from a Tank

APRIL 5–6   Death march from Buchenwald begins. More than 28,250
                   inmates are evacuated and 7,000 to 8,000 are killed.

The Photograph

APRIL 9   Evacuation of Mauthausen begins.

Resist in Everything!

APRIL 11   Buchenwald concentration camp is liberated by American
                   forces.

I Saw Buchenwald

APRIL 15   Nordhausen concentration camp is liberated by Ameri-
                   can forces. Bergen-Belsen is liberated by British forces,
                   who find the inmates in the midst of a typhus epidemic.

APRIL 19   American forces capture Leipzig, Germany.

The Psychologist
On the Way to Health

APRIL 29   Dachau is liberated by the American 7th Army.
    A Letter from Dachau
APRIL 30   Hitler and Eva Braun commit suicide in Hitler's bunker
                  in Berlin.
    The Golden Chain of Judaism
MAY 2   Soviet forces take Berlin.
MAY 3   The Nazis hand over Theresienstadt with 17,247 Jewish
                  inmates to the International Red Cross.
MAY 5   Mauthausen death camp and its surrounding labor
                  camps are liberated by the Americans.
    Gusen: A Nurse's Tale
MAY 7   The Germans surrender to the Allies.
MAY 8   V-E Day: the war in Europe is officially over.
    An Ending and a Beginning
JUNE 26   The United Nations Charter is signed in San Francisco
                  and goes into effect October 24, 1945.
AUGUST 6–9   The United States drops atomic bombs on Japan.
    Children from the Camps Going to England
AUGUST 20   Japan surrenders to the Allies. World War II ends.

Postwar
1945

SPRING–SUMMER   Many survivors are placed in displaced persons (DP)
                  camps until a country is found to accept them.
    The Aftermath
NOVEMBER 20, 1945– Nuremberg Trials. The first set of trials of Nazi war
  OCTOBER 1, 1946   criminals is held before an International Military
                  Tribunal made up of representatives from France, Great
                  Britain, the U.S.S.R., and the United States. This group
                  tries captured political, military, and economic leaders.
                  The second set of trials, known as the Subsequent
                  Nuremberg Proceedings, is conducted before the
                  Nuremberg Military Tribunals, established by the Unit-
                  ed States Government in Germany. Judges are American
                  citizens, but the Tribunal considers itself international.
                  Twelve high-ranking Nazi officials are tried, as well as
                  doctors involved in camp experiments and SS officers
                  involved in crimes against humanity.
    It Shall Not Be Forgotten Nor Forgiven!
    The Chief of the Gestapo
    Herr Schluemper

1946

JULY 4–5   Pogrom in Kielce, Poland: 150 Jewish survivors who
returned home are attacked by civilians and soldiers;
42 are brutally murdered, 50 are wounded.
2,000 to 3,000 Jewish survivors are killed by Poles in the
years following the Holocaust.

1947

DP camp populations continue to swell.
The United Nations establishes a Jewish homeland in
British-controlled Palestine.

1948

MAY   Many people living in the DP camps prepare to go to
Israel.

MAY 14   British mandate expires, and at midnight Israel declares
itself an independent state.

MAY 15   The United States recognizes the new nation of Israel.

JULY   First United States Displaced Persons Act is enacted.

1950

SEPTEMBER   Displaced Persons Act is amended.

1951

The Jewish Displaced Persons Organization is discon-
tinued.

1980s

The Sewing Basket
The Barber

Timeline developed by Sheila Chamovitz

Map of Concentration Camps in Europe

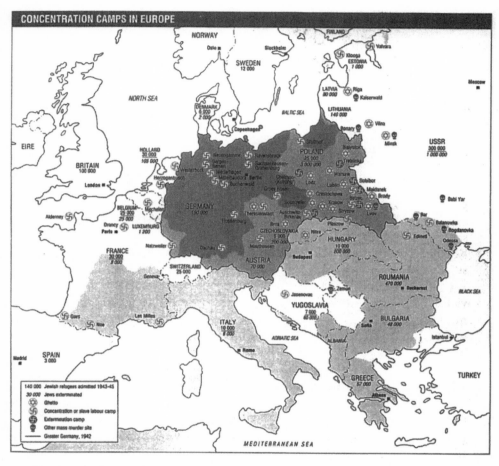

CONCENTRATION CAMPS IN EUROPE

Numbers on the map that are not italicized (e.g., 10,000) represent Jewish refugees admitted 1943–45. Numbers that are italicized (e.g., *10,000*) represent Jews murdered.

PREFACE

One quiet summer afternoon years ago, I was sitting in the tidy kitchen of a friend when she began to reveal a series of long-buried stories about her childhood during the Holocaust. It was obvious to me that while the telling was excruciating, so had been the silence. "Sometimes," she said, "I think I have been doing nothing all these years except shutting up the grief and pain and pretending it never happened."

But after attending funeral after funeral of Holocaust survivors, my friend said she felt a need and a responsibility to document her experiences. I shared her sense that this testimony must be preserved and recorded by the few who survived, most of whom had been teens or younger during the war.

Hearing her stories that afternoon, I felt for the first time what the life of a victim must have been like. Despite all the research I have done on the subject my understanding had never been so deeply personal. How are those of us who were born later supposed to comprehend the Holocaust? The numbers are too big; the images too frightening. I found I could absorb the experience only on a smaller human scale, by focusing on one single incident in one person's life.

The idea for this book began in that kitchen.

As a documentary filmmaker it would be natural for me to try to capture these stories on film, or, as an alternative, make transcripts of audio recordings. Both forms are widely and effectively used for personal Holocaust accounts. Instead, I chose to help Holocaust survivors write their stories themselves.

I chose autobiographical writing because it gives the survivors complete control of the work they create, unlike film, and allows the writers time for contemplation, unlike interviews. The process of writing gives the author time to reflect, revise, and dig beneath the first layer of memory. The reward for us, the readers, is a deeper, richer, more poignant story.

I was looking for the writers to be rewarded as well. I hoped that the process of writing would help the survivors to heal.

In 1994 I approached the Holocaust Center of Pittsburgh to support a book of memoirs in short story form, written by Holocaust survivors and liberators. Together we sent letters to about two hundred survivors. I then phoned them all and implored them to write. I also contacted several American GIs who liberated the camps, because it was important for them to give witness.

The survivor stories represented here come from most of the countries of occupied Europe and illustrate the varied experiences of Holocaust victims. Included are stories of children hidden by strangers, partisan fighters, people who posed as Christians, labor and concentration camp inmates, and resisters inside the camps.

The writers in this book recorded their stories at different times and under a variety of circumstances. Some had already written their memoirs and were seeking publication. Many had written their stories long before and filed the manuscripts away for their families. Others had never written but had joined a Holocaust speakers' bureau and talked publicly. Some, like my friend in the kitchen, had buried their memories and couldn't bring themselves to share them with many people.

To help survivors write, the Holocaust Center and I offered a series of writers' workshops. Dr. Lois Rubin conducted the first series, and Dr. Anita Brostoff conducted two more plus workshops for liberators. Over half of the authors used these workshops to develop their stories.

The writers were asked to focus on a singular experience, one that haunted or even warmed them, and write about it at home. Also, from the beginning, the writers requested and were promised that no changes to their material would be made, no matter how small, without their approval. All editing changes, including punctuation, grammar, and the minimal shaping that was done, were presented to the writers as suggestions and needed their consent.

Writing, for all of these authors, was difficult. A few needed one-on-one coaching but most wrote alone. They sat at home and wrenched up memory after submerged memory. They told of deep sadness and the return of nightmares. It took great courage, but they kept on writing. One writer described the experience of writing "like pulling off the scab of a poorly healed wound, causing the blood to flow again."

And what memories they exposed. A woman feels responsible for sending her sister to her death at Auschwitz. Another watches her mother die of starvation and exposure. A desperately hungry teenager fights with his conscience: must he share his last bit of soup with his father? His father would never know if he decided to eat it himself.

In private conversation the survivors would volunteer why, in spite of the pain and difficulty, they felt it was important to write. Time after time different writers said the same thing—they wrote so that the Holocaust would be remembered, so their loved ones would be remembered, and so that no one could say it didn't happen.

After this collection was completed, including my friend's contribution, she again sat thoughtfully in her kitchen and reflected, "Words are empty, vacant.

They have no heart, no soul. But they are the only weapons we have. In the long run there will be no survivors, no liberators, but the deniers will be there—and our words will be there. The truth will be there."

With gratitude to the writers,
Sheila Chamovitz

Introduction

"I never saw any of my family again," the speaker read aloud softly, looking up at last from the paper in her hand. Seated around a long wooden table in the book-lined library of a synagogue, a group of gray-haired Holocaust survivors listened, hardly moving. As the speaker finished reading her story, her hands shook visibly; her voice broke, she caught her breath, and sat down. Tears glistened in everyone's eyes. Nobody spoke.

This same scene happened again and again in the writing workshops which evoked most of the stories in this book. Among all the poignant emotions, that echoing sentence—"I never saw any of my family again"—seemed to stir the deepest ground. The moment of the last sight of their parents, sisters, and brothers is seared into the memory of each survivor. To an outsider, it was as if through all the stories which told about how they survived, the writers were really reliving, forever inconsolable, their loss of all those who did not.

Although some of the writers in this book did not attend the workshops, instead contributing stories previously written on their own, the book was essentially created by these Jewish Holocaust survivors working together to record their experiences. Unlike many Holocaust witness records, the book is not transcriptions of survivors speaking on audio or video tapes. And herein lies one of its strengths: all the stories exist here as the survivors wrote them, in their own words.

The Writing Workshops: The Process

A structured course consisting of six writing workshops was conducted twice for two different groups of survivors, by Dr. Anita Brostoff. In addition, two single workshops were presented for the first group by Dr. Lois Rubin. Most of the Jewish men and women authors in this book took part in the workshops. Subsequently, Dr. Brostoff conducted a set of workshops for a group of U.S. Armed Forces liberators.

The extent to which the workshop participants had previously communicated about their Holocaust experiences varied. A few people had written but not published parts or all of their stories, and several of the participants had talked about their experiences before groups or on tape. On the other hand, a few had not even told their stories to their families. The point is that most of the participants had not written before, or at any rate had not written the kind of story contained in this book. The workshops guided the survivors in the process of writing. The aim was to produce well-crafted stories about actual events that the writers had experienced.

The workshops had two main focuses, and each session was divided between these two activities. The first focus was to provide instruction in the process of writing brief stories—that is, in the standard literary conventions. At each session, participants concentrated on one convention of writing: describing people, places, and objects with specific sensory detail; writing dialogue; sequencing the action to create a coherent narrative; deciding where to begin and end a story, and how to provide enough context at the beginning. The watchword of the workshops was the use of detail and dialogue to "make it happen."

The second activity involved participants providing feedback to each other. The attendees were instructed to ask questions or give comments such as: "I liked the way you . . ."; "Can you tell more about . . . ?"; "Why did you include . . . ?"; "I don't understand . . ."; and "What's the point you are making about that event?" The writers then used the feedback to rewrite their stories, returning with the revised versions for further comments.

The process of writing was in many ways difficult for the survivors. For one thing, it often involved the recovery of long buried memories. And the word "recovery" here is two-pronged: the more one recovers memories, the more one recovers the unbearable trauma of those years. As time goes on, one survivor said, the pain only gets worse. Writers recollected in sleepless nightmares and woke up crying. They wrote "with tears in their eyes." One writer called the writing "like pulling off the scab from a poorly healed wound, causing the blood to flow again." And there were some memories so painful, it became clear, that the survivors couldn't write about them at all.

They spoke of being obsessed with the writing. For some, once the dam was opened, more and more stories spilled out, as if compelled by some subterranean force. And yet there must have been a kind of release or catharsis in this. Writers expressed a sense of closure to the pain of being unheard. Writing helped, one person said, "to bring out and come to grips with all the emotional and mental anguish that a survivor has to cope with." Another found a kind of relief in preserving in his story the names of relatives—and thereby the memory—of the millions who perished "at the hands of the fascist murderers." More optimistically, one writer said that writing "made me reflect on the capacity of people to experience the most painful, hopeless and traumatic situations, survive and go on with life."

The Writing Workshops: The Product

The effect of this workshop process went startlingly beyond our expectations in quantity and quality. Our intention was to evoke a collection of brief stories about single events, situations, places, or people—"flares" of memory. When the participants first began to awaken memories of their experiences, what often surged out, not surprisingly, was a rambling, generalized account of the writer's wartime experience—like the stories many survivors have told on tapes. The writers then selected some signal moments and events. By subsequently fixing their memory on those events, the writers brought out specifics that filled in the story and made it spring to life. This focusing of stories lends a kind of sharpness to the collection, an unusual pointedness to the overall effect.

As they wrote, novice writers found their stylistic voices within their memory of childhood trauma. Compared to oral testimony, writing and rewriting not only allowed writers to recall more specific and accurate memories, but also gave the writers time to consider their choice of words, to develop their style. One writer found her voice in a breathless series of one-sentence paragraphs; others used shifting verb tenses, moving somewhat illogically between past and present to reflect the blur and lumps of memory revisited; yet another built her stories around an intoned phrase, the words "Nazi murderers" ringing solemnly like a woeful bell beneath the action.

The feedback process, in particular, helped writers produce well-crafted stories. Although some participants were at first shy about giving feedback to others, they soon became aware of their ability to judge well, even if they were unsure of their ability to write well. Suggestions for adding detail or omitting needless detail, clarifying a narrative, or beginning in a different place helped the writers give form and meaning to inherently fluid and irrational situations.

The sharing of experiences also resulted in a richness of material. Listening to each other's stories and talking about the experiences they recalled helped participants to remember things that happened to them, and helped them remember details, which added to the stories they were writing or sparked yet another story.

Some writers at first didn't trust their words to tell the whole truth—didn't foresee the power of simple, everyday language to go further than expected, and seemed surprised by the impact of their stories upon the group. From an observer's point of view, what stood out about the feedback process was the deep respect and caring survivors showed for each other's words, as well as for the experience the writer had gone through.

Stories about Children

While the events of the Holocaust have been fully recorded by historians and countless individual survivors, the stories here have a particular focus: they document experiences of children and young adults. A majority of the writers were teenagers at the time of the events they describe here. A few were between six and twelve. (Our experience with survivors who were younger than this during the Holocaust was that they could not remember much specific detail about what happened to them.) A very few writers included here were in their early twenties, and two were adults whose stories are about children they took care of.

We have given the year of the writer's birth at the beginning of each story, to supply this childhood context. This enables readers, especially young ones, to more fully understand and share the writers' perspectives: their physical sufferings—hunger, thirst, cold, exhaustion; their helplessness, despair, and terror at the constant threat of death; their grief over the loss of their families, their homes, their whole culture. Thus the agonized moan of a writer who sees his synagogue burned on Kristallnacht and is marched off the next day to Dachau becomes more poignant as we realize that he was sixteen years old, just three years past his bar mitzvah. The six-year-old girl who somehow knows she must not "make waves" as she is shifted from one adoptive Christian family to another—who even learns to automatically cross herself when she passes a church—moves us deeply with her submerged longing for her parents.

Reading these stories, we must keep in mind also that before the war, these children had known for the most part sheltered and comfortable (if sometimes poor) lives, in devout, ordinary families. This perspective lends a starkness to the incredible bravery, endurance, and resourcefulness of these children. A twelve-year-old girl darts through the streets of Warsaw during a bombing raid to get milk for her baby brother. Another girl, fifteen, escapes Nazi captors to strike off alone, without supplies, in a frozen wilderness. A fourteen-year-old boy becomes a central link in a concentration camp resistance group through his ability to speak several languages. Such stories make us aware that whether in hiding, in ghettos and concentration camps, or in resistance groups, these children had to cope on their own in ways well beyond the expectation of their years; they had to grow up suddenly and fast, to face an encompassing evil greater than any adult had ever witnessed.

Historically, this perspective of children's experiences points up the fact that the Nazis had no mercy upon the children. The Final Solution was intended to exterminate all Jews, of all ages. Indeed, children caught in the net of the Holocaust stayed alive only as long as they were strong enough to work, or until the killing machines could get around to them. Although accounts differ, it is clear that the Nazis murdered at least one million children under fifteen.

A View of Holocaust History

This book does not presume to, and was not meant to, provide a complete geo-graphical and chronological history of the Holocaust. However, the survivors whose stories are collected here came from most of the countries affected by the Holocaust, and from many kinds of towns, from shtetls to large cities. The writer's place of birth is given at the beginning of each story to supply this con-text. The stories also tell how the writers were shuffled by the Nazis to many of the notorious camps and prisons, or fled to forest, farmland, and mountain land-scapes throughout Europe. Furthermore, the stories range over the period of time from the early 1930s through the 1940s, from before World War II through the end of the war. Stories by American soldiers who liberated the victims and saw the remains of the camps complete the descriptions of events. Thus the geo-graphical and temporal spread of the Holocaust in general is well represented.

Given all this information, readers of this book might ask whether all the facts of Holocaust events as they are told here are accurate—whether they are verifiable history. The answer, we suggest, is that if not always the precise facts, more importantly the *impression* of an event upon the memory and the psyche of the victim must be seen as reliable. That is, the stories achieve a fundamen-tal truth: the essence of the experience, its meaning, is absolutely true. Through writing about these events, these survivors have recorded, in their own voice and their own words, profound and true evidence about the Holocaust.

The heart of the book's content lies in the specific details, the writers' person-al anguish around particular (even if generally known) events. In one story, peo-ple standing knee to knee, freezing and hopeless in a cattle car, are uplifted by a man's silent prayer. In another story, the ordeal of a family's arrival at Auschwitz is made real through the writer's running back to retrieve some forgotten nuts. The brutality of SS soldiers is highlighted in yet another story by a child's terri-fied focus on the soldiers' spit-polished boots. Every story is different. By giving shape to events individually and personally experienced, the writers here help to shape our perspective on the Holocaust. The enormity of the six million dead can perhaps finally be comprehended only through these individual events.

Themes in Holocaust History

All of this material is arranged in this book in two ways. The stories are grouped in chapters by a commonality of the events that underlie and unite them, and the chapters are organized in the book in an overall chronological sequence.

The chapters, that is, move in time from Jewish life before the war to liber-ation and beyond. They illuminate crucial themes in Holocaust history: Ger-man actions intended to destroy Jewish life and society; the ruthless efficiency of the German system to achieve the Final Solution; the roles of chance and luck, hiding, family support, rescuers, and resistance efforts; the joy and suffering of survivors who were liberated; and the mixed emotions of survivors as they ponder the Holocaust in its aftermath. To put it another way, these groupings serve to define many kinds of experiences, which all victims had.

While the individual stories are interesting and moving in themselves, the thematic groupings also serve to enhance and enrich each one. These groupings help readers analyze and make sense of the stories, help clarify how each story faces up to and speaks to an aspect of the Holocaust. And the Addendum section, the stories written by liberators of the concentration camps, serves to reinforce the whole dark picture.

The thematic groupings also help to deepen readers' empathy with the feelings the writers express in retrospect. They shed light upon the subtexts of the stories. We share with the writers, over and over, gratefulness for the decency of rescuers and people who provided a grain of hope; grief and anger over the death, destruction, and loss; the effort to assuage grief through preserving the memory of one's personal dead.

The hellishness of the Nazi crimes gathers within each group of stories, accumulates and explodes in the collected whole. The book thus goes beyond individual experience; the whole is greater than the sum of the parts.

The Book's Purpose and Meaning

This book is intended first of all to serve as an educational agent. It is for Jews and non-Jews, students young and old. It is for those who want to know about the Holocaust, as well as for those who want to ignore it because the details are unpleasant, or because it is easier to do so. It is for people who have been taught incorrectly, having learned in school, for instance, that there was *something* good about Adolf Hitler. It is for the deniers who would distort truth and rewrite history.

Asked why they feel it was important to write these stories, the workshop participants responded on several levels. They alluded to the need to record the events of the Holocaust, to keep them in the world's memory. The writing, most said, is for future generations. For "if the past does not matter, why worry about the future?"

It seems clear that the writers intended as well to bring out crucial and pervasive questions about the Holocaust. Writers asked such questions openly or by implication in their stories. Sometimes questions were on a personal level: How was it that we did not see or believe what was coming? How could we know where to turn or whom to trust? How could such vagaries of fate have decided that this person lived while that person died? How was I to know what the right choice was in a given situation, or—worse yet—the moral choice? Ultimately the writers asked or implied the universal questions: How and why did the Holocaust happen? Or even, as a few asked about their darkest moments, the deeply symbolic query "Where was God?" The questions reveal the chaos, the illogic, and senselessness of Holocaust events.

The questions, like the basic incidents in the stories, are not new ones in the world: scholars as well as other victims have voiced similar ones. Such questions, unanswerable because the Holocaust was like no other event in history, point up some of the difficulties in the continuing effort to gain a historical perspective on it. Of course, atrocities and mass murders have been committed on groups of people before and since the Holocaust. What was different about this event was the openly expressed and thoroughly planned intent to eradicate not only certain "undesirables," but a whole people, *the Jews*, from the earth. What was different was that the Germans actually created a department of the government to deal with the "Jewish question." An efficient, institutionalized machine was invented to carry out this intent—from denial of rights to deportations, from humiliation to starved slavery, and on to the mobile killing vans, gas chambers, and ovens.

The survivors' questions, finally, point up the sheer incomprehensibility of the Holocaust. The Germans' ability to enlist the enthusiastic cooperation of *ordinary people* in many countries to commit extraordinary, indeed inhuman, acts of brutality against innocent victims young and old, largely based on pervasive anti-Semitism, seems beyond belief. What is almost as amazing and appalling is that for the most part, the rest of the world, including the leaders of the United States of America, *let this happen*—turned their faces the other way, and ignored it.

The stories in this book are important; they move us to imagine a reality, a truth, which is beyond understanding. And the survivors' questions within the stories constitute an essential contribution to education about the Holocaust. For the confusion and doubt they express teach us to be continually alert, to learn to recognize the faces of evil, and the harbingers of their reappearance.

Perhaps, finally, it is the passion with which the writers describe these events and raise these questions that matters. For the pain and hope that inform that passion compel us to care. When writers would read their stories aloud in our workshops, we heard the passion in their voices. As the world loses the remaining survivors, we stand to lose that first-person immediacy; we will have the facts of the Holocaust, but we will be in danger of forgetting the lesson of caring about the incredible suffering the Holocaust brought upon its victims.

Because the passion is written down in these stories, even though it is often subdued and restrained, it will continue to exist in the pages of this book. We must pay attention to the passion, for it resounds through the ashes of the dead. It keeps alive the haunting specter of cruelest murder, of endless loss.

Anita Brostoff

I. SNAPSHOTS: JEWISH LIFE
BEFORE THE HOLOCAUST

The Holocaust happened in most of Europe, including parts of the Soviet Union—wherever the Nazis and their allies touched the land and the people. But it happened in different ways and at different times. And it happened to Jews, as well as to other people, who came from different cultures and lifestyles.

The stories in this section of this book were written by Jewish survivors who were originally from Poland, Lithuania, and Germany. They begin with "snapshots" of some traditional Jewish lifestyles and loyalties. "War Arrives in Lithuania" emphasizes the religious orientation of a Lithuanian shtetl (villages that were predominantly Jewish). "Parting" and "Betrayal" give us a sense of the orderly regimen of Jewish life within small Polish communities. "A German Family" presents snapshots of the more assimilated Jewish families of Germany. Each of these remembrances of Jewish life before World War II, however, ends with an account of the beginning of the breakup of that life, as it happened to these individual writers, in their place and time.

The writers were children or young adults when these events occurred. The pictures they create of home and family life before the war will in some ways sound familiar; they are like those of most families, everywhere. The accounts of the sudden disruption of their lives, on the other hand, convey the terror and bewilderment that struck families that didn't know what to do or where to turn, children who were suddenly and cruelly ripped from their parents and siblings.

It is in these stories that the writers first voice the constant theme of all survivors who speak in this book, the anguished burden of never-ending loss—the loss of their home and culture, and above all, of their beloved mothers, fathers, sisters and brothers. They mourn for what was but now is no more, and never will be.

A. B.

Snapshots

Malka Baran
b. Warsaw, Poland, 1927

CHESTOCHOWA, POLAND, 1937–1938
Early evening in the city. My friends and I stroll
up the avenue. I am giddy, happy, joyfully
aware of my new blue coat lined with white fur, and
my smart little hat made of the same fabric.
Big white fluffy snowflakes fill the space
between the dark blue sky and the pavement.
The trees are covered with puffs of white.
We are carefree! The world so pretty.
"Excuse me, what time is it?"
my friend stops a passing lady.
The answer is politely given, sometimes with a smile.
We walk on, giggling quietly. It's my turn now.
"Excuse me please, what time is it?"
And so we continue up the avenue.
   • • •
My skirt matches my brother's shorts,
the same white tops for both of us.
We love our new clothes and walk proudly—
Mother waves from the window, her face bright with pleasure.
   • • •
My childhood . . . long ago . . . in that other life.
The avenues, the children, my loved ones—
   Where are they all?
In clouds of smoke and fumes they went
Buried in ditches filled with blood—
And only memories remain—
Snapshots, framed in pain and sorrow
Snapshots of a childhood murdered.

War Arrives in Lithuania

Leon Brett
b. Skudvil, Lithuania, 1922

Life did not change much in Skudvil, Lithuania. Each day had its own routine. Saturday was the most special day. On that day everything came to a standstill. The change really started on Friday, when the Jewish mothers and daughters cleaned and scrubbed every room in the house. The tables were covered with white cloth and shiny brass candlesticks. Anticipation was in the air, the smell of Sabbath food in the homes. Before sundown the shops would close. Everybody felt loved by God, blessed by God. On the four streets and five alleys, Jews dressed in Sabbath garments and walked from their homes to the house of God. And the same was done Saturday morning and Saturday afternoon. That day was to be for God and man, and nothing else.

It was not only on Saturdays that Jewish men of Skudvil went to our *shul*. Three times every day—morning, afternoon and evening—every male participated in a service to God. Afterward, if one did not have to rush home or go to work, he would linger and talk with friends. He might discuss conditions in the country or how certain events would affect their lives. He would analyze news items from yesterday's paper, news from foreign countries. Is it good or bad for the Jews? How could a pronouncement by the American President affect the Jews of America or even of other countries?

There were study groups that met every day. "To learn a page," they called it. They studied from a tractate of the Talmud, analyzed the validity of a ruling by our sages, debated the meaning of a word and sometimes even of a single letter. Their debating never ceased.

My father belonged to such a group. He usually took the moderate, lenient approach, where the others adhered to the stricter ruling. They would say, "According to you, Reb Shmuel, everything is permissible."

"Show me, prove it to me," my father would respond. "Where in the Talmud can you find a prohibition against such and such?"

"Your permissive rulings are a sin. They will cause others to sin, it will be the ruin of our traditions, of our faith," they would reply.

The argumentation would sometimes get heated, and they would accuse my father of apostasy. I heard them refer to my father as "the Berliner rabbi." That hurt me, especially when I was still young. Could my father, who was so gentle and unassuming, and whom I loved very much, be guilty of sin?

In our synagogue you could see not only scholars but also ordinary people, standing in a corner and reciting psalms. Perhaps they were troubled and that was their way of unburdening themselves.

The door to our house of prayer was always open. It was common for a wayfarer who happened to pass through our town to spend the night there. He would use a bundle for a pillow, cover himself with his overcoat and sleep on a bench near the entrance.

It was only on Tuesday that our synagogue was practically deserted, except for prayer time. Tuesday was market day and most people had to attend to their stores and workshops. Farmers from villages all around came in their wagons. They would bring butter and cheese, eggs and poultry, to sell in the market, and then proceed to the shops to buy salt and sugar, thread and cloth.

The Jankauskas family would park their wagon in front of our house and spend the day with us. We served them sweet tea and white bread. They liked a lot of sugar in their tea.

Their son, Petras, always came along. He was about my age. Sometimes he stayed with us for a day or so. In the summer, we would go down to a stream and climb the trees, looking for a long branch to get the longest possible rod. We would tie a string to it, then a fishing hook to the string, and try to catch a fish.

Sometimes I went along with the Jankauskas family after market and stayed with them, helping with the farm work. I slept in the barn on the hay with Petras. After a day or so, I walked home through the fields and along country roads.

Thursday night, from six to eight, was library night. People would come to the home of Meir and Feiga Krom to return books and get new ones. The Kroms set aside one room in their home for five hundred books of the library. Often library night would not break up at eight o'clock, but would last longer. It became a special event. Feiga Krom served lemonade and pastries. Some were round, thin and covered with sugar. Others were square, thick and filled with apples. Meir would read aloud a poem by Bialik and Feiga, a story by Guy De Maupassant. We would play the phonograph and quietly sing songs of joy, yearning, and hope.

The Kroms were one of the few families in town who had a radio. One day we turned it on while Hitler was speaking. His loud, hysterical voice was clear. The Jews, he said, stabbed Germany in the back and that's why Germany lost the World War. Jews are capitalists, communists, planning an international conspiracy. He spoke of the Aryan master race, of communism and the threat to the world from the east. He finished speaking but the thunderous cheering of a multitude of voices lasted a long time: "*Sieg Heil, Sieg Heil.*"

Meir clasped his hands and said in a fearful voice, "There will be a war between Germany and Russia and we are right in the middle, so close to the German border."

That night after we left Krom's house and walked down Tauragu Street, no one spoke. Everybody was thinking about what Meir had said.

When I came home, my father and Dr. Dolnitsky were sitting at the table, drinking tea. The book of Job was open before them. My father was explaining to the doctor passages of Bildad's response to Job. I told them of the voice on the radio and of the cheering, and that Meir had said there will be a war between Germany and Russia. Dr. Dolnitsky, who was very tall, rose from his chair, put his hands on my shoulders as he often did, and said, "Today's generation, so worried. I lived in Germany. I went to Heidelberg University. It will never happen there. Hitler is just an unpleasantness that will pass. Any other country, perhaps yes, but not in Germany . . . *Nicht in Deutschland,*" he repeated in eloquent German, as he was fond of doing.

My father walked to the window and looked out into the darkness of the night. "In the last war we ran all the way to Kremenchug in the Ukraine. At least I was young then. I could not run again."

"You will not have to, Reb Shmuel," said Dr. Dolnitsky, and bid us good night.

One morning in 1938, not long after that night, we found leaflets on the walls. They read: "Jews go to Palestine. We shall pave our streets with your heads." They threatened to burn down our homes. We patrolled the streets all night, hoping to prevent them from doing it.

As time passed, we lived each day with uncertainty. Germany occupied Poland in 1939, but that was far from us. Then in June 1940, the Red Army marched into Lithuania. It was a sunny Friday. Truckloads of Russian soldiers streamed toward the German border. The artillery followed, then the tanks. It seemed like an endless stream of power, but Jews felt relieved. We felt we were safe from Hitler's Germany. We knew our lives would change, but we thought that our lives would be safe.

The basic change under the Russians was that all Zionist organizations were banned. The Hebrew language was banned. We burned all Hebrew books at home and at the library.

Then came June 22, 1941. It was a Sunday. My father woke me. He was pale and looked scared. "It has started," he told me. "The war between Germany and Russia has started." Planes were flying overhead. We could hear the artillery. Truckloads of Russian soldiers were rushing to the border and the wounded were being taken away.

"Go, my child," my father said to me. "Eighteen is not a good age in time of war. You must go away."

My sister agreed. "What can they possibly do to us?" she said. "But you're only eighteen. You must leave."

Her two little girls were crying. The noise of war frightened them. They begged me to stay with them. My father gave me his round, silver pocket watch. "You will need it," he said.

We embraced. I got on my English bike and left. When I looked back, I saw my sister, big with child, standing there crying helplessly. Her two little girls, Shifrale and Rivale, were holding onto her skirt, sobbing. Tears were streaming down their faces. I saw my father standing there. His face was white, and his beard gray. Tears were in his eyes.

That was my last glimpse of them. I never saw them again. I disappeared into the uncertainty of war.

I went east on my bike. German planes were bombing the highway. I saw a lot of people in clusters along the highway. They thought they would be safer than in town. It was fairly obvious that the Russians did not want to fight. They were defecting. I met a man from my town who was fleeing on foot. I took him on my bicycle and we fled east together. Tired from fear and travel, we stopped at a barn to rest. It was full of Jews, many of them children. Some cried and some were too scared to cry. We didn't stay very long.

We continued east. Finally, we made it to Shavel. Shavel was a large city by Lithuanian standards, about 40,000 people. I came to my cousin's house. Bombs were falling. We took shelter in a basement. And then it became quiet. I went up from the basement, looked outside, and there they were! The Germans were on the street. The vanguard. They were on motorcycles, well-dressed and shouting orders to one another. I went to the basement and sadly told everybody, "They are here."

A German Family

Marga Randall
b. Lemförde, Germany, 1930

A Short Walk to Paradise

The side door shuts behind us. My Opa takes my hand and we walk down Main Street together. We walk past the blacksmith shop, past Town Hall. We cross a little bridge that spans the creek.

I always had to stop here. I loved the sound of the water splashing over the rocks. Opa let me pick some little white berries that looked like beads. I would lay them on the ground, stomp on them with my feet until they popped.

Our garden had an iron gate. I could look through the grillwork, down the straight path lined with strawberry vines. At the end of the path was a red-roofed gazebo.

For me, it was paradise. Here my grandfather—my Opa—and I became a team, co-workers and best of all, friends. There was a sandbox he built for me, right next to the gazebo. Inside the gazebo were the garden tools and a round table with two iron chairs.

The garden was about two or three acres of level ground, rich in minerals and sandy-soft in texture. Our harvest was always plentiful. New white potatoes, cabbages, carrots, leeks, and plenty of kale. Berries there were—strawberries, raspberries, gooseberries, currants—the sweetest fruit I can remember. Fruit trees—pear, apple, plum—yellow and purple. All of it was allowed to ripen to its fullest flavor. Our root cellar was always filled to overflowing. We gave to those who were needy.

For Opa and me in the late 1930s, the garden was, indeed, more than paradise—it was our salvation. He was no longer permitted to conduct his cattle-dealing business. I was no longer allowed to attend public school. In the garden, we felt happy, safe and productive.

When I return to the German town of Schermbeck now, I can still walk down Main Street. I can still cross the little bridge, still hear the water babble. The bush bearing the little white berries still grows. Only now when I get to the spot where the garden gate once waited to be opened, there is just sidewalk and a path leading to someone's front door. There are no more lined strawberry paths, and the gazebo is gone.

But the taste of the fruits is still on my tongue. The joy of those moments in our garden lingers on.

Opa

When I think of my grandfather I think of the pungent aroma of his cigar. I think of how on Friday night, it lay on an end table in our living room. Alongside it, a cigar clipper to cut off the end. It lay there until sundown Saturday when the Shabbat was over. He enjoyed his cigar.

Opa had breakfast before sun-up each morning, always fully dressed. Shirt and tie, vest, the gold chain hanging from his pocket watch. He was a dapper man, a cattle-dealer of status in our town.

In 1935, the Nuremberg Laws came to Germany. Jews could no longer deal at the stock market. The local butchers who used to buy from my grandfather were told to buy from someone else.

Inspecting his cattle in his pastures at the edge of town, he has to decide quickly what to do.

"Do I call Ridder now to transport a hundred head to market? If I don't sell soon, they'll take these cows away from me regardless."

The signs are all around him, humiliating and depressing. A prestigious group of men in town have a club, the Kegelclub, people who run businesses, tavern owners, the druggist, the dentist and my Opa. After the meetings they play cards. Opa is no longer welcome.

"What has happened?" he thinks. He remembers back to 1929, the big three-day festival, *Killian Schützenfest*. The king of the festival, the best marksman, chose a maiden to reign beside him in the town of Schermbeck for an entire year. The choice was Opa's daughter Paula—the first Jewish queen. He can still see the white horse-drawn carriage taking Paula past our home, up and down the street. She sits across from the mayor and his wife, and next to the king. A tiara crowns her beautiful black hair; it sparkles in the sunlight.

With the Nuremberg Laws, all Jews lost their citizenship. It was no longer safe in Germany. But where was he to go? He was too old to begin again. He spoke only German.

The incomprehensible November 9th, 1938—Kristallnacht—was the final blow. Every Jewish home was ransacked. All material things lay in pieces in the street. All houses of worship were destroyed. Our sacred Torahs were burned. Prayer books, prayer shawls and arc curtains were burned.

In our house, the *Kachelofen*, the tile stove, was totally destroyed. There wasn't a chair with four legs left whole for my ill grandmother to sit on. Coming back at dusk, we heard Opa say, "Who would do such a thing to my little canary?" The bird lay on the living room floor, trampled. The cage was smashed. Opa's bird, who sang our wakeup song every morning, who sat on his special oversized coffee cup on Passover.

Only one of our neighbors resisted the Nazis that night. He went after them with a pitchfork. Within minutes, all of the windows in his home were broken. The family suffered many harsh consequences as a result of being our friends, *Judenfreunde*.

"Come," Opa says to his family. His voice, the usual gentleness gone, is stern. "It's time to leave. We are not wanted here anymore."

We left Schermbeck in January of 1939, heading toward our cousins in Berlin.

My Place in the Park

Only a suitcase to take away from this place where once we had proud possessions. I clutched my doll.

There was still enough light for me to see the beautiful lake, only a short walk from our home on Main Street. The lake was frozen over. People of all ages were ice skating. They wore colorful, handmade hats and scarves.

We walked toward the railroad station past barren winter fields. In the summer, red poppies and blue cornflowers created a sprinkle of color throughout the vast wheatfields. I was leaving the natural beauty of this village to go to the noise and concrete of the big city of Berlin . . .

The part of Berlin where my aunt, uncle, and twin cousins lived was a quiet residential area. Beautiful Körner Park lay across the street from their home. The ivy-covered walls were the backdrop for the vivid colors of the flowers that changed with the seasons. Neatly trimmed bushes and paths wound around the high fountain in the middle of the park.

I would sit in the park with my cousins, Hanna and Ruth. They read wonderful stories to me, walked the paths with me, while I pushed the doll buggy that once belonged to them. After a while, since I was old enough, they would leave me—wave good-bye and go to meet their friends. I sat on the white wooden bench and rocked my doll in the buggy and felt very smug. I heard splashing water from the fountain, I looked at the colorful flowers. I lifted my doll out of the soft buggy and as I held her upright, her eyes opened. I felt a sweet love for this doll, my only real possession. She belonged to me. I needed her. I felt satisfied.

One day—it was now 1940—a sign went up on the gate: "*Juden ist der zutritt verboten.*" I could no longer enter this place—no longer take my doll for a walk, pretend that I was her mommy, gently take her out of the buggy, lay her over my shoulder, or cradle her in my arms. No longer the gentle sound of the splashing water of the fountain or the aroma of the flowers. Just like the walks I used to take with my Opa in our village, it was all taken away.

Our legal papers were in order; it was a miracle. We prepared to leave Germany in May 1941. We were each allowed to take fifty pounds of clothing and my mother was permitted to keep her wedding ring. I still held my precious doll *Püppchen* close to me.

Before we left, Mother and I stood at the gate of Körner Park for one more glance at the beautiful fountain and the green lawn, now dotted with huge anti-aircraft guns, their turrets aimed to the sky. I turned away from the park, reached for my mother's hand, and walked to the main railroad station. My family stood on the platform and as the train began to move, I cried. They waved their arms at us. We waved out of the window until they were out of sight—never to see them again.

Betrayal

Cyna Glatstein
b. Sochachev, Poland, 1928

The town of Sochachev lay forty kilometers from Warsaw. According to the census, the population was forty thousand. Twenty-five percent were Jews. The remainder were Catholics. Although the cultures, religions and languages were different, we were able to live amicably side by side.

Sochachev was quite a modern town with two train stations, one local and one express. There were Hebrew as well as rabbinic schools, parks, a hospital, a library, and two synagogues, one ancient.

My father was the rabbi of Sochachev. He was the spiritual leader beloved by all.

Our home was open to everyone. Jews did not go to secular courts of law in Europe, they went to the rabbi. So people came to our home with questions about what was kosher—dietary observances—about emotional problems, economic problems and for *Din Torahs*. In *Din Torahs*, the Torah was used as a source to settle all types of problems.

My father listened carefully, patiently, and with an open analytical mind to what was being claimed by the litigants, after which he consulted the Code of Talmudic Law.

Opposite us lived Mr. Tarnovsky, a well known and successful advocate. As a lawyer he was very interested in my father's legal work. He sometimes attended trials and stayed later to discuss the outcome. He admired the logic and humaneness of the Torah teachings. My father considered him a friend.

When the Germans occupied Poland in 1939, everything changed.

One afternoon Advocate Tarnovsky and an SS officer called on my father. They came bearing a large bowl with a liver in it. The bowl was placed on the table with malice, so that the blood splattered over the white tablecloth—an act designed purposely to humiliate my father.

"Is the pig's liver kosher or *treif?*" asked the advocate.

"Mr. Tarnovsky, you know very well that according to Jewish law, I cannot judge a non-kosher animal."

"You must."

"I cannot."

"You must. If you don't, you will soon hear from us."

They stalked out of the room, slamming the door behind them.

My father was shaken. He knew that he had to leave immediately.

Before leaving, he impressed my mother with the necessity of all of us going into hiding. My father left for Blonie where we had many friends.

Because I was close to my father and I was daring even at the age of eleven, I accompanied him.

My mother and two younger children went to a friendly neighbor; my older sisters went to another friend. And so, we were dispersed.

Parting

Dora Zuer Iwler
b. Chodoròw, Poland, 1923

My parents, Yehuda and Sima, worked very hard in our small fruit store and our home in Chodoròw, near Lvov, Poland. My brother, Moshe Lazer, and I worked in the store after school also. Father supplemented his meager income by collecting scrap metal with a friend. Once a week he went to Lvov to restock the store, while Mother took care of the customers.

Thursdays, market days in our town, were when my mother bought all the food to prepare for Shabbat. I stayed home to care for my younger brother Yitzhak and sister Miriam. We all looked forward to the treats Mother brought back from the market for us.

Fridays were spent cooking and baking bread. We made our own butter, and we each had a glass of milk on the window sill which eventually separated into layers of milk, yogurt, and cream. I still remember the delicious tastes and smells.

On Shabbat, the six of us walked to the synagogue together. My father looked at all of us with such pride in his eyes. Mother was a quiet, religious woman who had come from a family of eleven children. She had long brown hair which she wore in a braid wrapped in a bun and pinned to the back of her head. She dressed modestly, but she always looked beautiful to me. Her four children gave her very little free time.

My brother Moshe Lazer was handsome; the girls loved his black hair and tall build. Since he was only eighteen months older than me, we had lots of mutual friends. He was known to get in trouble pretty often and sometimes I got caught with him. Once, when we were quite young, we went to the circus without telling our parents. They were worried sick about us because we were gone so long. We got a good whipping with Father's belt when we got back, which I suppose we deserved.

My sister, Miriam, was three years younger than me. She was a beautiful brunette and quite shy and reserved, unlike me. She loved to stay home with Mother and our brother Yitzhak, who was six years younger than I. Miriam and Yitzhak went to school together every day and then to *Cheder*. I still picture Yitzhak going down the street spinning a wheel with a stick or playing dominoes at the table with Miriam.

This beautiful, simple life came to an end in 1942 when the Nazis declared that Chodoròw would be made free of Jews. My mother, forty-three years old, was taken away in a cattle car in the first action. That same day, my fifteen-year-old sister Miriam was shot by the Nazis. My twelve-year-old brother Yitzhak was taken away in the second action. Somehow, they didn't find my father and older brother who were hiding in a bunker which my father had made under our house.

I was working in the garden of a Ukrainian family outside of town and didn't know until I returned home about these actions. It was a horrible shock when my father, brother and I found Miriam. We buried her and placed a glass bottle with her name inside over her grave, hoping that someday someone would find this inappropriate marker and replace it with a more suitable one. None of us ever returned to that place.

It was now my turn to go to the rail station and be loaded into a box car. A Nazi who was a friend of the Ukrainian family I worked for recognized me and pulled me out of the crowd. I was saved for another day. That night I slept in a stable, full of fear.

The parting with my father and older brother, Moshe Lazer, remains one of the most painful moments of my life. Father had been ordered to go to Strij, a small town nearby. My brother decided to join the partisans. I wanted to go with him but he wouldn't take me. We had to say our final farewell. My father's face was ashen. He said, "Before I die, I would like to see the blue and white Jewish flag." It was this wish of my father's that has motivated me to work for the State of Israel, hoping to make my father's dream come true in a small way.

I never saw any of my family again.

II. The Destruction of a Society

A keynote of German social policy was racism. To the Nazis, the Jews were lowest on the scale of humanity. To create a racially pure Aryan society—to "save" Germany—Jewish people, Jewish society, had to be eliminated before any other undesirable group.

This policy was instituted gradually in Germany. It began in the early 1930s with book burnings and a skillfully conducted propaganda campaign against the Jews. In 1935, the Nuremberg Laws denied citizenship, property, and means of livelihood to Jews. A signal event was Kristallnacht: November 9, 1938, the "Night of Shattered Glass" in which Jewish synagogues, schools, homes, and hospitals throughout the country were destroyed. After that, the Germans began arresting Jews and shipping them to concentration camps.

The policy of racial hatred and destruction of Jewish society was carried out in other countries, such as Austria and Czechoslovakia, where Germany occupied the land or attained power in the late 1930s. Many local people, continuing their historical anti-Semitism, willingly collaborated with the German occupiers. But in these countries, the destruction was carried out in more sudden ways. Jews were quickly denied rights, humiliated, beaten, jailed, killed. They were resettled in ghettos and then deported to death camps.

When Germany invaded Poland in 1939, Poland fell at once and was divided between Germany and its then-ally, the Soviet Union. Soviet occupation was bad enough. But then in 1941 Germany invaded the Soviet Union, occupying the Russian part of Poland, the Russian-occupied Baltic countries—including Lithuania—and parts of the Soviet Union itself. The German regime of terror began immediately in these areas.

Many Jews, especially in 1930s Germany, found it hard to believe how serious the growing signs of imminent danger were. And many Jews, especially in other countries, simply didn't know what was happening. In any case, the early events of the Holocaust struck with sudden, cruel blows. The writers in this section tell of their shock and horror as they watched the emblems and institutions of their society being destroyed. In "An Action against the Jews," "Kristallnacht" is the moving cry of a boy witnessing the burning of his synagogue; he experiences the pain of all German Jews when sacred and secular

Jewish structures were senselessly trashed. In "The Sandwich" the same writer's reliance on religious law and traditional beliefs is wrenched away. "The Harbinger of What?" conveys the panic and terror among Polish Jews when Germany occupied their towns and they had no place to go, and only an idea of the potentials of Nazi cruelty. "A Shtetl's Life Is Ended" and "What Ever Happened to the Jews of Skudvil?" are stories of the deliberate and terrible destruction of vital Jewish communities in Poland and Lithuania: they give us a sense of the Jews' bitterness toward local collaborators, as well as the vast suffering in these broken communities.

Far too few people understood at the time—indeed, how could anybody comprehend?—that the Germans truly meant to erase Jewish society from the face of the earth.

A. B.

Herr B.

Fritz Ottenheimer
b. Constance, Germany, 1925

It was 1933. Herr B., our friendly neighbor, showed up with a Nazi party insignia on his lapel. My father was shocked.

"Herr B., would you mind telling me why you joined the party?"

"Not at all. We have a new leader now, and we have to show him that we'll support him. Besides," he added, "I picked up a few new jobs since I joined."

"What do you think about what the Party is doing to the Jewish people?" my father probed.

"Ah, yes—it's too bad," Herr B. sighed. "It's too bad that the good have to suffer along with the bad!"

"Which ones are we?" my father inquired. "Are we the good Jews or the bad Jews?"

Herr B. laughed. "What a question! You know you are good people. You are our friends!"

My father persisted. "You know most of the Jews of Constance. Which ones are the bad Jews that we have to suffer along with?"

Herr B. thought for a few seconds. He admitted that all of the Jews of our town seemed to be decent, honest people.

"Then where are these bad Jews you are talking about?"

Herr B. was angry now.

"You know damned well where they are," he shouted. "All you have to do is pick up a newspaper or turn on your radio!"

He turned away, then looked back. "Where there's smoke, there's fire!"

A Kristallnacht Journey

Herbert Silberman
b. Lemförde, Germany, 1920

At about 2:00 P.M. on November 9, 1938, a group of SS men walked into the meat market in Altena, Germany, where I was working as a butcher. They immediately began to destroy the store, breaking all the windows and contaminating the meat, all the while shouting anti-Semitic slogans. After they left, I decided to go to my grandparents' house in Schermbeck where my mother and sisters were.

I left after dark to catch the train to Wesel where I had to transfer. When I arrived in Wesel, I thought I would look up my uncle's parents who lived near the station. It was a short walk. But when I got there, I found no one in the house. All the windows had been broken and all the contents destroyed.

Walking back to the train station, I saw that the sky was lit up with flames; there was a lot of smoke. The synagogue was burning! The whole building was engulfed in flames. I was afraid to get too close because there was so much noise from the voices of the Nazis shouting. There was no fire-fighting equipment.

I fled the horrible scene, heading back to the station where I took the night train to Schermbeck.

My grandparents' house in Schermbeck was about a half-hour walk from the station. When I arrived, again no one was at home. A neighbor, who was a childhood friend of my grandfather, was standing in front of his house across the street.

I asked him, "Where is my family?"

"I am not allowed to talk to you," he said, and walked into his house, closing the door.

We had always thought of this neighbor as a good person; he was not a member of the Nazi party. But he was afraid to talk to me because I was a Jew.

I went into my grandparents' house. The front door was broken, the furniture inside overturned and broken. The feather beds and pillows had been slashed, and there were feathers all over the house. The windows were smashed and food had been thrown all over the floor.

Since my grandparents were elderly, I went to the nearby hospital to look for them. They were indeed there, together with my mother and two sisters. After about thirty minutes, the head nurse told us that a call had come from the *Bürgermeister* that we would have to leave there immediately. We all walked back to the house.

I had to move some of the furniture so that we could walk in the door. By order of the *Bürgermeister,* we were all under house arrest, so I spent the next two days working to make the house livable. I boarded up the windows and repaired the furniture as much as I could so that we had chairs to sit on and beds to sleep in.

On the third day, the Nazis took me to the *Bürgermeister's* office, where I was thrown into jail. After two days I was taken by auto to Wesel, where I was jailed again with many other Jewish people. Two days later, we were all taken to the train station where we were pushed into cattle cars and transported to Dachau.

An Action against the Jews

Arnold Blum
b. Nuremberg, Germany, 1922

Kristallnacht: November 9–10, 1938

I stood before the burning *shul* and watched as the firemen protected the surrounding buildings, being careful not to put any water on the isolated curls of smoke rising here and there from the devastated sanctuary that once was our *shul.*

I stood before the burning *shul,* unbelievingly, in deep shock, empty of strength, gutted, as was our *shul.* A murder had been committed, symbolic as it were, soon to be followed by the near annihilation of our people.

Slowly my senses returned in a wave of anger. I clenched my fists, my eyes filled with tears of outrage. My silence screamed: "*Kooma Adonai, veyafootsoo oyvecha* . . ." "Rise up, Lord, and scatter your enemies . . ."

But the clouds did not part, the *shofar* did not sound, the strong hand and the outstretched arm did not appear.

It was not the year of the Lord. He had averted His face.

The Arrest

On Friday, November 11, 1938, around six o'clock in the morning, they came for us.

We had lived in a state of apprehension since the previous day, when our *shul* had been burned to the ground and Jewish places of business destroyed. We had entered a twilight zone between memories of earning our keep at our occupations and the fear of becoming game during hunting season.

When I opened the window of my room and looked out into the mist-laden, dark street, I saw two men with flashlights approaching our house. They were dressed in long leather coats and felt hats, the uniform of the Gestapo. They entered the gate in the fence, approached the front door of our house and rang the bell. My mother and grandmother got up immediately and I went downstairs to open the door. A sense of foreboding hit me.

The men flashed their identification badges and one said, "*Geheime Staatspolizei.* Is there an Arnold Blum living here?"

"You are speaking to him."

"How old are you?"

"Sixteen."

"You are under arrest."

I was shocked and asked, "But why?"

"You are placed under protective custody," he said. Then he asked, "Does a Bruno Stern live here?"

"Yes."

"Show us the way upstairs."

While we were going upstairs my uncle, who must have heard the commotion, came down from his attic apartment. When the Gestapo men saw him, one asked, "What is your name?"

"Bruno Stern."

"You are under arrest."

The Gestapo men told my uncle and me to get ready to leave. My uncle took his time, had a cup of coffee and something to eat, but I had no appetite for food or drink. My mother insisted I put two pieces of bread in my pocket. She asked the Gestapo men how long we would be gone and one replied, "Not long." I kissed my mother and grandmother, who were both in tears, and we left, filled with fear.

My uncle and I walked in front and the Gestapo men walked behind us. They told us which direction to take, downhill toward the city. The sun was rising, the air was cold and damp. The light cast by the street lights was diffused by the moisture condensing in the air. We walked silently, following the occasional directions of the men behind us. After ten minutes, we realized we were being taken to the nearest police station, Am Vogelsang, in the western part of Stuttgart.

The station was staffed by the regular police. The Gestapo men made them sign a receipt for us and left. My uncle and I were taken to a prison cage which already held an occupant. He was Dr. Walter Strauss, an insurance man from our street, a widower with two young daughters. We greeted each other and Strauss said in English, "Some fun!" Neither my uncle nor I knew what "fun" meant, and Strauss said it meant *Vergnügen*.

We did not talk much. We could see the street through the steel bars outside our window. After some time a big, canvas-covered truck pulled up. We were taken from the cage and made to climb onto the truck which took us to the central police station in the center of Stuttgart.

We could look out of the truck on our way to town and, in return, could be seen by the people in the street. The media had been full of reports about the assassination in Paris of a German legation counselor named vom Rath, by a young Polish Jew, and about the "Action against the Jews." The burghers of Stuttgart must have been aware of our identity, but those looking at us showed no ill will in their expression and there were no hostile gestures.

We pulled into the fenced-in yard of the central police station where similar trucks had already discharged their passengers. Black-uniformed SS men herded us inside the building. We were made to line up and to answer to our names.

Afterward we were led upstairs and driven into a crowded, foul-smelling cell. The leadership of the Stuttgart Jewish community, including our family doctor, Professor Simmel, were there. I saw the members of the Board of Trustees of our congregation, mostly elderly men, and Herr Kupfer, head of the *Chevra Kadisha,* the Jewish Burial Society. I observed fathers and grandfathers of my teenage friends and felt awed, being in such close physical contact with them.

The foul odor, I noted, came from a pail in a corner of the cell. It was the only sanitary facility available to us and it had apparently not been emptied. We were confined in this crowded, stinking place for several hours, standing while being pressed together ever closer, as more and more Jews were added. There were whispered conversations, recounting the previous day's events, and speculations as to the fate in store for us. The cell door was opened only to admit more prisoners. Finally we again heard steps outside. The door was opened and we were led downstairs into the yard where the trucks had been replaced by buses.

An SS man addressed us to tell us we were going to Dachau.

As I was climbing aboard, the thought flashed through my mind that despite our differences in age, status, and wealth, and the degree of our religious observance, our Jewishness alone was of interest to our oppressors.

The Sandwich

After about one week in the Dachau concentration camp, there were daily callouts of names. Those called were told where to assemble. They did not return to us, and we thought they had been released.

My name was called after yet another week and a half, about the end of November 1938. By that time I had gotten used to the camp routine and the terrible food: breakfast of gruel and malt drink; the noon meal, consisting of pork-blood sausage, dark bread and water; and the evening meal of thin soup and bread.

Bad as the food tasted, it harbored a more serious problem. The blood sausage was in multiple violations of Jewish dietary law, which forbids consumption of blood in any form, of pork, and even of permitted animals slaughtered by means other than those prescribed. It had been my first exposure to nonkosher food and I had gagged as it crossed my lips. Eating had posed a moral dilemma to me, whether to starve or to live in violation of religious law. The problem didn't end when I left Dachau.

Those of us who had been called out were put on a train from Dachau to Munich, where we rushed to find trains to take us home to various parts of southern Germany.

A man named Sallie, husband of one of my mother's cousins, was on the trip with me and took a fatherly interest in me. We entered a compartment in one of the cars bound for Stuttgart. It already held two Stuttgart Jews, one the ghostly pale, orthodox rabbi, Dr. Simon Bamberger, and the other, Dr. Walter R., a former Stuttgart District Attorney. He was a pink-complexioned, tall, distinguished looking man, bald and bespectacled. The rabbi's beard had been shorn in camp and the stubble, which had replaced it underlined his cadaverous appearance.

Sallie said to me, "We still have time till the train leaves. I'll go and get us something to eat." He left and returned some time later, carrying two wrapped sandwiches, one of which he handed to me while keeping the other.

We were ravenously hungry and unwrapped the sandwiches which, on casual inspection, turned out to contain slices of ham.

Sallie started to introduce himself to the men sitting opposite us, when the rabbi noticed what we were eating. He became incensed and said in an agitated voice, "*HaKadosh, baruch hoo*, the Holy One, blessed be He, just liberated you from that terrible place and in gratitude the first thing you do is to eat pork. You ought to be thoroughly ashamed of yourselves." With this outburst he fell silent and did not utter another word the rest of the trip.

Neither Sallie nor I felt like arguing with the rabbi.

As for me, I had already broken the law by eating the nauseating blood sausage in camp. In the choice between starvation and living in violation of religious law, I had opted for life. Was it worse to eat ham now? I didn't know.

There was some casual conversation with Dr. R. until, hours later, we arrived in the dimly lit Stuttgart main railroad station, from which we went on our various ways.

I left for the United States in April of 1939.

Leaving Germany, Leaving Home

Gertrude Newman
b. Munich, Germany, 1928

Like many German Jews, my family lived in Germany for many generations. They were well known in the Jewish community in Munich. My father was a business man—a partner in the family business and a war veteran. He used to say that the Nazis would never harm a veteran who fought for Germany.

As the Nazi movement grew bit by bit, neither the German Jews nor the governments of other countries faced its growing strength. Anti-Jewish incidents were happening all over Germany as early as 1933 and 1934, but my family ignored them and felt it would pass.

In 1934, when I was six years old, I was not allowed to enroll in a German school, so I went to our Jewish school in Munich. Each year there were more incidents, such as boycotts of Jewish businesses and vandalism of Jewish stores. Some of my family members who lived in small towns were forced out of their homes by the Hitler Youth and had to relocate to a larger town.

I remember one summer day going to an outdoor restaurant where my father was slapped in the face and told, "Jews are not wanted here." Still my father insisted that this was not serious. "It will pass," he said.

Then in 1937 the main synagogue of Munich was burned down—utterly destroyed. Now there were family conferences about whether it was time to leave. It was so hard to decide. We were comfortable among our friends and family, and Germany was a beautiful country. The Alps were only a few hours away, and we spent winters and summers there. So far, our nice lives were not too inconvenienced.

But on November 9, 1938—Kristallnacht—the decision was made for us. That night, we heard on the radio that a lot of Jewish businesses were destroyed and Jewish people were rounded up. The next morning, my father received a phone call at five o'clock from a loyal employee of his business telling him to leave immediately, because the Gestapo was arresting all Jewish males in Munich. My mother agreed that he should leave and send for us later. So my father left with a friend for the country. I went off to school with my friend. We saw nothing unusual during our walk, until we came near the school, when we smelled smoke. Sure enough, our school was burning while the Hitler Youth watched and cheered.

At ten years old, I could not comprehend why anyone would do such a horrible thing. I was also very angry.

Then when I returned home, I found my mother very frightened. The Gestapo was at our house looking for my father and threatening that if he was not home shortly, they would take us away and punish us.

A little later, my father called to see how things were. My mother told him the Gestapo was looking for him and if he did not come back, we would be punished. He came back a few hours later. The Gestapo must have been watching the house, because they were there after a few minutes and took him away. We knew only afterward that they took him to Dachau.

The Gestapo was not finished with us. We went to a friend's home, so as not to be alone. They followed us there, looking for other members of our family. Our host was a brave elderly lady; she told them to leave us alone. Surprisingly, they left, but they kept watch on us. We did not sleep for many a night, and we prepared for anything.

It was now time for action. My mother went to the American consulate in Stuttgart where she waited hours to receive a number for immigration to America. She finally received a number in the low eight thousands. At the time she did not know it was a lucky number—but it was.

Father was released from Dachau after four weeks—on December 6, 1938. He was never the same again, nor would he speak about what happened to him in the concentration camp. My grandmother died shortly after that—probably of grief.

The Nazis left us alone until Yom Kippur, 1939 when they burst into our apartment and took all our jewelry and radios. They did not harm us physically. They knew we were leaving soon.

Finally, after passing our physical at the American consulate, we left on a snowy morning—October 28, 1939—with four suitcases among us and ten marks. Most of our beloved family members stayed behind. We went by train to Genoa and then boarded an Italian ship to America. It took seventeen days to cross the ocean. When we docked in New York, the Jewish Committee relocated us to Pittsburgh.

One image remains vividly in my mind: the twelve-hour bus trip to Pittsburgh. It was shortly before Christmas and as we passed the houses along the highway with their glowing lights, I felt so homeless and lost, and kept looking longingly at each house, picturing myself inside safe and secure.

I never regained what I lost, but I did find a new life and, most of all, freedom.

Escape to England

Marianne Silberman
b. Kassel, Germany, 1930

The day of departure from Germany for me and my family had finally arrived. It was August 30, 1939. For months, my father had been planning for our leaving, hoping that our quota number would be among those listed for emigration to America. Actually, he would have taken us to Palestine or South America or Shanghai just to get us out of Germany, but my mother only wanted to go to America because some of our family had already emigrated there.

When the notification from the American consul finally came, there was much jubilation in our house. Arrangements were quickly made for packing our furniture, linens, and china for shipments to America. The Germans did not permit Jews to take any valuables or money out of the country, but we were allowed to take any amount of household goods and clothing. I remember that my mother bought clothing for me in several sizes so that I would have it to wear once we arrived in our new home.

We traveled from Berlin to Bremen, where we were to meet my brother and together board the ship which would take us across the Channel to Liverpool. My father had made arrangements to take my brother shopping for clothes prior to boarding the ship. However, my brother was late and arrived just in time for all of us to go through German customs for a final examination before boarding.

My father was the first to be called by the uniformed SS men. They told him to take everything out of his pockets. When they opened his wallet, they discovered that it contained 300 marks instead of the 40 marks (10 marks per person) that he was allowed to take out of the country.

Without another word they grabbed him and took him away. My mother screamed and started to sob and, of course, I cried too.

My brother was too scared to move because he realized that it was all his fault. If he had arrived on time, Papa would have shopped with him and spent the extra money. Instead, Papa was so upset that he completely forgot about the extra marks in his wallet.

We waited. My mother's tears stained the lapels of the pale gray suit that she was wearing.

Meanwhile, my father was being stripped and searched. They even cut the soles off his shoes to check whether he had hidden any money there. My father never told me exactly what transpired between him and the two Nazis who took him away. But when he finally reappeared, he was pale and visibly shaken.

He grabbed my hand and my mother's arm and with my brother following behind, we all ran to board the ship. I remember standing on the deck watching the German coastline disappear.

We arrived in Liverpool the next day. With feelings of renewed hope and great anticipation of the new life which awaited us, we left the ship. As we stepped onto English soil, my father fell to his knees and kissed the ground, shouting in German, "*Gott sei dank, wir sind jetzt frei.*" (Thank God, we are now free.)

The Best-Laid Plans

Frederick Forscher
b. Vienna, Austria, 1918

It was April 13, 1938—my parents' twenty-fifth wedding anniversary. We sat around the sparsely set dinner table to "celebrate." Though it was early afternoon, our dining room with its beautiful cordovan mahogany furniture was dim, and the mood was somber. The curtains were drawn because one could never be sure what neighbors would see and report.

Only a month ago, the day after Hitler marched into Vienna, my father was told that he need not return to his place of business. He was the second largest painting and decorating contractor in the city. Yet his life's work was now in the hands of his employees, those who had clandestinely joined the Nazi party years before the Anschluss. His most senior foreman was in charge, telling my father what he was allowed to do or not do.

But this was not the time to bemoan the situation. There were plans to be made. First, schedules had to be prepared for Dad's "underground school" to help people with their emigration plans. There were many doctors, lawyers, accountants, and other professionals who realized that their knowledge, so useful at home, would be of no help in any foreign country to which they emigrated. Dad offered to teach them a skill—something they could do with their hands—to tide them over until they could reenter their profession.

Next we talked quietly about our emigration plans. We had received assurance from relatives in New York that affidavits for the whole family were on the way. Now it was time to arrange for exit permits, visas, passports. My mother's mother was not covered by the affidavits and my mother would not leave without her. So it was decided that my older brother Bruno and I would leave as soon as possible. My twelve-year-old younger brother, Walter, was to stay behind with my parents "till things blow over."

With tears in my eyes and the words choking in my throat, I lifted my glass of water to toast my parents, to thank them for all they had done for us three boys: for the wonderful home they had provided; and that I would never forget the advice from my Dad, "*Alles sollst du können, nichts sollst du brauchen.*" ("You should have the skill to do anything, but you shouldn't need it.")

I left Vienna August 18. My parents and Walter saw me off at the West-bahnhof.

It was the last time I saw my parents.

On November 9, Kristallnacht—when Bruno and I were already in the United States—my parents gave up hope for the future and reluctantly sent Walter with a children's transport to England.

With all our planning, we couldn't have anticipated how things would turn out.

A Life-Defining Impression

Ruth Lieberman Drescher
b. Stuttgart, Germany, 1934

There were always people staying in our apartment in Stuttgart. I always wondered why we had a bed in the bathroom. Only later did I realize that we had all this company because the American consulate was located in Stuttgart, and people were desperate to make arrangements to emigrate in 1938 and 1939.

My father, however, had no interest in leaving Germany. He thought, I later learned, that all these people were foolishly disrupting their lives. This Hitler madness was sure to blow over, he said. After all, he had fought in the Great War, and his picture in uniform hung in a place of honor in our apartment along with his well-earned medals. It was not until Kristallnacht, November 9, 1938—when my father came home from hiding in a villa that belonged to a non-Jewish friend of his, who had warned him of what was to happen—that he believed the disaster so feared by others could actually take place.

Finally, my parents agreed that they too had to leave, and the visas were applied for and received. We were to take the train to Rotterdam where we would board the SS *Veendam* to take us to New York.

There was one incident before we left Stuttgart which has become emblematic of my childhood in Germany. It occurred shortly before we left. I had been playing with four or five children outside our apartment building. One of the mothers came out and gave candy to the children. All the other children were given two pieces, I only one. Why, I wondered aloud, did I get one piece when everyone else got two? The daughter of the woman who gave us the candy said: "It's because you are Jewish." This, my first direct experience with anti-Semitism, has stayed with me all of these years.

The thing which symbolizes our departure for me was my little red shoulder bag, which I loved and wore diagonally from right to left. I was too young to understand why the men and women were separated at the train station, and I certainly did not understand why my mother and sister Margot (age twelve) were taken into another room. Later I learned that they were strip searched. I, however, was spared that experience, and was greeted by a Nazi official who asked me what was in my bag. As I began to open it, he said something like: "You are a sweet little girl—never mind, you can go." I can only imagine the relief which my mother must have experienced as she saw that her little five-year-old daughter was not subjected to any humiliation.

My parents both had mixed emotions about leaving. They felt relief at being able to escape the terrors which in 1939 they could only suspect, and at the same time, a great sense of loss at having to leave their home and their community. For me it was an adventure. I loved the train, and I could hardly wait to get on the ship. Little did I realize how painful this displacement must have been for my parents, then in their forties and fifties.

How could I, with these two small examples, have considered myself to be in the same category as people who had suffered anguish, pain, and humiliation at the hands of the Nazis? I was never able to. I am only humble in the face of their suffering. Yet, how will we ever know what the impact on a small child of such devastation can be. At sixty-three years of age, I still wonder.

The Harbinger of What?

Cyna Glatstein
b. Sochachev, Poland, 1928

The Nazis knew that first the spirit had to be broken, then the body would follow. In 1939 when they took over Poland, the breaking of the spirit started immediately.

They came for my father and brother, and my sister and I followed to see what was happening. My father and brother were taken to the marketplace which was opposite the church. Many of our Jewish men and boys were already there.

The Jews who had beards and sidelocks were the first to suffer.

The Germans slashed beards, cut off one sidelock.

The Poles, who had congregated, applauded. They jeered, they mocked and laughed hilariously.

What a joke!

The Nazis made the Jews jump, dance in a ring, while their photographers took many pictures which were to be used for propaganda purposes.

All the Jewish women and children who witnessed this sordid spectacle and humiliation were crying. We were told we were making matters worse and were ordered to leave. We did not leave, only retreated.

What they had done evidently was not enough for the Nazis. In the next scene of this "comedy," they ordered the men and boys to walk across the shallow River Bzura. It was November and the water was icy. The Jews were not dressed adequately to withstand the cold. Later, many developed pneumonia.

We believed all this was an aberration and things would improve.

We were wrong.

It was the beginning of the Final Solution.

The Beginning and the End

Jacob Wolhendler
b. Zawiercie, Poland, 1913

The first of September, 1939, was a Saturday. The Germans started the war against Poland very early in the morning. All day long we heard bombs from planes around our town, Zawiercie. We were scared that the Germans might be near our town. Toward evening, at the end of the Sabbath, the men started to leave town to run away from the Germans, heading northeast. My father and I joined the running people. We walked all night until we reached, on Sunday morning, a small town called Szczekocing, about 40 kilometers away.

The Germans reached Szczekocing on Sunday afternoon. We were hiding in a small house. Toward evening the soldiers burst into the house and ordered all outside. On the way out from the house, I was near my father. Suddenly my father fell on the ground; he had been shot by one of the soldiers. I fell on him and saw the blood bursting out from my father's body. He was dead in the next few minutes. I had to leave him there, and I started to run away, worrying that I would be killed too.

I hid in the nearby forest; it was a long night. Toward morning I met other Jews who had hidden in the forest all night. On Thursday morning I left, heading back home; I reached Zawiercie the same evening.

When I came into the house my mother immediately asked me where my father was. I said, "I don't know." I did not want to tell her what happened to Father right away. We went to sleep. Early in the morning my mother woke me and started to ask me where Father was. I could not keep it a secret anymore and told her what had happened. My mother threw herself on the floor and cried all day that Friday. Toward evening our Jewish neighbors came in to make a *Minyan*. My brother and I said the first *Kaddish* for our father.

And so did the Germans start to break up our family. The rest of my family—my mother, brother, and three sisters perished in Auschwitz in October 1943.

I ran away from the train that took the whole Jewish town to Auschwitz. I worked on a German farm to the end of the war, posing as a Polish citizen of the Catholic faith.

I am Jacob Wolhendler, son of Ephraim and Sarah, brother of my sisters, Chana, Jochened, and Hinda, and brother of Eliezer. We were a family of seven people very close to one another, and I am the only survivor to say *Kaddish* after them, who are in heaven.

A Family Gone, One by One

Simon Gelernter
b. Lodz, Poland, 1926

Before we landed in Auschwitz, my family lived in Lodz, Poland. All Jewish people in Lodz were forced to move to the assigned area of the ghetto. Our home was located in the ghetto area, so for a while we had a semblance of regular family life. But we didn't know what was going on outside the ghetto—we were not allowed to possess radios or read newspapers. Although in 1944 the tide of war had finally turned in favor of the Allied forces, I personally thought that by this time the Germans had conquered the whole world.

All we knew was that in the early fall of that year, the ghetto was being liquidated. My family now consisted of my father, brother, and myself. My eldest brother had died in the ghetto in 1943. My mother had died in 1938 of a stroke after the horrible news of Kristallnacht when all the synagogues were set on fire in Germany.

Since the ghetto was now ninety percent empty, my brother and I decided to look for food and coal in the abandoned buildings. As we were looking for something to eat, we got the shock of our lives. On a plate in an empty apartment we found several human ears.

We left the apartment in a hurry, disgusted and frightened beyond belief.

As we were heading for our home in the ghetto, we were surprised by an SS officer. At first he threatened to put us on the wagon, but he relented as I was pleading with him that we were only looking for coal. We were happy that he let us go, but the officer knew that in a few days we would be herded onto cattle cars on the way to Auschwitz.

My father, brother and I were in the last transport, because my brother was working for the fire department in the ghetto.

My arrival in Birkenau-Auschwitz in 1944 was a shocking eye-opener. I said to my brother, "We are going to die here." I had no time even to say anything to my father as the selection officer, "Gottesfinger," sent my father to the left. For all I know it may have been the notorious Dr. Mengele. When I asked the "Canadian" (Commando units which searched the new arrival transports) where my father was, he pointed to the billowing smoke from the crematoria and said, "That's where your father went."

My brother died in Ebensee, a concentration camp in Austria, about two weeks before the liberation by the U.S. Armed Forces. Had the liberation been one or two weeks later, I would not have survived.

To this day, I have been unable to find any of my relatives. The most painful and galling feeling is the fact that I don't even have a picture left of my mother, father or brothers. Everything was thrown in the mud on that fateful day at Auschwitz in the fall of 1944.

The Abandonment of Mielec

Jack Sittsamer
b. Mielec, Poland, 1924

Our town was occupied on September 6, 1939, by the Germans. I lived in a mixed neighborhood in Mielec, Poland, near Krakow. In this town also lived my maternal grandmother, four aunts and four uncles. Some were married and had children, and some were single. My immediate family were my parents, Moshe Ytumer and Perla Sima Sittsamer; one older brother, Yisroel; myself; one younger brother, Joseph; and two younger sisters, Devorah and Gitla.

On March 9, 1942—a cold, dank, snowy morning—all the Jewish people of Mielec were ordered from their homes at 5:00 A.M. without any warning. I was seventeen years old. We assembled in the city square, about three thousand of us.

After the SS checked and rechecked that no one was overlooked, we were marched toward the Mielec Airport, about ten miles away. We didn't have time to grab warm clothing, and we had no idea of our destination. Guards and dogs in automobiles and on motorcycles, as well as foot soldiers, escorted us.

Many people could not keep up with the pace of the march. They were shot to death and were left in an open ditch. About two to three hundred people were shot, including my father. He could not keep up because of a leg wound he had received in the First World War, when he was a soldier in Emperor Franz Joseph's Austrian Army.

We arrived at the Mielec Airport in the afternoon. In an unheated airplane hangar, we were immediately divided into groups. Women and young children and older men on the right-hand side; young, able-bodied men on the left. My older brother and I went to the left. The people to the right were herded into box cars, like cattle. That was the last time I saw my beautiful mother, my two little sisters and my younger brother.

Shortly after the train pulled away, the seven hundred of us that were left were divided into groups and were shipped out to various camps. My brother and I were separated, and I never saw him again.

I am the sole survivor from my family.

A Shtetl's Life Is Ended

Moshe Baran
b. Horodok, Poland, 1920

On September 17, 1939, the Soviet army crossed the border of Poland from the east, while the German army entered from the west. The Polish army collapsed. The Germans and Soviets, by previous agreement, divided Poland. Our shtetl, the village of Horodok, fell to the Soviets.

Life as we knew it came to an end. All Jewish activities stopped. People active in the community and those belonging to the bourgeois class were arrested and deported.

The Communist Party with the help of a few local, and until then clandestine, Jewish communists took over the town. Mass meetings with communist orators spewing propaganda were held to "brainwash" us. Occasional arrests continued. Secrecy and spying on neighbors became a way of life.

Little did we suspect that the Russian occupation was heaven compared to what followed. In a surprise attack on June 22, 1941, the Germans broke the resistance of the Soviets and within a few days reached Horodok.

A period of terror began. Jews in leadership positions disappeared. The yellow star was to be worn front and back. Walking on the sidewalks was forbidden. No schools, no trade, no free movement. We were forced to do denigrating labor—with bare hands, pulling grass from between cobbled stones in the market square. Military vehicles roared through the town, sending some into hiding while others trembled or scurried aimlessly, looking for an escape. There was no place to go.

The Germans demanded that we establish a committee, the "Judenrat," to carry out their orders. Extortions—demands for specific amounts of gold, silver, and valuables—followed. The Jews complied, under the illusion that temporary safety might be bought.

The Germans enlisted local gentiles into the police. They became loyal and eager collaborators. A schoolmate of mine who joined the police was "kind" enough to take my watch during a sudden night intrusion into our house.

Early in 1942, a ghetto was established at Horodok. Eight hundred dehumanized souls were herded into an area where approximately three hundred had lived. Among them were my family—father, mother, brother, and two sisters. Barbed wire was strung around the ghetto and guards were posted. Entrance and exit were restricted.

Hunger and sickness set in. People exchanged their diminishing possessions with the few gentiles who were willing to provide clandestine food.

Eventually the Germans allowed our gentile neighbors to take over our abandoned homes and possessions. Thus, they became accomplices, often active collaborators in the persecutions and murders—to make sure that the former owners never returned.

Survivors from neighboring towns reported the annihilation of whole communities. Our ghetto was one of the few remaining ones in the area. We realized that the end was imminent. A few of us began to plan an escape, or as a last resort, resistance.

We searched for money and weapons. When this news reached the "Judenrat," they called us in. They had the difficult job of trying to postpone the inevitable. On a daily basis they struggled to maintain a balance between brutal German extortions and threats, and some bits of Jewish life.

"Do you realize what the consequences will be if you resist or escape?" they asked. "Do you know what will happen to the rest of us, including your families?"

We had no answer but silence.

The organized effort ceased. Many young men left the ghetto for the surrounding forest. Others were ordered, through the Judenrat, to work in neighboring work camps. My brother Josh was sent to Molodeczno and I to Ghetto Krasny, where my younger sister, Musia, joined me a few weeks later.

By July 1942, rumors reached the Horodok ghetto of German troop movements on the outskirts of town. Some people hid in previously prepared bunkers—my father, mother, and other sister among them. Some slipped out under cover of darkness. During the night the roar of trucks and motorcycles was distinctly heard. The ghetto was surrounded by SS troops and local police—our former neighbors and classmates. A large convoy of empty German military trucks pulled up to the ghetto gates. The soldiers and police entered the ghetto, shouting for everybody to leave their houses.

"*Heraus, heraus,*" they harangued.

As the people stepped outside, they were pushed toward the trucks and loaded into them. Children were torn from their parents, older people who fell to the ground were shoved onto the trucks like cattle.

The loaded trucks, accompanied by the SS on motorcycles, headed out of town. The destination was a large barn on an isolated hill. Here the people were unloaded and forced inside the barn.

Once inside, they were machine-gunned and set on fire.

Thus came the brutal and hideous end to the town of Horodok, a thousand-year-old, vibrant Jewish community.

Those who escaped into the nearby forests eventually joined the partisans. Later, one group returned to the town. They burned down some areas, primarily the town center, which had belonged to the vanished Jewish community.

Literally and figuratively, local collaboration was thus to some degree avenged.

What Ever Happened to the Jews of Skudvil?

Leon Brett
b. Skudvil, Lithuania, 1922

Esther Levy used to live on our street. She hadn't changed much in the years of hiding, except that she was pale and her countenance had hardened. We talked for several hours; she told me what had happened to the Jews of Skudvil, Lithuania.

I went to see her right after I heard that a Lithuanian man who lived near Skudvil was hiding a young woman from our town. At the time, I was with a Jewish partisan group moving about in the Lithuanian countryside. I went to my Lithuanian friend, Praniukas, and asked him to take me there. As always, he readily agreed.

I felt safe in his wagon—two peasant boys going to market. We timed it to approach the vicinity of the town when it got dark.

The Germans had occupied Skudvil the day in 1941 when the war between Russia and Germany started. At my father's insistence, I had fled east.

The Lithuanians immediately had begun to terrorize the Jews. My father was one of the first victims, Esther Levy told me. Petras Staniunas came to our house looking for me. Because my father said that he did not know where I was, Petras slapped him and tore his beard. "I can still see the blood running down his face," Esther said.

I vaguely remembered Staniunas. He was a teacher. He was always well dressed, in gray suits. He once said that he liked gray suits because that's what the American president, Roosevelt, wore.

On the 23rd day of the month of Tamuz, all men were ordered to assemble at the market place. Staniunas was in charge and gave orders to his Lithuanian helpers. Our teacher, Oshrin, approached the German who seemed to oversee everything and asked him why only Jewish men were ordered to assemble here. Without any hesitation, the German shot him. He then asked if anyone else had any questions. Obviously no one did. He promptly motioned to the Lithuanians and they marched all men to a wooded area several miles away and killed them. "Your sister's husband, Meir Sherf, also died that day," Esther Levy said.

For some reason my father wasn't there. But three days later, he and the rabbi from the neighboring village of Upine were taken away and forced to dig their own graves.

Several weeks later all women and children were taken away and put in barracks without roofs. "You can imagine what it was like when it was raining," she said. She was with my sister, Feige Sherf, and her two children, Rivale and Shifrale. To calm her children, my sister would tell them that their father would come soon and take them home.

There my sister gave birth to her third child, a little girl. They named her Chaya, which in Hebrew means life. Esther Levy said, "She was a beautiful child and the marvel of the camp. We took it as a good omen. Certainly God would not bring forth a new soul and let it be destroyed. Our spirits were raised."

Rebbitzen Masha recited from the *sidur,* which she was always carrying: "God is gracious and merciful." She promised that for Rosh Hashana everybody would be home, and even the men would come back. How could a rabbi's wife be wrong?

On the 23rd day of Elul, exactly one week before Rosh Hashana, they were all taken out and killed. Even tiny Chaya wasn't spared.

"How did you survive?" I asked Esther Levy.

She said that several days before that happened, she ran away. She also knew of three other women and one young boy who were hiding out. "Including me," she said, "as far as I know, only six of the thousand Jews of our town are still alive."

The last thing she said to me was: "Your Mother Shifra was smart. She died a long time ago. Way before this war."

We parted hoping to see each other after the war.

On the way back, Praniukas and I went through Skudvil. It was still dark.

I stood in the middle of the town where I was born and had lived for nineteen years. I knew every house, every door and window. Jews had lived in all these houses. They were all killed, and Lithuanians lived there now. You murdered and also inherited. The destruction of my community was real. What did not seem real was that I was still living.

There in the corner, the church was still standing as secure as ever behind its massive stone wall. And it always will.

I went to our synagogue. They had converted it to living quarters for the Lithuanians. Our *shul* where we "learned a page" every day and prayed three times a day is no more and never will be.

We went to my house. Lithuanians lived there now. You murdered my family and inherited my house.

Staniunas came here, beat my father; blood was running down his face. My father suffered because of me, because I ran away. It was not an evenhanded struggle. Staniunas was born with a gun in his hand and hate in his heart. Reb Shmuel was born with a book in his hand and compassion in his heart. You see, a gun and hate are stronger than a book and compassion.

I was deep in thought, but Praniukas nudged me and said, "Day will break soon, we must leave." So we left Skudvil in the early morning darkness.

III. Ruthlessness as a System

The German government developed an extremely efficient system for handling the Final Solution. The pattern set in Germany in the 1930s was repeated in occupied countries later: Jews were identified, civil liberties restricted and property confiscated, work denied; then Jews were forced to wear the Jewish star and forbidden to use public facilities. Finally, Jews were dislocated: assembled in ghettos, cities, or transit camps and deported to death camps in the east, where they were murdered en masse.

What this brutal system of dislocation and slaughter was like for its victims has been told by many survivors. Holocaust history books and survivor testimonies have shown us about life in the ghettos under the Nazis: the starvation, disease, crowding; forced labor; SS "actions" where young children, old people, and sick people were taken away and killed. We have heard from many witnesses what it was like to be transported: the cattle cars—people crowded, stifling, enduring hunger and terrible stench, dying while standing on their feet; the "selections" upon arrival at the concentration camps, which only the young and unencumbered might pass, while the rest were sent immediately to their death; the incredible life in the concentration camps, with hours-on-end roll calls, brutal labor, starvation, crowding, disease, and the constant threat of death.

However, these stories cannot be told too often: not only because history demands that we know the truth, but also because we can only begin to understand this truth in terms of the personal ordeals of the victims.

Stories in this section provide those truths in detail. "In the Dark" makes us aware of how helpless Jews felt upon being deported, never knowing where or what was intended for them, seeing family members mysteriously taken away. "Dachau" gives us a graphic picture of what it was like to arrive at and become an inmate of a concentration camp. "The Tenth Woman on Block Ten" quietly describes the plight of women victims of inhuman medical experiments at Auschwitz, where many were sterilized. "The Gypsies" strikes upon one woman's experience of another infamous event: the overnight liquidation of thousands of gypsies at Auschwitz. The pattern set up for handling the "Jewish problem" in Germany happens again, in "The Law in Lithuania." The ruthlessness of Romanian gendarmes who carried out German policies in the Ukraine, after the German invasion, is meticulously detailed in "Horrors of War." In this story we experience through another writer the agony of dislocation, transport on cattle cars, death marches, forced labor and ghetto existence. Although there is some rare expression of hope in these stories, most end with despair—the scar, as one writer has put it, which can never fade.

What is most important about these stories is their ability to convey, in simple and restrained language, through individual eyes, that which is essentially inexpressible. We cannot help but ache with (even though we can hardly imagine) the physical weariness, hunger, thirst, and extremes of heat or cold the victims went through. We can feel how chaos and humiliation, sudden and unpredictable changes, and arbitrary murders made victims feel helpless and hopeless in the ghettos and camps. What must it be like to get through a daily selection, only to believe that death was merely postponed until the next one? As readers, we must stretch behind and under the words, which are in themselves, as the writers knew, inadequate to tell the horror of these nightmares.

A.B.

In the Dark

Ernest Light
b. Uzhorod, Czechoslovakia (became Ungvár, Hungary), 1920

 T he Germans were excellent at deception, at keeping us in the dark.

They invaded Hungary in March 1944. After Passover, on April 18, Jews were ordered to pack up to fifty kilograms of the most important necessities and gather at the synagogue. They told us we were being sent to Germany to work, because the German men were fighting in the front lines.

They took us by train to a nearby city. That evening, my family—my father, mother, brother, sister and her child, and I—found ourselves in an abandoned brick factory, in cramped quarters. Every day more people arrived from the surrounding commmunity.

All kinds of rumors circulated about where we would be taken. Some said to Austria, some said to Germany. On May 24, all of us were told to pack up again, that we were being "relocated."

The next day we arrrived at Auschwitz. We had no idea where we were or what to expect. As we got off the freight wagons, SS men with dogs and a whole crew of men in striped uniforms hollered, "*Heraus, heraus, schnell, schnell.*" Most of us were in a daze—children crying, holding on to their mothers' skirts and dresses; older people had to be carried out.

The women were sent to one side, the men to the other side.

Then came the selection. I alone from my family was sent with the young men who seemed to be in good health. The older men and children—my father and brother among them—were sent to the other side.

Those who were selected to our side were ordered into a big barrack where we were told to undress, put our clothing in order, and remember where we left it, so that when we got back from the showers we would have no difficulty finding it. When we came out of the showers we didn't have to look for our clothes. Each of us got a striped uniform and a pair of clogs.

In the morning came the same reception, "*Heraus, heraus, schnell, schnell.*" As we assembled in the courtyard, we inquired about our families from those who had arrived a few days before us. They answered us, "Look up." We saw smoke and smelled the stench. "This is where your family went to," the prisoners told us.

We were handed cards to fill out the vital information—date of birth, name, home country, and occupation.

At that time Jews from Hungary were arriving daily at Auschwitz, by the thousands. The Germans had to send some of us to other camps to make room for the new arrivals. About the third day, the stronger ones were put on a train and taken to Warsaw. Here we met prisoners from Bohemia, Slovakia, Belgium, and Greece. They told us where we were and what our job would be.

The next day I filled out another card. Again they wanted all the vital information. Only one thing was different this time: they used the cards of those who had perished during the early spring, after a severe winter. The used side of the card had the name and number of the deceased one. I wound up with the number 3339.

Two days later, about twenty of us were told to line up separately, that we would be taken somewhere else to work. A military truck pulled up, and we got on. A canopy was put over us so we couldn't see where we were being taken to.

The dark under the canopy was nothing new to us.

Theresienstadt

George Lauer
b. Hamburg, Germany, 1907

A Professional "Career"

In early 1943 my wife Edith and I were deported from Prague to the concentration camp Theresienstadt (Terezin), located about 60 miles north of Prague in the heart of Bohemia. Because of my background as a chemist I was attached to the Sanitation Department, called *Entwesung*—a peculiar German word. This department was concerned with general hygiene and with fighting insects.

My first job was to distribute baited rat poison and, the next day, to collect the rats. Amusing as it may sound, this job saved Edith's and my life!

Terezin was an intermediate camp. Transports, usually about a thousand people, were brought in frequently from all over Europe, and just as frequently transports were sent out of Terezin.

During the time of my "Rat Patrol" Edith and I were ordered into the next transport. But the head of the *Entwesung* stormed to the "Elder" in protest, claiming that nobody knew where my rat poison was distributed, and that they would have mass poisoning! We were taken off the list as being indispensable for the camp.

Soon after this I was made second in command of the department and assigned to more serious work, like the gassing of the large barracks when the plague of fleas and bedbugs became intolerable. The gassing was done with Zyklon, which was essentially hydrogen cyanide, a volatile liquid whose vapors cause death within moments. Wearing gas masks, we applied several hundred kilos to a building, which within less than twenty-four hours was free of insects.

I was also in charge of the delousing bath, a measure to prevent typhus outbreaks. Typhus is a bacterial disease which was prevalent in eastern Europe. It frequently results in death. It cannot be transmitted directly from one person to another; the bacteria have to go through the body of a louse to be effective. In other words, if a louse stings a person who has typhus and then stings another person, the latter is almost certain to be infected. Since lice were frequent where people were crowded together, as in army barracks or in concentration camps, only vigorous exclusion of lice would prevent a deadly epidemic.

Somehow, the original five thousand "pioneers" to Terezin were able to instill the fear of typhus into the Gestapo. The Gestapo then supplied us not only with all materials necessary for a delousing bath, but also with buildings, including a former brewery complex with a steam plant. They then ordered that all persons arriving in Terezin be kept in quarantine until they were deloused.

Our delousing procedure, following Czech army rules, was as follows. New arrivals were marched from their holding halls in groups of thirty to the bath, men and women in separate groups, and led to a large room with benches. They undressed and all their belongings were hung on pallets. Helpers carried these belongings out and stacked them in gas chambers in the court yard where they were treated with Zyklon. Fans blew everything free of gas in minutes.

The naked people lined up to have their body hair shaved off by our two physicians, who used long, old fashioned razors. To my knowledge, nobody was ever cut, but the doctors didn't like their jobs very much. One day I got them some help. We were treating a transport from Hungary, when a pretty young woman came to me, told me that she was a beautician and would like to help. She got the job and for many months shaved men and women all over and seemed always happy.

After being shaved the people went under showers. We had about twenty, with hot and cold water. The people got some war-time soap, and for their heads they got some very harsh soap. Then they each walked into a small booth where our specialist checked their heads for lice. They were given towels or robes to wait for their clothes.

My job was to keep everything flowing. I wore a white doctor's coat and walked through all this commotion, dissolving bottlenecks by getting extra people, supervising the gas chambers, and mediating quarrels between our key workers. Mainly, however, I talked to the new arrivals who were understandably very nervous, reassuring them and listening to their stories. Since it took twenty-four hours to process a thousand people, we had several shifts, except for me who had to be there for the whole time. Considering our malnutrition, it was surprising how much the three hundred or more people engaged in this could achieve.

One day my foreman ran over to me, saying that the Gestapo commandant, *Obersturmbannführer* Rahm, was stalking around there. I went out and introduced myself. He asked what these "machines" were for. I explained, but he mumbled that this was all over his head. Then he said "*Danke Schon, Herr Doktor*" and with Gestapo bearing walked off. Facing him I was scared, but his politeness eased my fear. I suspect that my height (6 feet, 3 inches) and my North German accent impressed him.

During the last few weeks of the war we were put to a real test. Within a few days the Nazis pushed into the camp about twenty-five thousand prisoners from other camps. They intended to kill everybody with Zyklon gas, of which they had large stores. The rapid advance of the Russian army forced the Nazis to flee in a hurry and we all survived. However, since we were unable to delouse so many people upon arrival, and many of them were full of lice, we developed a great epidemic of typhus which took several months to eradicate. The Russians who liberated us were well aware of the situation; we reversed our procedure so that people went through delousing just prior to repatriation. Because of that and because of the difficulty of transportation it took several months to liquidate the camp, much to the disgust of Russian officials. Edith and I and some of our key people remained during that time, officially as employees of the reinstated Czech government, which even paid us a little salary.

To the East

The inmates in Terezin changed constantly as transports came in from Germany, Hungary, and other countries and, just as frequently, went out "to the East." We knew that going East was not good, but we assumed people would go to labor camps where they might be worked to death.

Sometime in 1944 I learned what "East" meant. One night I was awakened and told to come to the delousing bath. There were two women, mother and daughter, from a prominent Jewish family of Prague. My orders were to delouse them. And they were really full of lice, more so than I had ever seen. The two women were taken through our procedure, while their clothing was treated in one of our gas chambers. After the bath we gave them some robes and then started to talk.

The women had been taken from Auschwitz, a camp in Poland (we did not know why or how, nor did we ever learn what happened to them after they were delivered back to Gestapo headquarters). They told us what Auschwitz was: an extermination camp! The people arriving there in the transports were marched past a few Gestapo men who separated out some able-bodied persons; the rest were marched, in groups, into a delousing bath similar to ours. There was a difference, though: out of the shower heads, instead of hot water, came Zyklon. In a few minutes everybody was dead, soundlessly! After venting, some prisoners came in and dragged out the bodies and threw them into huge furnaces while a new group entered the "bath." The whole operation was so well organized that five thousand people literally disappeared in twenty-four hours. This then was what "transports to the East" meant!

The three or four of us who were present were of course stunned and kept it secret, except that I told Edith and reported it to the Jewish "Elder."

In 1992 when we visited Prague with our sons we made a bus tour to Terezin. The town had returned to civilian life but there was a large memorial area beautifully maintained by the state. Where the railroad track had been, there was a bronze plaque with the following inscription:

FROM THIS PLACE THOUSANDS
OF PRISONERS FROM THE TEREZIN GHETTO
STARTED ON THEIR LAST JOURNEY.

Dachau

Arnold Blum
b. Nuremberg, Germany, 1922

After three hours of travel on the Autobahn, our bus turned into the town of Dachau, fifteen miles from Munich. The date was Friday, the 11th of November, 1938. A few minutes later we pulled up along a railroad siding where other buses were parked. SS men approached. The driver opened the door.

Stiff-limbed from our trip, we had some difficulty obeying the shouted orders of the SS to get off the bus and line up.

While standing in formation I observed other buses being unloaded. One man, who had apparently lost consciousness on the trip, was removed from his bus by an SS man pulling him by the ankles. This caused the man's head to hit each of the steps leading down from the bus. The shock and pain revived him. After being dumped on the ground he flailed his arms and legs through the air, thereby inadvertently kicking his tormentor. The latter, in a blind rage, jumped on his victim, stomping and kicking him into submission with his hobnailed boots. The other Jews from this bus also bore marks of abuse. Black eyes and raised welts on their faces were commonplace. I learned later that these people came from Vienna, where the treatment accorded them had been particularly brutal.

After being counted we were marched in the direction of the camp. I saw a large quadrangle, surrounded by an electrified barbed-wire fence, perhaps ten feet high. Machine gun towers were manned by helmeted SS. We approached a gate house with a tall double gate made of steel. One of these bore the legend: *ARBEIT MACHT FREI,* Work Makes Free. The gate was opened and closed again after we entered.

Our guard escort marched us onto a large field we would soon learn to call *Appellplatz,* the drill field. It separated the prisoner barracks on our left from the administration complex on our right. The prisoners were housed in wooden, one-story huts, arranged evenly on both sides of the *Lagerstrasse,* the Camp Street—eighteen huts on each side.

We were marched to the barrack side of the field and were ordered to stand at attention facing the barracks. It was about mid-afternoon. We were cold and hungry. Worse yet, we had not been able to relieve ourselves since a foul-smelling pail in the Stuttgart cell had been available to us, many hours ago.

As far as I could tell out of the corners of my eyes, there were thousands of Jews standing at attention on the *Appellplatz,* to our left, our right and our rear.

In about an hour the sun went down and our discomfort increased. Moving my head ever so slightly, I noticed that some of my fellow prisoners had wet their pants. I waited for a guard to pass, quickly opened my fly to relieve myself outside my pants, and quickly closed it again. The odor of urine blended with that of burning peat moss which pervaded the entire area. Dachau is located at the edge of a large swamp from which peat was dug by the long-term prisoners.

About 9:00 P.M. we were marched down the camp street and ordered to break formation in front of a barrack located within a separate barbed-wire enclosure, a camp within the camp. We were ordered to remove our shoes outside the barrack and to place them in neat rows so we could find them again the next morning. We entered the hut in our stocking feet, to be received by a Kapo, a prisoner trustee who assigned us to our quarters. There were two rooms, each perhaps twenty feet square with double-decker platforms arranged in a U-shape along three walls. The two rooms shared a single washroom, housing a number of commodes and a circular, ceramic fountain on which cold water taps were arranged in a circle.

The platforms were straw-covered, the lower being about one foot and the upper about four feet off the floor. The Kapo had his own bed with a straw mattress and a blanket. He proceeded to initiate us in the working of the camp.

He explained that his barrack was a recidivist camp, housing prisoners who had been incarcerated for political "offenses," then had been released and arrested again. He explained the markings on his uniform. He had a red triangle and a red stripe on both his trousers and his jacket, the red triangle denoting a political prisoner and the red stripe his recidivist status. He also had his prisoner number on a white background on his trousers and his jacket. His head was shorn.

All prisoners were color coded, according to the Kapo. Green denoted a felon; purple, a *Bibelforscher* or a Jehovah's Witness; black, a shiftless person; pink, a homosexual; and yellow, a Jew.

He told us he was a Communist tailor from Bad Cannstadt, a suburb of Stuttgart, then asked for a show of hands of men over ninety years of age. There were two, one ninety-two and the other ninety-six years old. He wanted the oldest to use his bed, indicating he would sleep on the floor that night. He then cut up his own bread ration and passed it around. For most of us this was the only nourishment since morning or even the night before.

The washroom seemed a luxury after the episode on the drill field. We hurriedly washed ourselves with cold water but without soap and dried ourselves with our handkerchiefs. Then following the example set by the Kapo, we urged the elderly among us to sleep on the straw-covered platforms, while the younger ones would sleep on the floor.

We were packed very tightly. There was not even room for everyone to sleep on his side. I lay across other people's legs. There were no blankets, but the barrack was heated and the body heat was enormous. During the night those of us on the floor were stepped on by those going to and coming from the washroom. Yet we consoled ourselves with the realization that we were at least under a roof and not standing in the chill of the drill field.

We were awakened at five o'clock in the morning. Everyone crowded into the washroom. It was an achievement to be able to rinse one's mouth, not to speak of washing.

When we went out to recover our shoes we discovered that they had been thrown into one big heap, probably by the SS, their idea of a joke. The idea was not a novel one. Anyone familiar with *Till Eulenspiegel's Merry Pranks* will recognize this as one of the pranks described in the book. There was a tremendous scramble with everyone trying to find his own shoes. An SS man oversaw the proceedings with great mirth and urged us to hurry and fall into formation. I had big feet even at the age of sixteen and thus only had a limited choice of shoes from the pile. I wound up with two unmatched shoes, each much too small.

The day was to be dedicated to "processing" us into full-fledged prisoners. There would be no time for eating. We were first marched into one end of the administration building to be photographed and fingerprinted. The walls of this room were decorated with photographic enlargements of prisoners' faces, selected for their ugliness. From this room we were taken to an adjacent one, where we had to strip. Our clothes and their contents were collected and a receipt was issued, yet another example of the Nazi penchant for legality, regardless how atrocious the action taken.

I was shocked seeing my relatives and acquaintances standing naked before me. But we were not yet done with humiliation. Next the SS ordered us into another room to be shorn of our hair. Political prisoners acted as barbers. We were made to sit on wooden benches while our heads were shaved with electric clippers. The man attending me was a Social Democrat from the Sudetenland. He had been imprisoned when the Sudetenland was occupied by the Nazis after England and France sold out Czechoslovakia in the Munich Agreement.

Then we were herded into the shower. As we emerged, the SS guards took pleasure in hosing us down fore and aft, full blast. We were taken into yet another room for a "medical examination." We stood in line and were ordered to come to attention about eight feet from an SS "doctor" who looked us over from top to bottom, ordered us to do an about face and waved us off to get our prison clothes.

We received no underpants—only a nondescript shirt, a pair of socks, trousers and a jacket. These were of cotton twill, vertically striped black and white, and marked with a yellow Star of David and a white tape to which our camp number would be applied.

No attempt was made to fit the uniforms to our bodies. I drew a jacket and trousers made for a much shorter and stouter man, in that the trouser legs barely covered my knees and the sleeves came about one hand's width below my elbows. I had to take up mightily on the trouser drawstring to keep the pants from falling down.

We looked at each other and sadly shook our heads. We were made to form up and were marched to our "permanent" barrack. I drew Block 12, *Stube* (Room) 3. A Kapo from Berlin whose uniform was marked with a green triangle, the symbol for a felon, was in charge. A rough character addicted to picturesque obscenities, he had been convicted of armed robbery. Each of us drew a spoon, two of us shared an aluminum pot to eat from, and four of us shared a toothbrush. We were all assigned a spot on the sleeping platforms.

The Kapo lectured us on the camp rules. There was a grass strip about eight feet wide on the inside of the fence. Anyone stepping on this strip was liable to be shot without warning from the towers or by a guard on the ground. The Kapo told us never to step on the strip, even if ordered to do so, as there had been cases when such orders were obeyed with fatal results.

We would be marched to the drill field every morning and evening to be counted. There would be no food until the count was accepted by the SS. In the unlikely event of an escape, no prisoner could eat until the escapee was caught and returned. Anyone dying during the day or night had to be carried to the drill field for the count.

We would not be allowed out of the barracks after dark. The streets between barracks were scanned with searchlights from the towers. Anyone found outside was liable to be shot.

In the presence of an SS man we were to stand at attention until told otherwise. Our names were not to be used. Instead we were to refer to ourselves as *Schutzhaftjude,* Jew in Protective Custody, and our camp number. We could request money from home and spend it in the canteen.

On the evening of our second day in camp we were ordered to fall in outside the barracks. The Kapo made us count off. He then ordered us to march toward the camp street where we were ordered "Column Right," which brought us in line with the drill field. The entire camp street was filled with columns of prisoners, marching to the cadence counted by the Kapos. At the field we took our position for the count.

It was dusk, the air was damp and chilly. The odor of burning peat moss hovered over us in an all-pervading cloud.

We shivered in our thin cotton uniforms and our stomachs growled. During the preceding thirty-six hours most of us had eaten only a small piece of bread, donated by the kindly recidivist Kapo the night before. A feeling of weakness overshadowed most other sensations. Yet we had to stay upright and alert. My surroundings seemed unreal as I stood at attention surrounded by my fellow Jews in their striped uniforms with shorn heads, shadows unmoving as the sun went down.

Off in the distance we heard the Kapos report to the SS, shouting the number of *Schutzhaftjuden* in their units. The SS guards, in their warm uniforms, strode up and down the columns, trying to reconcile the Kapos' count with their own. The count had to be repeated a number of times.

There was a commotion in our rear, but none of us dared to look. After some minutes there were whispers that a man had dropped in formation. We heard shouts from the same direction, addressed to the fallen man's neighbors who had broken formation to come to his aid. Finally, an order was given to carry the casualty to the rear where he was kept lying on the ground till the count was accepted by the SS. The man was later taken to the dispensary, a place we would soon learn to avoid at any cost.

The evening count completed, we were ordered to march back to our barrack, our Kapo counting cadence and yelling obscenities at those out of step. We were halted in front of our barrack, given a "right face" and dismissed.

We each wrote a brief note home, trying to sound cheerful and requesting money for use in the canteen. We spent the evening talking with our fellow prisoners, trying to learn something about them. Several distant relatives were in my room and our common fate drew us together. All of us were weak from hunger and had no trouble falling asleep.

We were awakened before dawn and streamed into the washroom which was less crowded than the one in the recidivist barrack where we had spent the previous night. Some had risen early and had used the facilities while the rest were still sleeping, thus lessening the crush later on. We folded our blankets, straightened up the room, put on our shoes and jackets and got ready to fall in.

I still wore the unmatched pair of shoes which hurt my feet. We marched to the drill field with the Kapo counting cadence. The entire drill field, from one end to the other, was full of prisoners.

As we stood at attention for the count, the horizon gradually reddened and the top of the sun's fireball slowly appeared. I had never seen such a spectacular sunrise. The sky was clear and the air was cold. Though we shivered in our thin prisoner uniforms and our stomachs growled, this beautiful, natural spectacle gave us hope and almost a sense of triumph. There was, after all, a force in this world far superior to our oppressors. I was sure this force would ultimately prevail.

An orthodox Jew pronounces a blessing over all manifestations of the deity. I was not in this habit, but I wordlessly gave thanks to my maker for having given us this sunrise as a sign of hope. We would, I felt certain, survive this place of humiliation and degradation and defeat our oppressors.

Auschwitz, 1944

Jolene Mallinger
b. Hrabovo, Czechoslovakia, 1923

I arrived in Auschwitz around May 1944. The SS men were waiting for us. As we got off the train, there was panic, screaming and crying. After we were separated, we were taken to a place where we were shaved and changed into gray dresses.

What happened to our families, we did not know at the beginning. But we soon found out what the big chimneys were for.

We were put into overcrowded barracks with very little food. We were completely stripped of human dignity. Every morning we awoke at 4:00 A.M. to stand in the cold, rain, and all kinds of weather, while we were counted. It took hours.

There were selections every week during the six weeks I was in Auschwitz. The sick and the weak were selected and gassed. After the six weeks we were taken to Kristian Shtat to work in the ammunition factory, where we made guns.

The living conditions were a little better, but the work was a lot harder. We built railroad stations by cutting down trees in the woods.

Since the Allied and Russian fronts were closing in on us, we had to leave. We started to walk in January and walked for about six weeks. The weather was very cold, and we had no winter clothes. Most did not survive.

We marched to Bergen-Belsen. The Nazis had dumped all the prisoners there from all the other camps. There was no food or water; we were just waiting to die. We had to drag the dead bodies to one mass grave. We got sick from typhus. If the English army had not liberated us within a few days, none of us would have survived.

I was taken to a military hospital with malnutrition and typhus. I stayed in the hospital for three months. Then the Swedish Red Cross took us to Sweden for rehabilitation. Finally, we had new hope for life.

The Tenth Woman on Block Ten

Esther Haas
b. The Hague, Netherlands, 1919

When the Germans brought me to Auschwitz in the fall of 1943, I came with nine other women. I can't remember all of the names or even all the faces, but I remember that there were nine and I was the tenth woman in our group. We were all young married women in our late teens or early twenties. We knew each other from our *Hachsharah* (a group of young people learning to work the land in order to leave Holland and emigrate to Palestine). We planned to stay together if we could because we would have more strength together than each alone.

The SS trooper separated the young married women and made us stand at one area together. Then he marched us to Block Ten, which was in the middle of the men's barracks. It was a long gray building made out of stone. Inside there was a big stove built of tiles that served as the only source of heat for one hundred and fifty people. This was to be our home and our hell for the next two years.

We ten women managed to stand in a small group, so that we ended up with our bunks together. The wooden bunks were stacked three tiers high. The top beds were the choice picks because there was air up there; we could breathe. So we rotated bunks—we ten women gave what we could to help each other.

The Polish girls who were there already told us what was going to happen to us. We were to become, like them, a part of Dr. Mengele's experiments. He had bought us from the German government and he could do what he wanted to us. We were his property. We were to be his gynecological guinea pigs, and if we became sick or disabled, then came the gas.

We knew then that we had to stay strong—stay clean—stay together. We made each one wash every day. Only cleanliness could ward off typhus and cholera. The strong washed the weak. I was one of the strongest. With ice cold water and soap that felt like clay, I washed the women's backs and had them wash the front of their bodies when they could. Some of the girls had already given up and did not want to be washed. One girl in particular, Marta, already knew that her husband, a rabbi's son, had been gassed. We had to force her over to the buckets of water to wash. We made her stay alive.

We lived with a numbing routine. After roll call every morning came the watery tea for breakfast. Then most of the women went to the fields to work; but some were selected to go to the operating rooms that were located right in the barracks.

Because I had nursing experience, I stayed behind in the barracks to try to make the women who were used for the experiments comfortable, after their ordeal. Some did not want to talk; some were crying; some were moaning. I had no medicine; I could only comfort them, massage them and wash them with water.

I was picked only once to go into the dreaded operating rooms to be worked on, and I can only remember being injected internally. I never learned what they did.

No one ever said anything, but we women knew that these men who did terrible things to us were not doctors. They were barbers; they were technicians; they were ordinary men picked by Mengele to carry on his work.

One day the SS men decided that our lives were "too luxurious." We each had our own bunk, we each had a skimpy sweater and a used overcoat. We were Mengele's girls and these were our privileges. The SS men came and herded us out of the barracks and walked us to the gas chambers. We knew where they were taking us. We knew what the buildings meant. They walked us up to the very door of the gas chambers. We stood in shivering fear for what seemed like forever. I don't think we talked. I know we didn't cry. We were over crying by this time.

Then suddenly, they walked us back to Block Ten. My guess is that one of the "experimenters" must have called Dr. Mengele in Berlin, because their jobs would be over if they gassed Mengele's property. The doctor must have commanded the SS to hold onto us.

We were a door away from the gas chambers, but that day we ten all lived to go back to our bunks. In our barracks, our home, we ten women collapsed in joyous relief. The terror of Mengele's experiments seemed like nothing compared to the terror of the endless nothingness that came with the gas.

The Means to Survive

Ruth Weitz
b. Podhoritzin, Poland, 1929

Hitler's troops came to my village in Poland in the fall of 1941. Before that, retreating Russian soldiers had warned the villagers to flee with them to Russia. Unfortunately, many Jews did not believe the Russians and refused to leave Poland.

My father was a cattle broker who owned a farm; we lived comfortably. We, too, stayed in Poland.

The German troops moved swiftly. They forced all able-bodied Jews to work laying asphalt for the highways and sent them to live in concentration camps. My younger sister Rhoda, my younger brother Harold, and I were sent to concentration camps. Since I was older than the other two, I was sent to a different camp. Our parents were able to bribe the German soldiers with money and remain on their farm. In March of 1943, our parents were shot dead by drunken German soldiers.

Hoping to escape from the concentration camp, I had sewed coins inside the waistband of my dress before going there. Within the hem of my dress I sewed my mother's engagement ring, and I secured a gold chain inside my long braid of brown hair. I knew the consequences were death if I were caught, but I wanted to be prepared.

In the camp, I learned to use the money to advantage. It was known throughout the camp that certain soldiers could be bribed. Occasionally, when temperatures soared into the high nineties, some of the Jews, including me, would give solders money for a cup of water.

One day while I was laying asphalt for the highway, a German soldier approached me on a bicycle. He had been a friend of my father's before the war and was working for the Polish underground. He told me he had overheard the Germans saying they had no more use for the Jews and planned to execute everyone in both camps in a few days.

I quickly went to one of the soldiers who accepted bribes and offered him money so that I could visit with my sister and brother. He accepted the bribe but warned me to return to the camp before 6:00 A.M. the following morning so that I could continue working on the highway. A soldier escorted me on foot to the other camp, and I was able to warn my sister and brother.

When the opportunity for escape came, approximately two hundred out of the four thousand Jews in the camp escaped. I was engaged to marry a young man chosen by my family, named Saul; I escaped with him, his mother, brother, and his mother's sister.

My thirteen-year-old brother was caught during the escape and thrown into a truck to be taken back to camp. Along with the rest of the Jews in the camp, he was executed and thrown into a mass grave at the top of the hill. I was told that the earth moved for several days, as some were buried still alive that July day in 1943.

After escaping, I returned to my village and claimed my mother's coat and diamond earrings from a neighbor. I knew that if necessary, I would be able to sell them for food in the woods where I planned to hide.

Jews camped mostly in groups of ten inside the woods. My sister had fallen in love with an older man inside the concentration camp, and I wanted to be with Saul and his family, so we decided to separate and live in different camps.

To survive, we purchased food from the Ukrainians who came into the woods with supplies such as bread and potatoes. A loaf of bread might cost as much as $45.00, but we had no choice but to pay the high prices. I was forced to sell my mother's engagement ring for food to a Ukrainian man who was getting engaged. On his next visit to my camp, he told me that within three days his fiancee had lost the ring. He felt maybe my mother did not want him to have it.

Not all of the Ukrainians could be trusted. Some would befriend the Jews and ask where they were camping. As soon as they found out, they would turn the Jews over to the Germans. One Ukrainian woman invited a group of Jews to her home where she said she could provide them with supplies. Four men went with her; they never returned. The Gestapo was waiting inside her home.

That December, the Germans found my sister's camp. Everyone, including Rhoda, was executed.

My group, however, was never discovered. In the winter when the trees were bare we dug a grave in the snow and lived in it. By March the grave collapsed, and we needed to find a new hiding place.

In July of 1944, the Russians came into the woods and liberated the surviving hidden Jews. They sent the women, elderly, injured, and children back to their homes. All young, able-bodied men were sent to the Russian front in Germany to battle the Germans. My fiancé, Saul, was sent to the Russian front, where he was killed.

Finally, I returned to the village where my family had once lived. Neighbors were shocked to see me. They felt certain the Germans had killed me.

I gathered what little was left from my family, some linens and small belongings, and left, heading for the American zone of Germany.

The Gypsies

Ilona Weiss
b. Kosino, Czechoslovakia, 1923

In May 1944, my sister and I arrived at Auschwitz. They took us to the gypsy camp within Auschwitz. There were about twenty thousand gypsies there, and about ten thousand Hungarian girls in separate barracks.

It was a terrible place.

We had to get up at 2:00 A.M. for the *Appell,* the roll call. The Nazis would come and we would stand in line until seven, eight, or nine o'clock in the morning. At 2:00 A.M. it was very cold because we had only rags on, and we were freezing. Then when the sun came up, it beat down on us. This was very hard on us because we had shaved heads and were used to having a lot of hair. Many of us fainted. The Kapo slapped our faces so we would come to.

We envied the gypsy girls. They had their long hair and wore their own clothes, long dresses with ruffles. To us—shaven, in rags—they were beautiful. There were gypsy men, too. Cruel they were, slapping and teasing us whenever they got a chance. We would hide from them.

The rumor was that this was some sort of an experiment with the gypsies, this keeping young men and women together in a sort of "normal" environment, unlike the rest of the inmates.

And in what must have been their usual way, the gypsies were very noisy. We heard them singing and arguing at all hours. Then suddenly one morning, it was quiet.

I asked the Kapo, "What happened that the gypsies are so quiet?"

She pointed to the crematorium. She said that the gypsies were there, up in the crematorium. All twenty thousand of the young men and women gypsies were gone—all of them, in a single night.

The Nazis were very efficient.

Nazi Murderers

Violet Weinberger
b. Uzhorod, Czechoslovakia (became Ungvár, Hungary), 1928

The Killings

I saw it. I am an eyewitness.

Thousands of people arrived at Auschwitz every day. The Nazi murderers couldn't burn all the bodies in the crematoriums—they weren't big enough. They quickly came up with a solution. They burned the bodies in pits. And this went on twenty-four hours a day, seven days a week, for years.

The flames were sky high, like a towering inferno. The smell was awful, throughout the camp.

As if this wasn't enough, they shot people. They shot them outright, for no reason.

They hanged people.

Many times when we walked back from work to the concentration camp, we saw gallows erected. We knew there would be an execution.

The Nazis picked people to be hanged randomly. They made us watch the executions, and they left the bodies hanging there until the next morning. Then as we walked to work, they made us stop, and they told us to look at those bodies.

Each day, they selected people and killed them. They selected lots of women, young ones and not so young ones. They put them on open wagons. All the women believed that the Nazi murderers were taking them to be killed. I see them even today, crying and begging us to pray for them.

The Selections

Don't think that if you weren't killed the first day, your life was spared. Each day we stood in line for roll call while those murderers counted heads.

Sometimes they selected people to be killed, and sometimes they selected people for work. But they never told us where they were taking us.

One day the Nazis counted eight hundred people—and my mother, my four sisters and I were among them. We were sure they were going to kill us in the gas chambers. We walked, getting closer and closer to the inferno. We were so scared, so frightened. People were crying, praying, and saying goodbye to each other.

And then, suddenly, the Nazis detoured us. They took us to the railroad station.

For the time being, our lives were spared. They sent us to a different concentration camp in Latvia, where we worked for a few months. Then they took us to work in another concentration camp, Stutthof. So our daily hell continued—the selections and the killing and the dying.

How Many Made It?

Ernest Light

b. Uzhorod, Czechoslovakia (became Ungvár, Hungary), 1920

In the last days of July 1944, as the Russian troops were approaching Warsaw, the Germans decided to evacuate the Warsaw labor camp.

Orders were given to be ready for the next morning's trip. Old and sick people were not to take part in the march; they would be taken by wagons. (Of course, those who stayed never left the camp. They were shot and disposed of.)

In the morning about thirty-five hundred of us were assembled, counted, and recounted. We were on our way. As we walked we saw the Poles looking at us from their balconies, windows, and streets. "You *yids* will not last long. It's about time to get rid of you," they shouted.

One or two said, "Don't give up, the war will end soon."

We marched without food and without water. The sun beat down on us. Those who fell or couldn't keep up were gotten rid of by the Germans on the spot.

At midday we reached a river. We were permitted to drink from the slimy, stinking water. While we were in the water, the German guards watched us from the bridge. After a short while they shouted at us, "Get out of the water, *schnell*." Most of us ran out. Those who either didn't have the strength or didn't hear the orders were machine gunned. One of the victims, I remember, was a young man who was deaf.

The river ran red with blood.

Arriving finally at the town of Kutno, we waited for cattle cars to pick us up. The heat continued to be unbearable.

The train trip was the worst experience of all. Squeezed together, we endured more heat, hunger, and above all thirst. Thirst is almost impossible to describe: it does things to you, both mentally and physically. Many hallucinated, went berserk. After a day or two many died.

Those who survived at least had more room to lie down. Either they lay on top of the dead, or the dead were piled up in a corner to make room.

I don't know how we managed to get out of the cars when we arrived. I felt barely alive. I haven't the slightest idea how many of the thirty-five hundred who left Warsaw, marching before the Russian Army, reached our destination at Dachau.

The Law in Lithuania

Leon Brett
  b. Skudvil, Lithuania, 1922

The Jail on Traku Street

It happened in the middle of the night. It was not a knock at the door, it was a bang at the door. Two Lithuanians with rifles burst in. They went from room to room and pulled everybody from their beds. We want all men, get dressed. They shouted, "*Skubek!*" which means fast. They took me and my cousin with whom I was staying after fleeing from my own home.

My cousin's mother wanted to give us food. "They won't need any more food," the Lithuanians yelled. Why shouldn't we need food? What if we get hungry? I was puzzled.

We were on the street. It was dark. Lithuanian police, serving the German occupation forces, were chasing Jewish men from their homes. There was a pogrom atmosphere in the street.

A woman begged for her husband. She wanted to go with him. "Right now we want only men. Your turn will come later."

A woman begged for her young son. He is sick. "We'll cure his sickness in a minute." How do you cure someone's sickness in a minute? I was puzzled.

We were brought to the market place. There were a lot of Jews sitting on the cobblestones with their hands up. Lithuanians with rifles were rushing back and forth, counting their prisoners. *Vienas, du, trys,* they counted in Lithuanian and took them away.

When a father was separated from his son, he begged that they should stay together. "Don't worry, you'll wind up in the same place." And the Jewish father thanked God. They will wind up in the same place together after all.

And then my turn came. Many of us were marched off to Traku Street. There the gates of a big jail opened and we were marched inside the courtyard. After an orgy of beatings, we were ordered to give our name and occupation. Then they started counting again: *vienas, du, trys,* ten, fifty, seventy. We were taken to a cell in the jail. Seventy men were put in a cell of about twenty-five by twenty-five feet.

There were seven cots, or rather steel frames, with steel nets in the middle, on each side of the wall. A total of fourteen cots. They were attached to the wall by means of a hinge and could be put up against the wall. It was obvious that seventy men cannot sleep on fourteen cots. So the cots were up against the wall

all the time, and we slept on the floor. Even the floor was too small for seventy people.

The jail in Shavel, Lithuania was my home for the summer of 1941. It was the only life we knew.

The summer of 1941 was not a good summer for me and the other sixty-nine Jews in my cell. It was a hot summer. The room was closed with no ventilation. We were never allowed to work and never allowed to wash. There was a barrel in the middle of the room. There we would urinate and eliminate our waste. We were not given toilet paper. Sometimes they would send the barrel back without a lid and sometimes even dry without water. The smell was unbearable. Lice traveled from one man to another. Lice thrive in filth. They settle in your clothes and in your hair. There is no way to get rid of them.

It was a hot summer. The heat in our cell was unbearable. Seventy people in such a small space. It was stifling, suffocating. There was precious little air coming in from the outside through the one small window. The window was also rather high from the floor. Obviously, everybody wanted to be close to it. To be fair, we formed a line and marched along the walls of our cell so that everyone should have the same chance to walk by the window and get a breath of air from the outside. If one lingered, the others would urge him to move on— "Don't be selfish, we also have to breathe."

After a while, we lost count of the days and were not sure what day of the week it was. However, someone always claimed to keep track of time—of days, of weeks.

Our cell was on the third floor. When we looked down through the only window in the cell, we could see the courtyard. There was a mass of people— Russian prisoners of war. The courtyard was the only life they knew. I never saw them getting any food. There they slept. There they urinated and there they eliminated their waste. When it rained, they got soaked. You couldn't even call them human beings. When you looked down, all you saw was a mass of military greatcoats. There was a wagon in constant motion, and when a greatcoat seemed to move no more, other greatcoats picked it up and dumped it into the wagon. That went on day and night. It never stopped. And that was how thousands and thousands of war prisoners died that summer.

One day we were told to line up and were taken outside to weed a garden. We were warned not to eat from the garden, not even a blade of grass. If one of us was suspected of putting something from the garden into his mouth, the Lithuanian guard would hit him with his fist. A lot of teeth were knocked out that day. When we were finished, we had to open our mouths so that they could see that no trace of food was there. Not even a blade of grass. But as humiliating as it was when we were brought back to the cell, the weeding raised our morale a bit. There was still a world outside.

My thoughts often wandered back to my home town, which I had escaped the first day of the war. What is happening there? Does my family know that I have been locked up in a terrible jail all summer? Is it possible that things there are not very bad; that I just had the bad luck to be in the wrong place at the wrong time, where the local Lithuanians acted on their own? Perhaps any day the heavy door to our cell will open, and a German officer will appear, tell us that it was all a mistake, and let us go to our homes. He might even apologize.

One day the cell door did open and a German officer entered. He was mild-mannered and polite. He asked if anyone would volunteer to go to work on a farm. He apologized for conditions in the prison cell. In Germany, he said, it couldn't happen. Only the primitive Lithuanians could keep us in conditions like that. Yes, he would take five men to work on a farm. *Geehrter Herr*—honorable sir, the Jews begged, please take me. The next day, he came back and took five more men. The Jews volunteered. They were eager to go and waited for him to come back. He came back many times and our cell became emptier and emptier.

Then one day at the end of the summer, the cell door opened and my name was called, Leibas Bretas—I was freed.

Why was I freed? A Jew named Fomberg, who was in charge of jewelry shops, used to make jewelry for the German officers. My cousin gave him money to bribe one of the Germans. He said that he needed me to work in one of his shops. I was freed, and my nightmare was over.

When I came to my cousin's house and looked in a mirror, I did not recognize myself. I was pale and had a long beard. I couldn't enter my cousin's house. I had to shave off all the hair from my head and body in the backyard. That was the only way to get rid of the lice. I washed and became clean again.

Among the thousands of Jewish men who were taken out of their beds that terrible night when the Germans first came, several hundred wound up in that jail on Traku Street. The rest were promptly killed. From the several hundred who wound up in that jail, about one hundred were freed. The Jews who volunteered for farm work never got to a farm. So that was how the Jewish men of Shavel, Lithuania, were dealt with.

Traku Ghetto

How was life for the Jews in Shavel, Lithuania, under the Germans in 1941? One ordinance after another was announced:

(1) Jews must wear yellow stars on back and chest.

(2) Jews cannot walk on the sidewalks. They must walk on the street.

(3) Jews cannot engage in business or professions.

(4) Finally, by a certain date, all Jews must move into a ghetto.

(5) Any Jew found outside the ghetto will be shot, and any Lithuanian caught hiding a Jew will be severely punished.

So all the Jews of Shavel moved into the ghetto. And so did I, walking with two bundles of my belongings. One in each hand. I was walking on the street next to the sidewalk as I was supposed to. Two German officers stopped me. "Hat off, *Schwein*," they shouted. "We'll teach you to respect a German officer." They slapped me with their hands and kicked me with their boots, and my two bundles of the only possessions I owned scattered on the cobblestones. Lithuanians, men and women, young and old, gathered around and cried, "Officer, you've got a gun, use it. The only good Jew is a dead Jew!"

I finally broke away from the mob. The bleeding stopped and the wounds healed, but the fear caused by the shouting was with me for a long time: "Officer, you've got a gun, use it."

What was the ghetto like? The ghetto was surrounded with barbed wire. There was one gate through which we could enter or leave to go to work. There were armed guards at the gate. Watch towers with armed guards were around the ghetto. The guards were mostly Lithuanian and sometimes Ukrainian. The ghetto was named Traku, after that section of town.

The police inside were Jewish. They had rubber clubs and white armbands.

Every family was given one room. If a house had five rooms, it was for five families. There were six people in the room that I was assigned to. There was space for only three beds, so we slept two in a bed. We never became used to the congestion and hunger.

Of all days, Sunday was the worst. Soldiers and officers came to the ghetto with cameras and took pictures to send to their parents, wives, and *Fräuleins*. See what we accomplished—men, women, and children in ghettos, scared and hungry with six-point yellow stars on their chests and backs. *Untermenschen*. I did not like my picture to be taken, so I stayed indoors on Sunday.

The ghetto was next to a leather factory. It was said that the Germans established the ghetto and let it exist for such a long time because leather is so important in war, and the Jews could keep the factory going.

The Judenrat, the Jewish council, was in charge of all internal matters. They would assign where people went to work. They would make up the lists. Everybody had to go to work. In the morning, thousands of men and women assembled at the gate, formed lines and were marched off, accompanied by armed guards. The largest number worked at the leather factory. Everybody had to wear a yellow star on chest and back.

The first winter I was assigned to work for Urmanas, a Lithuanian jeweler. He also owned a farm. He sold food on the black market in a back room. Although he knew that I was hungry, he enjoyed eating in front of me—meat, bread, and butter. He never gave me food. He said that it was against the law. He said that he liked me. It's too bad that all Jews are not like me. The Jews are communists and capitalists. Hitler is really a medicine that they need. If it weren't for the Americans, the war would be over fast. It's the fault of their Jewish president. His name is really Rosenfeld.

One day Urmanas said to me, "The Jews of Sidluva were forced to dig their own graves and then were shot."

At the end of the day I was taken back to the ghetto. At night when I was in bed, I spoke to God. Oh God, I do not understand your quarrel with me and your wrath. And still less can I understand why it must be done in such a cruel way. To dig my own grave. The deeper the hole, the less there would be left of my life. I saw myself digging with a shovel. The Lithuanian would be standing there with a rifle. Would he yell *"Skubek!"* "Hurry," or would he want me to dig slowly, to prolong my agony and his pleasure?

In the still of the night, my heart would fill with fear and my eyes with tears. It must not happen to me, I would say to myself, and was silently terrified.

When we came back from work, everybody was searched, mainly for food. It was against the law to bring food into the ghetto. One day Furster, the German *Gebietskommissar,* showed up. He also searched for food and found some bread in the pocket of a young man, Mazavetski. He was promptly ordered to be hanged. The hanging was scheduled for the following Sunday after church. Lithuanians by the hundreds, with Bibles under their arms, came to watch a Jew being hanged because bread was found in his pocket. The gallows were erected inside the ghetto and all Jews were ordered to watch the hanging. The Jewish policemen were ordered to see to it that everybody came.

Mazavetski told the two Jews who were assigned to hang him, "I know that you are forced to do it. I forgive you." His last words were, "In one minute from now I will be in heaven. I will pray to God for you. Perhaps your troubles will be over." I'll never forget his words.

Then he saw in the distance that his young wife and small child were being brought to watch the hanging. He kicked away the stool from under him and was dead. When Furster saw what happened, he became outraged. He shook his fist at the dead man who was swaying from the hanging rope and yelled, *"Verfluchter Jude,"* "Cursed Jew." You see he wanted a long show. Mazavetski deprived him of a long show.

Although Jews were being killed by the thousands, the hanging of Mazavetski had an impact on the people of the ghetto. He became a symbol, a martyr, because he died with dignity. That hundreds of Lithuanians came to watch a man being hanged because of a piece of bread found on him was a fact never left out in the retelling of the event. People talked of Mazavetski for a long time.

Some time later when I went to work for Urmanas, the Lithuanian jeweler, he told me that he also went to watch the hanging and it broke his heart. His advice to me was not to do anything against the law. "Obey the law," he told me, "and everything will be fine. Really, Leibas, does it pay to get hanged because of a piece of bread?" he asked. I wanted to ask him whether a man should be hanged because of a piece of bread, but I did not dare.

Not long after, Furster came back. This time not to hang anybody but to apologize for congested conditions in the ghetto. He said it wasn't suitable for children. He would resettle them into a resort, a place where they will be well taken care of.

Kartun, from the Judenrat, stood up to him and said that he would rather have the children here.

"*Das ist nicht möglich,*" Furster said. "That's not possible."

"*Herr Gebietskommissar,*" Kartun said, "when the ghetto was established you told us that we shall be allowed to manage our own affairs. All we have to do is provide you with workers, which we do. I appeal to your German word of honor, *Herr Gebietskommissar,* don't take our children away. Please let us keep our children here."

"That is not possible," Furster said again.

"In that case, I am not letting you through." And Kartun attempted to block his way.

Furster pointed to the armed SS men and said, "If you are so concerned about your children, *you* will come along."

So Kartun was ordered into the waiting trucks. This was the highest form of resistance any of us had witnessed.

Furster, very angry, ordered the SS men to enter the ghetto. The armed SS men entered the ghetto, went from house to house, from room to room and took the children away. We called that *Kinder Aktsia. Kinder* means children, and *Aktsia* means you kill them.

Shortly, Furster came back again, not to hang anybody and not to apologize. This time because he was concerned about sick people living in the ghetto. So his SS men entered the ghetto and proceeded to remove anybody who was sick or looked sick. We called this the *Kranke Aktsia. Kranke* means sick people. *Aktsia*—you know what that means.

Not long after, he came back again. This time to remove all old people. They entered the ghetto and removed anybody who was old or looked old. We called this *Alte Aktsia. Alte* means old people. *Aktsia*—you know what that means, by now.

Horrors of War

Rubin Udler*
b. Braila, Romania, 1925

The Image of Terror

In July 1940, in order to avoid the dangers of fascism and Nazism, my father, mother, sister, and I left Romania for Bessarabia, my parents' native country. One year later, in July 1941, we fled to Odessa. To go further east became impossible. The city was almost completely encircled by enemy armies.

There were frequent aerial bombardments and artillery barrages. Then suddenly, on the 12th or 13th of October, Odessa became oppressively silent. The noise of airplanes, of falling bombs and shells, ceased. Auto, artillery, and dray traffic stopped. The radio announced that because of military considerations the Soviet Army was leaving Odessa.

Three days of anarchy followed. Then the Romanians and Germans entered the city. They came in stepping stealthily and with obvious caution, walking close to the walls of the houses with rifles at the ready.

My memory often returns to one episode that happened shortly after this. On the 22nd of October, there was an explosion in the headquarters of the Romanian occupation forces. The blast killed many Romanians and Germans, among them the commandant of Odessa, General Glogozheanu, and officers of his staff. The terror of reprisal began immediately. People were arrested on the streets and in their apartments. Many were killed on the spot; others were dragged to jail.

On the morning of the 23rd, a few boys from our apartment house came together in the doorway behind the tightly closed outer gate. We heard shots, yells, and moans.

Curiosity overcame fear. We opened the wicket-gate and looked into the street. Two houses down the street, on the corner, stood a gallows that looked to me like a carousel. It consisted of a vertical pole with four horizontal beams extending from the top of it; the end of each beam had a noose suspended from it. Near the gallows stood a Romanian guard. On Karl Marx Street, from the direction of the railway station, away from another gallows on which hung four dead bodies guarded by Romanian soldiers, a line of twenty to twenty-five men moved slowly. It was apparent that they had been severely mistreated. Their clothes were torn; some walked without shoes and some barefoot; all were bareheaded.

---

*Translated from Russian by Alexander Zwillich.

Their faces showed black and blue signs of beating and were covered with blood. When they came abreast of us, we noticed their eyes looked not like those of the living, but empty, not showing any thought behind them, apathetic. Seeing how others, perhaps their relatives, possibly people they knew, had been hanged; knowing that the same awaited them on this street corner, or in some other block; overwhelmed by the inhuman cruelty that had befallen them, they meekly became resigned to the verdict that was pronounced against them—or maybe craved death. They did not look forward nor sideways. They dragged themselves mechanically as if sleepwalking.

At the gallows the line of people stopped. The Romanian sentry and those who escorted the line of men began to talk to each other and to smoke cigarettes. Finally, they said something to the first doomed man in line. He came closer to the gallows, placed a stool that he carried underneath the noose, stood upon the stool, placed the noose around his neck and waited quietly. The Romanians gave an order to the next man; he submissively came forward and kicked the stool from under the first man. Thus, quietly and sadly, the first man was hanged.

The Romanians continued talking, and after waiting a while, ordered the second man to do the same as the first one did. He also, obediently, as if his life were not at stake, placed his head through the noose. He did not say a word, did not beg for anything; he just stood and waited. Then the third man in line was ordered to be the executioner of the second man, who after a few moments hung as motionless as the first man.

One of the doomed, realizing the tragedy which awaited him, and instinctively yearning to live, suddenly left the line and ran. He was able only to cross the street before being overtaken by the bullets of the guards. No one went to look at him. He remained lying in a pool of blood.

All of us youngsters recoiled from the gates and closed them tightly, shaken by what we saw. We sat down on the steps in the doorway, moved closer to each other and did not talk for a long time.

This was only the first time we witnessed executions, directly collided with the horrors of war, and understood what the fascists could do.

Strength of Prayer

February 12, 1942. A train of freight cars guarded by soldiers with German shepherds waits for us at the Odessa–Sortirovochnaya station. The guards are obviously apprehensive about attempts at flight, since all of us are convinced that what awaits us is death from the cold and hunger in the cars, from the bullets of the gendarmes and policemen during the trip or, in the end, from sickness, slaughter, and malnutrition in a ghetto.

Loading us into the freight cars, Romanian guards curse, harry us with rifle butts and set their dogs on us. Because the doors of the cars are high off the ground, people cannot enter, and are shoved and rolled in like potato sacks. Their packs, knapsacks, and bags are thrown after them. Yelling in anguish, people call the names of their loved ones and friends, and in the terrible scantiness of space push to be near them. Here and there it dawns on some that members of their family—a husband, a wife, or children—have been put into different cars, or maybe are being killed. Mothers with outstretched arms beg to have their children, who were left outside the train, join them. People cry, sob, and faint. The door of the fully loaded car is closed and locked from the outside.

The train starts to move. It is very cold. A strong wind, caused by the train's movement, blows through the openings in the walls. All of us have to stand one against the other; there is no room even to turn around. No one can sit down or lie down.

Soon the unavoidable begins to happen: old people, small children, people with weak hearts, and the sick, begin to die. They perish where they stand and remain standing because there is nowhere for them to fall. Many ask for water, but there is none to be had. We have to relieve ourselves wherever we stand.

Those who have lost all hope cry constantly. Others, the stronger ones, curse themselves, the Bolsheviks, and the Fascists. Near us a few middle-aged people begin a discussion about what is happening to us. Why so many Jews—in Odessa alone there were more than one hundred thousand—did not resist when they were put into jails, hanged and shot, chased into the ghetto or deported. Why they went to their death without a murmur of protest, scared and meek like little sheep. Why such intelligent, talented, energetic, shrewd, enterprising people, who at all times and everywhere in the world used to help each other by all methods and means, became at this frightful time demoralized, disunited, unable to defend nor save themselves.

Some say that the Jews did not believe that Hitler and his adherents could be capable, in the twentieth century, in civilized and democratic Europe, of reawakening in people a senseless animal-like hate, a blood lust, a bloodthirsty racism. Others think that many opponents of fascism were hypnotized, paralyzed, at a loss and scared, not believing nor understanding that this horror was possible. Also, the Jews were unprepared to resist such atrocities. They were defenseless.

Among the people in our car is a tall, imposing looking Jew, over sixty years of age, who appears not to listen to the ongoing conversation, but reverently cites several fragments from our holy books. He assures us that God will severely punish the present persecutors of the Jews for their villainous deeds, just as He punished our previous persecutors, and that His people will be reborn and will overcome all their obstacles. He continues to pray silently, rocking back and forth in the orthodox manner. The aspect of this man and his unexpected speech somehow inspire us with renewed hope.

The train voyage lasts for three days. During that time the train stops for long periods at many stations, but the doors of the cars remain closed. The condition of the people grows worse and worse.

On February 15, we arrive in Berezovka, in Southwestern Ukraine. The gendarmes force the men to unload the dead bodies. The frostbitten, the frozen and the sick are carted away as if to a hospital. Their belongings become the property of the gendarmes. The rest of us are arranged in formation and driven to the ghetto. We spend a night there, in an unheated barrack.

Next morning we see the old inhabitants of this ghetto. The view is frightful. Hungry people in rags shuffle along between tumbledown barracks. All their threadbare and ragged clothing is infested with lice. They have not been fed for a long time. For a piece of bread they have bartered all their possessions. Feeling doomed, they try to find out anything about their relatives from whom they have become separated.

In spite of all this I do not despair, because I recall the remarkable man who gave us a glimmer of hope. In the freight car on the way to the ghetto, he reminded us of the infinite power of the Almighty.

A Road of Death

The road over which my parents, sister, and I marched from Berezovka, in Southwestern Ukraine, through Mostovoye to Domanyevka was truly a road of death.

We were so worn-out from our horrible train journey that we slept while walking. We progressed very slowly. A sharp, strong wind was blowing over the borderless, snow-covered flat steppe. We could barely see the road.

About ten kilometers away from Berezovka we began to see, on both sides of the road, corpses of people from previous transports, shot and left where they fell. The corpses were naked, swollen, and had a strange, fluffy orange color. My mother ordered us not to look. The sight was like a nightmare.

About midday, we discovered on the snowy steppe black dots moving quickly toward us. The Romanian escort-guards stopped the transport and ordered the people at the rear of the stretched-out column to move closer to the people at the beginning of the column. It was the first time they showed any concern for us. They went so far as to warn us that what we saw in the distance coming toward us were the German inhabitants of nearby villages.* This concern was partly because the Romanians hated the Germans, and partly because they were afraid of them.

---

*Descendants of the German colonists that Catherine the Great invited to settle in Russia in the 18th century.

The escort-guards were correct. Sleighs full of German colonists overtook us quickly. We saw well-fed young men with red cheeks, dressed in long, good quality sheepskin coats and high boots. They looked at us haughtily and with hate. The word *"Juden,"* pronounced in undisguised malice, could be heard. Their sleighs began to accompany the transport from each side, the left and right. The Germans had trouble keeping their fiery horses in check. The Romanian guards found themselves between us and the Germans, and with rifles at the ready they told the Germans to move on. As an answer, they got insolent laughter, verbal abuse in German, and harassment by the sleighs being driven very close to them.

The Germans burst into the column and with whips in hand, forcibly began to pull off the Jews any clothes that looked to them of good quality: overcoats, fur hats, shawls, gloves, scarves, overshoes, shoes and high boots. Those who tried to protest were whipped over their faces, hands, or wherever the whip fell.

Having looted what they wished, they turned around and drove off in the direction from whence they arrived.

The escorts began to breathe easier now because they did not have to use their weapons or scuffle with these insolent allies. We, on the other hand, felt very sorry for those who were robbed of the last items that protected them from the cold. People cried and their tears froze on their cheeks.

To the ones who lost clothing, shoes, and hats, others gave what they could. They shared their last belongings.

Beyond that, people thanked God that the Germans did not take us from the Romanians and drive us to their colony.

As hard as it seems now to imagine, we were lucky, because the German colonists in the region of Odessa, through which passed the roads of death to the infamous ghettos in Bogdanovka, Domanyevka, Ahmechetka, and Mostovoye, were true murderers.

Recently I discovered in the library of the Pittsburgh Holocaust Center, in "Documents Concerning the Fate of Romanian Jewry During the Holocaust," Volume V, edited by Dr. Jean Ancel, informative notes made by inspectors of the Romanian Gendarmerie of Transnistria, a district of Southwestern Ukraine. These notes state that between the 9th of March and the 30th of May, 1942, the German colonists in the villages of Kartayka, Novo-Kandeli, Bernandovka, Zavadovka, Lichtenfeld, and Reichstadt robbed 3,223 Jews of their valuables and clothes, save their shirts, then shot and cremated them. That number did not come near the total figure of the victims. No one ever kept count of the Jews killed by the German colonists: Jews who, after arriving in Berezovka by train, walked in convoys along the road to Domanyevka. It is known, however, that those who mostly suffered from these attacks were the Jews of the initial transports.

Death at Domanyevka

On the 20th of February, 1942, my parents, sister, and I arrived at the ghetto at Domanyevka, in southwestern Ukraine. As the convoy guards handed us over, we were counted and taken to a big building that used to be the district club, and before that, a synagogue.

The temperature in the enormous hall, where there were many broken windows, was as low as outside. The wind gusts shook the broken window frames so they knocked sinisterly all the time. Many of the wooden floor planks were missing. Possibly they had been used as fuel for heating or for cooking over makeshift fireplaces made out of broken bricks. We could see the ashes and traces of those fires among the exposed joists.

We, the newcomers, searched for a place where we could find shelter from the draft, and where there was planking on the floor. Finding such a corner, we managed to sweep it and clean the rubbish and rags left by prisoners who were there before us and had disappeared into the unknown.

In these quarters were many people constantly in motion, who went and returned to and from somewhere. It was noisy: the sick moaned asking to be helped, children cried, and the women complained or argued.

Alongside us, someone died. Relatives of the dead person began to cry, mourn, and read prayers. Afterward, they carried the body in their arms to the assigned place.

By morning—like every morning, we later learned—the hall contained many dead bodies. They were taken away to the cemetery in carts or sledges. This being winter, the frozen ground was too hard to dig graves, even with pickaxes. The relatives of the dead had to put the stiffened corpses into a common grave previously dug for others.

I do not know whether today there stands a headstone that narrates the tragedies of the ghetto at Domanyevka.

The Ghetto in the Vine Garden

All of us were brought to the ghetto in the Vine Garden by the Romanians: some were the remnants from the ghetto of Bogdanovka following the mass execution of more than fifty thousand Jews, while others were from Domanyevka where eighteen thousand Jews were annihilated.

This ghetto where my parents, sister, and I were held was in a hamlet called Vine Garden, in Russian Vinogradniy Sad. The name of the hamlet was invented by some optimistic manager, who thought to transform the bare, hilly landscape into a luxuriantly fertile vineyard. The irony of this name never failed to ring in our ears, even years afterward.

75

The hamlet was located approximately seven kilometers southward from Bogdanovka, in Southwestern Ukraine, along the river Southern Bug. The hamlet consisted of two short, straight streets, running parallel to the Bug, connected by a few perpendicular alleys. I never walked in the streets of this hamlet because it was forbidden.

Between the hamlet and the ghetto there was a field onto which, every morning, the women of the hamlet drove the cows before moving them to the pastures. On one side of the field were a cow barn, a horse stable and a piggery.

The ghetto, which was adjacent to the side of the field used for animals, was in a squalid building previously used to house calves. It had a low ceiling daubed with clay, a clay floor and clay-daubed walls with three narrow windows. In the middle of the space, about five by nine meters, stood a small potbellied stove with a black flue. It had two elbows, in order to increase the heating potential of the stove. On either side of the narrow aisle were homemade wooden plank beds, the width of which depended on the number of people in each family. Between the rude beds were small spaces. Some of the plank beds were covered with old shabby reed mats, others with palliasses. When it was cold, all of us slept fully clothed, covered with overcoats, cotton-filled jackets or sacks. Everyone's meager possessions were stored under their plank beds.

The only entry to the building opened into a small lobby that served as a kitchen. The kitchen's crude hearth had two cooking places: one to cook food, and the other to warm water. For fuel we used dried cow pats either au naturel or hand-formed into cakes and air-dried before use. The fuel gave off its characteristic odor and permeated our beggarly clothes and even our emaciated bodies. A single, poorly constructed door led out of the building into the street. This door, after some time, ended up as fuel.

The former calf house faced a deep ravine. In its course, the ravine became wider and deeper before reaching the river Bug. This ravine channeled runoff waters from spring and fall rains, snow thaw, and our communal latrine, to which we marched in a queue.

In this calf-house ghetto, guarded by Romanian gendarmes, lived for more than two years (from 1942 to 1944) six families and six single people, twenty-seven souls all told—men, women, and children.

Together we did heavy slave labor, ate, slept, often were ailing, experienced pain, surmounted obstacles, and even were happy on very rare occasions. We were a large family created by common unhappiness.

Almost all of us lived to see our long yearned-for liberation.

Scars

One morning, an urgent summons came for Philip, the elder of our ghetto in the hamlet of Vine Garden, Transnistria. He was to report to the commandant of the Romanian gendarmerie.

The commandant had decided to hold an immediate search of the ghetto. This came about because the higher levels of military police administration had gotten wind of partisan activities, such as circulation of leaflets and spreading of rumors about German and Romanian retreats before the Soviet Army. The police feared that the Jews were supporters of the partisan operations.

The commandant assigned two gendarmes to the task. They and Philip soon arrived at our building.

The gendarmes not only searched, but used the opportunity to torment us even more than usual. They were still at it when we returned from work. They would not let us into our living quarters and pretended that they had not finished the search. From outside we could see what the two gendarmes had done to our meager belongings. Mattresses, their sacking ripped and their straw strewn all over the place, were off the bunks. On the floor, turned inside-out and their linings torn, lay our old overcoats and padded jackets. Our underwear, our threadbare dirty laundry, children's clothes, and even the items from our sacks and knapsacks were thrown all over the floor. What's more, it looked as if throwing our clothes about and mixing them up in every way imaginable was not enough. Our clothes also showed imprints of the gendarme's dirty boots. Wooden spoons and earthenware plates, which could not possibly hide anything, were thrown on the floor.

We were shocked, but not because of the search itself. We had undergone searches before and gotten used to such hardships. However, this search, surpassing all the previous ones, showed us in the strongest terms the contempt the police felt for us.

The two gendarmes who conducted the search were short, skinny, with haircuts like prisoners, low foreheads, and shifty thief-like eyes. Drunk with power, they appeared eager to humiliate us. Their dialect was that of illiterate peasants from the province of Oltenia. They behaved like believers of the propaganda of the Iron Guard—a fascist organization in Romania whose members canvassed the countryside before elections in search of votes. The Iron Guards, along with the gendarmes' warrant officers, filled the heads of peasants with virulent anti-Semitic ideas. The Jews, they said, deserve every possible punishment.

Eventually, they ordered us to enter our sleeping quarters. In the narrow space between the bunks people began to collide with each other while trying to pick up their belongings from underfoot. Our impotence to do anything about what was happening to us must have shown in our faces, and this must have given the gendarmes much satisfaction. However, our stubborn self-control angered them. With choice curses they expressed their annoyance with the futility of the search. They did not find any weapons or leaflets, nor, what is more important, anything worth stealing.

One gendarme noticed a bag I held over my shoulder. Pleased at finding a cause for venting his anger, he began to curse terribly, took his rifle from his shoulder and started to move toward me. He shouted, "Why, you mangy Jew, you didn't let your bag be searched! What are you hiding in it: leaflets, arms?"

I answered calmly: "I am the herdsman, just now returned from the pasture, and in the bag are a few potatoes, two eggs and a chunk of bread given to me by the women farmers who came to take their cows back from the herd. I'm not hiding anything."

The gendarme did not believe me. He grabbed the bag and emptied it on the floor. Visibly disappointed at being proven wrong—the bag did not contain anything forbidden—he nonetheless continued the assault. Holding his rifle above his head, butt forward, he stormed toward me, yelling even louder than before: "You dirty thief! You stole this! I'll punish you!"

My mother, who heard and saw it all, in a protective impulse instantly stepped between the charging gendarme and me. The rifle-butt strike, meant for me, fell heavily on her head. My mother, her head covered with blood, lost consciousness and collapsed on the floor. We, thinking her dead, began to yell. The gendarme, the bloody rifle in his hand, froze.

In desperation and rage, my father grabbed the villain, pushed him toward the exit, and with a powerful shove threw him into the street. The heroic gendarmes quickly ran away.

After a while my mother came to; we lifted her off the floor and laid her down on the bunk. We tried, but could not stop the bleeding. Someone ran for the doctor who arrived quickly. After asking all of us, except my elder sister Fira, to leave the room, he began to tend my mother's wound. First, he stopped the flow of blood. Next, Fira brought a basin of water which the doctor used to wash the blood from my mother's head and face. Then with Fira's help, the doctor made my mother more comfortable. He cut mother's hair around the wound and bandaged her head.

When my father and I returned we saw that my mother looked very pale; her face was swollen and her eyes were mere slits surrounded by blue-colored skin. We began to cry. Mother in a quiet voice tried to soothe us. She tenderly embraced me, happy to see that I had escaped injury. We prayed to God to give Mother strength to get well. The doctor left some medicine and instructed Fira in what was to be done. He asked all of us to be quiet, so that my mother could sleep. Promising to come back in the morning, the doctor left.

Philip, my father, and I followed the doctor and once outside the room we explained to him what had happened. The doctor thought that my father was in serious trouble. Philip suggested that my father should hide, until the anger of the gendarmes quieted down. The doctor advised against this, because he believed that my father would be quickly found and then punished even more severely. After all, the doctor explained, we were hostages. No matter how horrible the gendarmes acted, according to them, they followed orders. He promised to see what he could do to reduce the consequences, by going to the gendarmerie to see the commandant, telling him what happened, and asking him to consider the circumstances under which my father acted and to show mercy. We became hopeful because the commandant treated the doctor better than the rest of the Jews. He liked to talk to him about various subjects in order to relieve the boredom of a castaway's life in the Ukrainian backwoods.

That night we did not sleep. In the morning we all were very tired, especially my father. We left for work, but my father stayed with my mother.

As he promised, the doctor went to see the commandant and found him very angry.

The two gendarmes had told the commandant that they were forced to defend themselves, because my father started a riot that prevented them from finishing the search. They demanded that my father be severely punished to restore the dignity of a Romanian gendarme, and as an example for the Jews.

The commandant originally thought of arresting my father and sending him under guard to Golta, the district center, for trial. However, after the doctor told the commandant our side of what happened, the commandant reconsidered. Because of possible consequences to us, to the gendarmes, and to his prestige, he decided on a punishment which would satisfy all except my father.

At approximately nine o'clock the next morning a gendarme came for my father. Not knowing what awaited him, my father said goodbye to my mother and sadly left with the gendarme. An investigation at the gendarmerie followed; my father was accused of leading a riot which forced the gendarmes to defend themselves. My father tried to tell his side of what happened, but it was no use. They did not hear him out. First, the commandant threatened my father with a military tribunal if he did such a thing again. Next, he ordered my father to suffer twenty-five lashes with a birch rod.

My father was pushed roughly out of the commandant's office and bound in a face-down position to a wide bench that stood before the gendarmerie. The same gendarme who hit my mother with the rifle butt carried out the sentence. He scourged my father's back with all his strength and sadistic pleasure. The other gendarmes counted each hit loudly and urged the executioner not to weaken in his duty. They also took the opportunity to hurl abuse at my defenseless father, and all Jews.

The punishment finished, the gendarmes untied my father's bonds and left laughing and feeling vindicated, their national and personal pride restored. His back covered with blood, hurt, not able to move, my father remained where the gendarmes left him. Philip had to help him return to the ghetto and lie down on the bunk. My father remained tight-lipped about his injury and about the undeserved punishment, so that my mother would not suffer even more than she already had. Fira, for some time, managed to avoid going to work and remained in the ghetto to care for our injured parents.

Eventually both of my parents recovered physically. However, for the rest of my mother's life she carried on her high forehead a visible, deep scar—a memento of the animal behavior of the Romanians. After the war, when someone asked my mother about her scar, she used to look at me in her special way, as a mother looks at her darling son, and with a sigh, say "Praised be God for this also." The wounds on my father's back healed too, but left deep imprints on his soul. Whenever he heard words such as gendarme, fascist, or legionary my father became gloomy, and his eyes took on a dark, peculiar look.*

All my family, who spent long years in the forced-labor camps in Transnistria, were deeply changed by the experiences we lived through. Our wounds may have healed, but our scars did not fade. They remained and will remain with us forever.

---

*Legionaries were members of the Romanian fascist organization led by Corneliu Zelea-Codreanu.

IV. The Lottery of Death and Life

What determined whether a person lived or died—today, tomorrow? What should Jews and other victims do to escape the bullets of Nazi hunters and their collaborators?

In a very real sense, survival was often a matter of luck. As some of the stories in this section suggest, being born in the right place, being in a certain place at a certain time, running into a Nazi who might be "a decent human being" or who might be, for whatever reason, in a nonkilling mood—these things might have made a difference at one point for somebody.

Making the "right" choice in a crucial situation might seem an important factor in survival. But were Nazi victims ever actually able to choose what to do? The answer is that they frequently had to make choices, but these were totally blind choices since the chooser in this lottery had no way to predict what the outcome might be. To paraphrase one writer in this section: you took a chance; then you lived or died.

This theme of the impossibility of knowing how to choose what to do arises in several stories in this section. In "German Roulette," a man must make a life-or-death guess about the intentions of his Nazi captors. "My Sister Rieke" tells of the heart-rending dilemma of making a moral choice, upon which depends someone else's life, without knowing the possible consequences. Among the series of stories in "The Concentration Camp Lottery" we find a girl who was "selected" for death seeming to choose death, when in fact she had no choice—and on the other hand, another girl, in "Happy Christmas, Sir," improbably choosing to confront a very cruel Nazi, risking death for the sake of some stale bread.

Given this atmosphere of total disorder and unpredictability, a few writers simply wonder at the inscrutability of fate. "A Definition of Survival," "An Unforgettable Passover Seder," and "Bread" (in "The Concentration Camp Lottery") pose unanswerable questions about why or how someone survived—or, as in "The Skull With the Golden Braid," did not survive.

Thinking back upon the lottery of death and life, a few writers in this section point out the terrible irony of some events. In "Trying to Go Home," "The Filbert Nuts," "Taken to the Smoke," and "Fancsy" (the latter three, part of "The

Concentration Camp Lottery"), the writers contemplate the contrast between what was meant to happen and the life or death result of a certain action.

In spite of their despair over the chanciness of life, concentration camp inmates on rare occasions found something to sustain them and give them hope. "The Child" tells how prisoners imposed a kind of victory in the game the Nazis forced them to play.

We must remember, however, that the odds in favor of Jews living rather than dying were never fifty-fifty; the numbers were always rigged against them.

A.B.

German Roulette

Fritz Ottenheimer
b. Constance, Germany, 1925

My father was shaving when they came for him.

"Can I finish shaving?" he asked.

"Wipe it off and get moving," they growled.

It was November 10, 1938, the day after Kristallnacht, the Night of the Broken Glass. They had blown up the synagogue early that morning, our beautiful synagogue where I had celebrated my bar mitzvah just six months before. We had heard of many other Jewish men in Constance having been arrested by the Gestapo before they came to us. Now, my father was gone.

The two Gestapo agents took him to their car, drove a few blocks and stopped in front of a tobacco store. They ordered him to stay in the car while both agents went into the store to buy cigarettes. This was very irregular behavior, especially since the Swiss border was only a fifteen-minute walk from there. Either the agents wanted my father to escape into Switzerland, or they wanted him to make a run for it, giving them, or hidden accomplices, justification to shoot their prisoner "while trying to escape." My father also considered the possibility that the border might be heavily guarded on this particular day and of the likelihood of punitive action against the family if his escape were to succeed. All these thoughts went through his mind. Only thoughts. No facts. He decided to sit still. After a few minutes, the agents returned and drove him to headquarters without any further conversation.

Most of the thirty thousand Jewish men imprisoned in camps on that day were released again one to six months after their arrest. But many, especially the old and the sick, did not survive the ordeal. My uncle in Stuttgart was neither old nor sick when he was sent to Dachau. After two months, my aunt received an official government letter informing her that if she would send one hundred marks to a specified address, the government would send her the ashes of her late husband.

One evening, at the end of December, there was a soft knock on our door. It was Papa! He had been released from Dachau concentration camp. He was very sick, had lost a lot of weight, was barely able to walk. With rest, he did recover during the following weeks.

Did my father make the right choice while waiting in the Gestapo car? Today, looking back, we have tons of wisdom about what should have been done. But at the time, we had to make life-or-death decisions without the slightest idea of what our options were. We guessed. Then we lived or died.

My Sister Rieke

Esther Haas
b. The Hague, Netherlands, 1919

My sister Rieke was the most beautiful of the four Blok girls. She had dark blonde hair, sparkling brown eyes, a delicate nose, full round lips and a smile that flashed as bright as her future should have been. Her personality also had that bright quality. She attracted loads of friends to our house and she was invited everywhere that a young Dutch-Jewish girl would want to go—gymnastic club, youth concerts, swimming parties and even movies. At seventeen she was married; at eighteen and a half she was sent to Auschwitz.

Ironically, tragically, it was her brightness, her joy and her beauty that led to her being transported. She drew unwanted attention that ultimately ensured her a place on one of the cattle cars leaving every Tuesday for Auschwitz, Poland, from Westerbork, Holland.

Westerbork, close to the German border, was the gathering place for the Jews of Holland after the Nazis forced us from our homes. Built on low, flat land, it contained rows and rows of long barracks and a large railroad siding. It was a damp, muddy, grayish brown place.

Every day Jews came to Westerbork from all over Holland to stay until their selection for the Tuesday train to Poland. Cattle car after cattle car would leave filled with frightened, gray-haired grandparents, clinging middle-aged couples, disoriented young men and women and bewildered, crying children. They left on a strictly adhered-to schedule. The train was never early, never late, always filled with people who carried with them a nagging fear of the unknown. No one knew, no one could know that the trip ended in slavery, sickness, death. We all thought we would be forced to work for the Germans; we had never heard of the Final Solution.

Every Monday the selection took place for the next morning's train. One of our own, a Dutch Jew named Samson, was in charge of making the selection for the train. He was fairly young, fairly good-looking. I suppose he had to deliver a full trainload of people in order to save his own skin, but he took advantage of the power of his position to satisfy himself. We were all afraid of Samson, for he had complete control over us.

When Rieke and her husband David came to Westerbork, I had been at the camp for three months, kept out of the selections because I was a nurse. I knew the ropes, so every Monday night for four weeks I gathered my courage and went to beg Mr. Samson to keep Rieke and David at Westerbork. On the fourth Monday, Samson answered my pleas with "I'll keep her out if she'll go to bed with me." He had spotted her among all the hundreds of women. He saw the freshness of her youth and the innocence of her beauty. She shone even in this terrible place. She had attracted his attention.

I answered him as I had to, being brought up in a certain time by certain good people who taught us to be faithful to ourselves and to our vows to others. "My sister is just a young girl. She is married for only a year and she would never, never sleep with you." I walked away from Samson with nothing more to say.

I think now that I should have asked Rieke what she wanted to do. In my heart I felt that I answered as she would have. I knew her love for David. I knew the rules we were taught. What I didn't know was what the journey's end would be. I only knew what Auschwitz meant when I took that journey myself a few months later.

Rieke left on the next selection. I was at the train with her and I wanted to leave with her and David. She would not hear of it. She wanted me to stay to nurse and help the new people to adjust to the world they were just entering at Westerbork. She said we would find each other after the war—after our hard work at the camps.

I never saw my beautiful sister again. She died at Auschwitz. Somehow, I can never forget that I answered Samson for her.

A Definition of Survival

Walter Boninger
b. Hamburg, Germany, 1928

For most of my life I have not considered myself a Holocaust survivor—not a real survivor, anyway. After all, I was not in the camps or the ghettos. I had no experiences of torture or starvation, of cold, of forced labor, of hiding, of seeing loved ones brutally killed before my eyes. Yet I have come to realize that I am indeed a survivor, though there may be a difference of opinion as to just when I actually survived.

Was it when my head came out of the water and I grabbed onto a log? It was instinctive. A few seconds earlier I had been standing on the deck of the *Simon Bolivar,* holding my parents' hands. Now I was alone, an eleven-year-old boy. My parents were nowhere in sight among the oil-stained waves and floating debris.

It was Saturday, November 18, 1939, two and one-half months after the start of World War II.

We were Jewish refugees from Germany, some of the 260 survivors among the 400 people on board. We had been passengers on the *Simon Bolivar,* a Dutch vessel headed for Santiago, Chile, which was to become our new home.

I do not remember the ship's crew conducting any life-saving drills. No one was told where the life jackets were or how to get into the lifeboats. The Netherlands were neutral, we were assured, and thus there was no danger.

It was revealed later that we had hit two German mines, deliberately laid in neutral merchant shipping lanes. With the second explosion, a few minutes after the first, there was only confusion. Some people who had managed to get into a lifeboat were tossed overboard with the force of the explosion. I had been on the deck with my father, and he had noticed German planes following us. Somehow we were reunited with my mother. There was nothing to do but wait as the boat fairly quickly listed and sank. The three of us held hands as we slid into the water.

In retrospect, I suppose we were among the lucky ones who got out of Germany. We were spared the agony and almost certain death in ghettos and concentration camps. My father had been among those in Hamburg who were arrested during Kristallnacht. He was released two months later, perhaps in part because my mother had been able to make arrangements for us to leave the country.

In February 1939, I was sent with a children's transport to Antwerp, Belgium, where my mother's parents and other relatives lived. Then in July, my parents came to Belgium to pick me up and prepare for our big journey. On November 15, we left for Amsterdam, our port of embarkation.

I didn't float in the water long. I was pulled onto a boat and then onto a fishing trawler that took us to Harwich, England. On board we were urged to drink endless cups of tea with milk to make us throw up and cleanse us of the polluted ocean water we had swallowed. I remember the taste to this day and have never since liked British tea and milk. My parents were not on board.

We were taken to a hospital, where my picture was taken with one of the surviving crew members. My face and pillow were still oil-stained. The picture appeared in newspapers all over the world.

Later we were taken to a hotel in London. My parents were not there either. I was in this hotel for a week. Part of my stay was very pleasurable. Because of the published photo, I received all kinds of mail, gifts, and many boxes of candy. I had been cleaned up, provided with new clothing, and the food was very good.

I kept hoping that my parents would somehow show up. I did not cry, nor was I afraid. It became clear many years later that I just shut out all my feelings. At the time I simply could not understand why a good boy like me was being punished by God. The only sin I could think of was that we had started our journey on a Friday evening, the Jewish Sabbath, something that is forbidden according to orthodox tradition. I must have been quite angry at my parents and at God, because at my very first breakfast in the hotel, I ate a piece of ham. I wasn't sure what it was. It just kind of looked like I thought ham might look. I didn't ask. If I didn't know, then how could I be responsible?

Within a day after I arrived at the hotel, my aunt and uncle, who were servants on a nearby estate, came to see me. They had also come from Hamburg. We had spent vacations, most holidays and birthdays together. I was very fond of them. It was a fondness not entirely shared by my parents. After all, my aunt and uncle were Reform Jews who did not keep all the dietary laws. They would drive and ring the bell when they visited us on the Sabbath. They were "bad."

The day after my aunt and uncle came, we learned that my grandparents in Belgium, who were very orthodox, wanted me returned to them. They did not want me to stay with those "bad" relatives. My aunt and uncle wanted me to stay in England.

This was perhaps the only decision that I had an opportunity to make, and it was not a difficult one. By now it was becoming clear, even to me, that my parents had been lost when our ship sank. I wanted to stay in England. A behind-the-scenes legal battle ensued, as my grandparents had hired an attorney, a tall, mean-looking Dickensesque villain with one large, swollen-shut, misshapen eye.

It was a nervous time for a few days. At last we were all summoned into an official looking room. We were informed that permission had been granted for me to stay in England. My grandparents' attorney stood up, announced angrily that we would be hearing from him, and stormed out of the room.

That was the moment when I really survived. We never saw him or heard from him again.

My grandmother died a natural death four years later. My grandfather was deported to Auschwitz and died there in 1944. After I was in England for ten months, my aunt and uncle arranged for me to immigrate to the United States. Though they were never able to have me live with them in England or in the United States, they truly saved my life and assured my survival.

An Unforgettable Passover Seder

Ernest Light
b. Uzhorod, Czechoslovakia (became Ungvár, Hungary), 1920

April 8th, 1944: Passover.

The table was set with our special dishes, wine, herbs, and matzos. Elijah's cup, filled with wine, rested at the end of the table where I was. Our family around the table consisted of my father, mother, sister, her two-year-old daughter, and my three brothers.

It was just about seven weeks since the Germans had occupied Hungary. You could see on everyone's face concern about the future. But reading the prayers in the *Hagadah*, we temporarily forgot the present.

Suddenly our neighbor's daughter burst into the house. Almost hysterical, she screamed, "Hide me, hide me! I just ran away from a German soldier. He tried to grab me!"

Without thinking about the consequences, we pushed her into the next room, where she hid herself. Everyone sat calmly and continued reading the *Hagadah*. My father led the prayer.

Following Passover tradition, we had not locked the doors, so that the Prophet Elijah could come in and join us at the Seder. This is how it was that a German soldier could just walk in, a gun over his shoulder.

Since I sat at the end of the table, he stood closest to me. I could feel his breathing behind my back. We continued to read as if we didn't notice him. He stood there for a while—I don't know whether it was two minutes or ten minutes. Then he turned around and left.

For the last fifty years, I've been wondering what made that soldier leave without inquiring about the girl, or threatening that we had to tell him where she was. I've come up with several possibilities:

—He thought that people who were hiding someone could not sit so calmly, conducting services.

—The German military command warned the soldiers not to commit any unnecessary violence, not to alarm the local population.

—He just might have been a human being.

• • •

I'll never know the truth.

Trying to Go Home

David Katz
b. Sapinta, Romania, 1919

This story starts with an escape, my escape from a prison in the city of Kamyshin, near the Volga River. How I got there is another story. That story began back in 1939 when Russia marched into Bessarabia, which was a part of Romania, and following that, when the Hungarians seized Transylvania from Romania in 1940. I was drafted into the Hungarian Army and put in a work battalion. My sergeant in that battalion, to avoid being executed for stealing money (but that's yet another story) marched us across the border into Russia. The Russians captured us. And although many men from my group were immediately executed, I was merely shuttled from one cruel prison to another, finally ending up at Kamyshin.

When I escaped from Kamyshin jail, I walked all night through the Russian countryside, through the fields and woods. While I was walking, I thought of a story I would tell. That I was looking for my uncle from Bessarabia. I went into a town and saw an old man traveling with a horse and wagon in my direction. I asked him to give me a ride. We traveled together for about twenty kilometers. When I told him the story I had invented, he said that he knew a family from Bessarabia, and that they lived in the place where he was going.

When we arrived he showed me the family which he thought might be my uncle. They asked me many questions about Bessarabia and I told them everything was fine.

The next morning the man asked me if I had heard the latest news—that just an hour ago he had heard on the radio that war had broken out between Russia and Germany. He looked happy about it, he did not like the Communists. We finished our breakfast and he told me that he had a neighbor who worked on a locomotive. He would ask him to give me a ride. In the meantime, his wife packed me a lunch of bread and herring.

His neighbor was leaving for the station immediately. He had been called to work ahead of time because of the war. He could take me to Veranezh.

From there, I walked hundreds of miles, stopping only to eat. I was thinking about the overwhelming happiness when I could arrive at home. Oh my family! My dear family! I made plans to hide out at home from the Hungarian authorities. I figured that every step was one step closer to home.

When I came to the Ukraine, I saw many pedestrians with sacks over their shoulders, wagons, and occasionally a truck with people fleeing from the war. I realized that I would soon meet the Russian–German front. I could not plan anything except to hide somewhere with a family until the front went by. I was not far from Kiev, in a small town named Skvira. I heard shooting nearby.

Here, I changed my story. I became a Russian soldier whose unit was destroyed and I was the only survivor. At a nearby house I asked a lady if I could stay until the front passed. She was happy to have me. Her husband had died in a labor camp and she had a son in the war. She said he was my age, he looked like me. I stayed there for a week. When things quieted down, I kept on going toward home.

My hopes were high that soon I would be back in Romania with my parents. Then the Germans, who were now occupying this part of Russia, caught me. They took over where the Russians had left off—in other words, more prison. They took me to the German camp. After a week of torture, without asking any questions, they threw me into a camp where there were only Jews. I was kept there, starving, for almost a month. I felt that we would either die or be killed.

In the camp, several young girls and boys got together and planned to escape. Little groups formed. We had a lottery as to who would be the first group to escape. Six of us, five boys and one girl, pulled the first set of numbers. We decided to jump the fence, one at a time, in different places. Each person was to take care of himself. We knew that we were taking a dangerous risk, but we felt we had nothing to lose and a lot to gain. We considered that even to be killed would be our gain. I selected the place I would jump, under the watch tower.

In a hail of machine gun bullets, I escaped. Then another boy, Philip, showed up. Three boys and a girl were gunned down. We watched from a distance for a while, but nobody ran after us. We assumed that they thought they had killed all of us. But Philip and I escaped. We ran to a wooded area, sat beneath a tree in the dark and talked about tomorrow, about our plan for where to go and what to eat.

Since Philip was a local boy, I asked him if he knew of any of his neighbors who would help us. He said he did; but the next morning, when we went quietly to one of his neighbors, they were very hostile to us. They told us they were going to call the Germans right away, so we ran away. We were hungry; we decided to try another neighbor. We were met with the same hostility. Then Philip said that he knew of a very religious family. Philip called them *Subotniky,* which means that they kept Saturday holy instead of Sunday. He said it was worthwhile to try, so we tried and succeeded. We told them that we did not come to stay, just for some food. They fed us and gave us a loaf of bread, onions, salt, tobacco, and matches. But they told us we should leave right away. Realizing that we were putting their lives in jeopardy, we thanked them for their kindness and went back to the woods.

We sat down to talk over what to do next. Philip said that perhaps if he were alone, his neighbors would not be so hostile toward him. I did not want him to die because of me, so we decided to divide everything equally, and I would go east and he would go west. We gave each other our home addresses so that if one of us survived, we could let the other's parents know where and when he saw the other person for the last time. As Philip was leaving, I vowed to him that the Germans would not take me alive. That was the last time I saw Philip.

Toward evening, I left the woods for a nearby city. At the edge of the city I saw destroyed buildings; nobody was living in the neighborhood. I assumed that the Germans had met resistance here and destroyed the area. I found a badly demolished house with a good ceiling. I went into the attic, carrying up all kinds of junk to hide myself. I wanted to make sure that I would not be caught sleeping and taken alive by the Germans. I laid down behind the junk and slept. When I awoke the next day, the sun was shining. I ate a piece of bread. Then I explored the whole attic, looking out and observing what was going on around me. I could see people walking around. The German army was there, moving their tanks, trucks, and other equipment. Occasionally I heard shooting.

I tried to work out a plan to get out of there. But however I tried, I could not see any suitable way. No escape.

Three days later, I finished my bread and onions. I still had my tobacco. I felt that the doors had closed for me. I felt very depressed; I felt that everybody was after my life. It was no use to struggle so hard, just to have a little longer life. The time had come for me to make an end of myself.

I found an old sack and worked several hours making a rope. I said to myself that I had made a good struggle. I had accomplished many things in my life. Now I had a choice: to fall into the hands of the evil power and be tortured to death, or hang myself.

I made my choice, and hanged myself. But after a while I regained consciousness. The rope had torn and I had fallen down. I was still alive.

My way had not worked. Then from the attic I saw a high bridge. If I were to jump down, maybe onto a moving train, surely I would die. The decision was made. As I walked to the bridge I saw many people coming and going. I noticed two officers on patrol, one smoking a cigarette, looking suspiciously at me. Then I took out my tobacco, rolled a cigarette, went over to them and asked one officer for a light. He gave me a light and I kept going.

On approaching the bridge, I saw four people coming toward me. They wore civilian clothes, with military caps on their heads. As they passed, I heard them speaking Yiddish. I asked them to save my life if they could.

"Yes," they said, "come with us."

They were members of a Hungarian work battalion, as I had been at one time. I went with them to their barracks.

Here I washed, changed my clothes, and ate. I felt better. They promised to take me home. Home, to my beloved ones.

Bar Mitzvah Boy

Sam Weinreb
b. Bratislava, Czechoslovakia, 1928

My bar mitzvah was only a few weeks away. Waving a casual goodbye to my family, I went off to my lesson.

When I returned home, I found the house locked and no one there. A neighbor who was not Jewish pulled me into his house and told me that my parents, two brothers and my sister, along with quite a few other people who lived on our street, had been taken away. Where they were taken he did not know. That afternoon was the last time I ever saw any member of my family.

The neighbor said he knew of some people who lived close to the Hungarian border and were helping people who were being persecuted to leave Czechoslovakia for Hungary. He got in touch with them and was told to take the first train with me, that they would meet us.

We left that same evening, arriving about midnight. Two men were waiting for us. They said that we had no time to waste and must leave immediately, so that I could cross the border and reach the safe town in Hungary before daylight. One of the men started walking with me toward the border. After about one hour, he said this was as far as he could go. He gave me directions and instructions on how to avoid the border guards, and told me what to do when I reached the town in Hungary. I walked and at times crawled on my stomach, so as not to be seen by the guards, for the next four to five hours.

In the town, I located the person I was to see, and he knew all about me. He told me that he would help me and assured me that I would be okay. He asked if I had any relatives in Hungary. I told him I had grandparents in a small town there and an uncle in Budapest. He said that to go to the town where my grandparents lived would be much too dangerous—that if I was caught there not only I, but also my grandparents, would be arrested.

We went to Budapest and found my uncle. I stayed with him for a few weeks. One day he received a call telling him that someone had reported to the police "that he was hiding a foreigner in his home." We had to make other arrangements immediately. We got in touch with a cousin who lived in the outskirts of the city, and he agreed that I should move in with him. I stayed with him too for only a short time, before someone reported him to the police.

I went back to the city to look for work. In some restaurants, I offered to clean the place in exchange for food, but no one would hire me. I was afraid to get in touch with my uncle for fear he would get in trouble.

After living outdoors, and looking for food mostly in garbage cans, I decided that I could no longer live like this and would go to the police and tell them the truth. I thought, "What could they possibly do to a thirteen-year-old kid, whose only crime is that he was born Jewish?"

So I went to the police. I told them why I was there and why I left Czechoslovakia. I told them that I had grandparents who lived there, and would it be possible for me to stay with them? Before I finished the sentence, one of the policemen slapped me. "There's only one place you're going, and that's straight to prison." I spent the next two years in prison. I cleaned, scrubbed floors, cleaned bathrooms—did whatever was asked of me.

After two years I was released into the custody of my grandparents. I was told that I would have to report to the local police twice a week, every Tuesday and Friday. I moved in with my grandparents.

When I went the first time to report to the police I was beaten and called names. "You stinkin' Jew, we have too many of your kind in our country," they said. They told me that if I said anything to anyone about the way they were treating me, I would immediately be sent back to prison.

Six months later the Germans entered Hungary, and what happened to us in Czechoslovakia a couple years before, was now happening in Hungary. All the Jewish people in town had to report. We were taken to a nearby city where people from different communities were brought in.

After a few days we were put on cattle cars and sent to Auschwitz. Upon arrival there I was given a number, "A4659," which was tattooed on my left forearm. While in Auschwitz I worked on construction, mostly carrying brick from one place to another. At times it was so cold that the skin on my fingers came off when I touched the brick. I also worked in a coal mine, where I had a difficult time picking up the huge empty shovel, let alone one with coal on it.

Shortly before the war ended, we were awakened in the middle of the night. We were told that we were being transferred to another camp, and to get ready at once. There were five to six thousand people in our group when we started marching. We were always surrounded by SS soldiers with machine guns. After three or four days of marching, of the five to six thousand people that started, we may have had about four to five hundred left. All the others died. Anyone who could not walk or stopped for whatever reason was shot immediately.

I decided that I would try to escape. I knew I would not be able to continue marching much longer. It was the middle of the night and I knew that my chances of escaping were very slim, but at that point it really did not matter. I ran out of the line. I have no idea how far and how long I ran. All I remember was waking up in a Russian Military Hospital. Later I was told that the Russian troops found me, lying unconscious on the ground.

The Skull with the Golden Braid

Rubin Udler*
b. Braila, Romania, 1925

Once, toward evening, as I was returning to the ghetto in the Vine Garden, I came across a skull, and lying near it a wealth of golden curly hair, plaited in a thick braid. It was near a large rock on the high, right shore of the river Southern Bug, which divided the Romanian occupied territory of Transnistria in Southwestern Ukraine from the territory captured by the Germans. I was dumbstruck! The skull was white as if painted with slaked lime; had empty eyesockets and a hole where once there was a nose; with two rows of white, straight teeth. The skull lay slightly turned sideways, as if inquiringly looking at me.

I was overcome with a painful feeling of horror and fright. In that state, I became aware of a question within me: "Why only the skull and braid are here near this rock?" Mechanically, almost at a run, I searched the areas around that rock and the other rocks nearby. I looked into the ravines and bushes without finding any trace of human bones, nor a shred of clothing.

I returned to where the skull lay, sat down nearby and kept looking at it. "Who was this young girl?" I asked myself. "Who is crying after her and still hopes to find her? What tortures did this innocent girl go through, and what did she suffer before dying? Who will answer before God, before humanity, for the loss of this life?"

One could easily imagine that the girl escaped from convoy guards or from the nearest ghetto of Ahmetchetka or Bogdanovka. Far away from the village, in danger of being beaten and persecuted, she perished possibly from hunger, exhaustion or sickness. Possibly greedy, cold-blooded marauders pulled off the clothes from her corpse, or hungry dogs mouthful-by-mouthful tore apart her body. Maybe stray dogs brought the head of the girl to this rock from some other place. There was no end to such thoughts.

Deeply shaken by what I saw, that evening I told the others in the ghetto about the skull with the golden braid that I had discovered. I hoped that someone among them may have heard about a missing girl. No one could remember anything.

The next day I dug a shallow hole near the rock and buried the skull with the golden braid of the unknown martyr. On the rock I scratched a six-pointed star to mark the grave site. I thought that someone, sometime, would inquire about it.

However, during the time of my stay in the ghetto, no one searched for a girl with wavy golden hair.

---

*Translated from Russian by Alexander Zwillich.

The Concentration Camp Lottery

Ilona Weiss
b. Kosino, Czechoslovakia, 1923

The Filbert Nuts

There was a store where they accepted ration clips for food. It was owned by an anti-Semite. He always made anti-Semitic remarks when we went in, but what could we do, we needed the food.

The store was next to the social hall where they gathered us up to be transported—where, we didn't know.

I was the oldest of my siblings and felt responsible for all of them. Before I went to the hall I stopped in the store to get as much food as I could for the journey. As I was leaving, the owner gave me a bag of nonperishable filbert nuts, saying, "I don't like you but I didn't wish this on your people."

We walked from the collection point to a field that had some railway tracks. There was a train of box cars waiting, and they put us on the train: my mother, younger sisters, two little brothers, six and eight, and me. My father had already been sent away.

After several days, the train stopped and we were forced out. Everyone was being separated. Some people were sent right and some left. I started going right and then realized I had forgotten the filberts in the train. I ran back to get them for my little brother because he was so hungry. On the way back a Polish boy said, "Grab your little sister and don't go left, go right."

So I went to my sister. "Edie," I said, "you come with me."

"No," she said, "I'm going with Mum."

I said, "You have to come with me."

My sister was hanging onto our mother and crying. I tried to take her to the right, but she pushed me away and hung onto my mother. Finally I just grabbed her and dragged her, fighting, into the group on the right.

My mother and my little brothers were made to go left. They were probably killed that day at Auschwitz.

My sister was angry at me for years and years because I pulled her away from our Mum. Maybe forty years. But just a few years ago she called me from Israel and said, "Thank you for saving my life."

Now she has ten grandchildren and two of them are just starting their service in the Israeli army.

So you see, if it wasn't for the filberts given to me by an anti-Semite, I would not have gone back toward the train and seen my sister hanging onto my mother and heading toward her death. I would not have seen her and been able to drag her to the right side.

The Girl Who Was Selected

One day the Nazis came to the barracks and made a selection. A girl from a barrack across the street was selected. This girl ran to our barrack, where we were sitting out. My sister Irene recognized her. She was the daughter of Dr. Krause.

Actually, it was not the Nazis who selected her; it was the *Blockälteste* who was putting her on the cart that took people to the gas chamber. Anyway, she knew what this meant.

So we said, "Here, stay with us."

But the Nazis knew there was one more person to go. Dr. Mengele came back and demanded that another person must appear. And you know what? The girl ran back to the other barrack. And so she didn't survive.

For trying to shelter her, Mengele directed that we all be closed up in the barrack. He locked us all in the hot barrack for one week. Once a day we could get a little bit of water, a little bit of food.

Taken to the Smoke

I asked the *Blockälteste*, Alice, what was going to happen to us.

She said, "It's like this. If they come at night, they get you undressed, believe me they take you to the smoke. But if they bring you clothes and they give you some food, it's a possibility that they take you to a work camp."

One night they came, they undressed us. We were walking. There were about a thousand of us walking. My sisters Irene and Edie were crying.

"We are so young; must we die?"

I told them that I didn't feel that we were going to die. I had a feeling we might live.

My sister said, "We can't even say a prayer. We are naked, how can we say our prayers? My God, we are going to die."

I told her, "You call this living? This is not living. But there is still hope."

My sisters said it was hopeless. They were crying.

"Please, O God, help us, how can you let us young girls die." We were mostly young girls.

It was a long walk. It was one of the longest walks of my life.

The gas chambers were so busy that we had to sit down near the railroad tracks to wait. It was already dawn. What was there to do? Just wait. You cannot describe the feeling when you are young and you feel that this is the last minute of your life—that they are going to kill you.

Suddenly, a train arrived and some elderly German soldiers jumped out of it. The Nazi head of the camp came up. A soldier said, "You promised us a thousand girls. We just opened up a new work camp in Bavaria."

The camp head said, "I don't have time. Don't you see how busy we are? I can't help you."

The soldier looked at us. He said, "They look healthy. I'll take those girls."

The camp head said, "You want to take them, you can take them."

So instead of going to the gas, we took a real shower. The gas chambers were made like showers. They gave us some half-decent clothes. They gave us shoes. They even gave us some rags for our heads. They gave us soup and bread, and we embarked on a train. It was a cattle car, but they left the door open.

A Brief Respite

It was in July 1944 that my sisters and I were sent to the work camp, not far from the town of Kaufering, Germany. It was a new camp, administered by the Nazis who administered Dachau.

In comparison to Auschwitz, we were not treated badly. We worked at the railroad station digging ditches. The guards were not strict and we had some freedom of movement, but there was nowhere to go. We were still dressed in rags.

There was a little house next to the railway station. One day, I rang the bell. A little old German lady with white hair answered the door. I asked her if I could use the outhouse. She said yes. I asked her for some water. She brought me a glass of milk and a slice of bread with butter on it. She told me that I spoke such nice German and looked so "normal." She told me she was good to the soldiers and the guards. She felt sorry for them because they were away from their families.

I called her "Gracious Lady." She would smile when I called her that. I asked her to ask the guards if I could help her with the housework. For three weeks I helped her with the cleaning, cooking, and washing. She fed me well.

Then I was told to stop working for her. I had to wash uniforms for the soldiers.

In the Germans' dining hall where I washed, ironed, and sewed the uniforms, two Austrian soldiers were painting scenes from the Austrian Alps. They asked me what I used to wear.

I described a polka-dotted dress with white puffy sleeves and a white apron. They painted my dress and face on the mural.

The German officer was angry at the painters for talking to me. He punished them by sending them out on night patrol. After that, the painters wouldn't talk to me.

Happy Christmas, Sir

In December 1944, my "beautiful" life in the Bavarian work camp came to an end. When they transported us away, the commandant gave us three days' rations of bread, margarine, and cheese. We were put in cattle cars. During the trip my two sisters and I ate most of our food, but we kept about six loaves of bread for whatever lay ahead. The train took us to Bergen-Belsen.

The day after our arrival, we were taken to work in the kitchen. It was an enormous room filled with huge kettles where the food was boiled.

The work in the kitchen was hard. We got up early and worked very late.

A group of non-Jewish Polish women also worked there. As we were let out from the kitchen, many of the girls would try to take something—a piece of onion, a potato—back to the barracks with them to feed to their relatives or friends.

One day the Polish women were crying and singing Christmas songs, so I knew it was Christmas. As we were leaving the kitchen that day, Kramer, the Commandant, stood at the door with a whip and a vicious German shepherd dog next to him. He was a fat, middle-aged Nazi. He checked the girls and found the scraps of food. He started to beat the girls. For an onion, for a piece of potato, he beat these girls half to death. The blood was running all over. No wonder he was called the "Beast of Belsen."

My sisters and I were scared because we had the six loaves of bread with us. They said surely Kramer would shoot or hang us.

I didn't want to give up the bread. So each of my sisters took three loaves. I pulled myself up straight and went to Kramer; I didn't want to show any fear.

In a mean voice he demanded, "What do you want?"

I told him I didn't want anything. "Sir, I just want to wish you a happy Christmas."

Then I explained that we had six loaves of bread because we had worked at a farm from which we saved the bread. I told him we fed hogs.

He said, "You must have *fressed up* the food from the hogs."

"No," I told him, "we were fed by the farmer so we would have strength to work." He stared at me. He looked at my sisters.

"Go," he said quickly.

We walked away as fast as we could.

Bread

In Bergen-Belsen, people were dying everywhere. Those who did not die of typhus were dying of starvation. One day I smelled bread baking. It was near Passover. I told my sister, Irene, that I had never eaten bread on Passover and was not sure what to do if we were given the bread.

But the bread was not given to us. It was burned. The bread was burned in huge piles outside. Starving, we watched them burn the bread.

The bread was Commander Kramer's great idea to get rid of all of us without firing a bullet. The bread had cyanide baked into it. But there was a German doctor at the camp and he determined not to distribute the bread. I will never know whether he felt that as a physician he had taken an oath to save lives or whether he knew that the war was coming to an end and he wanted to save himself.

Fancsy

There was a girl named Fancsy in Bergen-Belsen. When she arrived, she was a heavy-set girl from the Carpathean region. She was good-natured, always smiling.

We were very ill, except for Fancsy. I told Fancsy that we would all die before the liberators got around to us, but that she would survive us. Fancsy would have to greet the liberators and be the witness for the evil perpetrated against us.

Fancsy had a good appetite and a cast iron stomach. At night, she would sneak out of the barracks, go to the area next to the cookhouse and scrounge through the garbage. She would eat the raw potato peels and any edible garbage.

About a week before liberation, the Nazis left the camp and the Hungarians took over. They were even worse than the Nazis. While the Germans would not waste bullets on Jews, the Hungarians who took over the watch towers would shoot at anyone who dared to venture out of the barracks.

Poor Fancsy staggered in with blood running from her chest. The Hungarian soldiers had shot her. She died in my arms. There went our witness.

After the war these very soldiers got refuge and political asylum. They were allowed entry into the United States prior to the entry of survivors.

The Girl with Wooden Shoes

Irene Berkowitz
b. Uzhorod, Czechoslovakia (became Ungvár, Hungary), 1920

After our work mending Nazi uniforms at the Stutthof concentration camp warehouse was completed, we were sent on a forced march. As we were starting out, I heard a young girl begging for somebody to help her walk. She was offering a slice of bread in exchange for help.

The problem was that the girl's wooden shoes were falling off her feet. Because I had been working repairing military clothes, I had made myself mittens which were on a piece of string. I tore off my mittens and with the string, tied the girl's shoes to her feet as well as I could.

Unfortunately, her wooden shoes kept falling off. When I tried to tie them on again, the German guard asked me what I was doing. I tried to explain to him that her shoes were falling off. He shoved the girl into a ditch and shot her.

He ordered me, "*Lauf,*" run. I ran, expecting a bullet in my back. Surprisingly, the guard didn't hurt me.

I never knew that girl, but she is still in front of me.

The Wagon

Dora Zuer Iwler
b. Chodoròw, Poland, 1923

There were only five or six hundred inmates left at Jonowski camp. The camp was to be liquidated and we were gathered for a roll call before going on a death march. We stood in the *Appell* place in rows of four.

The woman on my left had been in the camp for a long time, but the woman on my right was a newcomer, inexperienced in survival. The woman on my left had an injured leg and she couldn't walk. The Nazi guard knew that she would not survive the death march and he asked her if she wanted to ride in a wagon. She shook her head, and although knowing that she would not be able to survive the walk, she replied, "Please, sir, there is nothing wrong with my legs. I can walk."

The woman on my right, the newcomer, asked if she might be able to ride in the wagon because her legs hurt her very much. I tugged on the back of her shirt, signaling her to be quiet, knowing that if I were caught I would be shot on the spot. The Nazi looked at me and our eyes met; he gave me an understanding smile. We both knew what would happen next. As I stood between them, he killed them both.

The Child

Malka Baran
b. Warsaw, Poland, 1927

The women in the gloomy large room were preparing for the night. Not that there were any real preparations possible; there was no water to wash with, no clothes to change. Only a mind which, though tired and numb, was not ready to rest. All the questions, unanswered and troubling, kept coming, persistently searching, probing. . . .

I was fifteen then, one among hundreds imprisoned in a concentration camp. Once, long ago, I was a happy child. Now, after a horrid whirl of events in which I lost everything, I existed merely as a number. But my mind remained and it was not ready to sleep.

Slowly the room became silent. Here and there a groan, someone cried, somewhere a lost soul was muttering meaningless words; a voice was praying. . . .

Suddenly I heard a child's cry! I was horrified—am I losing my mind? It can't be real! There were no children among us! Every child in the ghetto was killed! Yet here it came again, louder, angrier!

A hundred heads lifted. Deadly silence accompanied every step of a woman who walked toward the voice. Our hearts, our eyes followed her. Near the entrance she stopped, bent, and with trembling hands lifted a bundle. Slowly, silently the woman returned to her place, gently rocking the sobbing child. An unspoken agreement was reached through the language of hearts. The very well-known decree to deliver every child to the Nazis became meaningless; to hide, to protect this child in our midst was a command. Thus it was that little David, at two and one-half, came to barrack number 13 to stay.

If there is a ray of hope in a place where one waits for death, David was this ray; if there is laughter in a life that is reduced to mere existence, David brought it; if there were dreams where there was no past and no future, David was their cause.

I loved the child dearly. Again and again I told him stories I knew from that other life of mine. I sang songs to him, recited rhymes. We played together. David laughed and I was happy. Happy? In this camp? Yes! For those precious moments I was not in a cold, dirty barrack, hungry and sick, waiting for the end. We were together in a world full of dreams, warmth, love—and reality disappeared.

Days, months, years passed. David was a little over five years old. Tall, pale and very bright, he grew accustomed to our way of life. It was normal to stay forever indoors, to hide and remain silent whenever an officer came to inspect the barrack; to live on starvation diet; to wear the same clothes forever.

He was a gay child, jumping, dancing, and chatting with his many aunts. He was ours and we were his.

Then came another day. The air was crisp, clear. The sky blue. We were standing in the little square before the barrack ready for the morning call, cattle to be counted. How well we knew the procedure! Stiglitz, the lame, horrible man will come on his bicycle and receive the number from our Kapo. His eyes will look us over carefully and he will perhaps choose one or two for a special job. This might be a beating or hard work or anything his brutal imagination would move him to.

But on that day he did not choose anyone. He turned to leave and changed his mind.

Motioning to the Kapo he said, "I want to inspect the barrack." This never happened in the morning. We all froze. . . . David! Will he be able to hide? An eternity passed. . . . I could hear the hammering of a hundred hearts . . . and then a stifled scream. . . . Stiglitz appeared and behind him our little David! The hearts, so accustomed to shocks, trembled once again. Another moment and the German will scream, beat, shoot.

But none of these things happened. Stiglitz, looking at the boy sternly, asked him suddenly, "Would you like to go for a ride?" "Yes," David nodded. Poor child, how could he know? The lame brute lifted the boy, and placing him on the bicycle seat walked away, leaving us without the usual command, "Dismissed." Anyway, we did not move. I do not know how long we stood, but I do remember seeing the impossible. For *they* came back. They! David alive!

Stiglitz dismissed us and without a word left, his shorter foot limping markedly. There stood our boy, his cheeks tinted red with the brisk air of the morning, his eyes watching the sky as if seeing a miracle.

A few months later we were freed and hesitantly walked through the open gate to the world. Little David, the only child brought up in our concentration camp, was among us. Holding his hand tightly, I moved toward life. . . .

V. Disguise as a Way of Hiding

Given the near impossibility of other means of evading the Nazis, the Jews and other victims tried to hide from them. Above all, they tried to save, by hiding, their most precious possessions: their children.

Frequently, children were hidden by disguising their Jewishness. Such concealment was filled with danger. And whether these attempts at hiding through false identities succeeded depended on many factors: luck was important, as were planning, quick-wittedness and sheer bravery. The stories in this section reveal how arbitrary success was, as well as the burden of terror and confusion that being disguised and hidden placed upon the children.

Perhaps most incredible among these stories are those about young people who had to fend for themselves. Alone in an alien world, they needed to find work and a place to live while keeping up the lie of being someone other than themselves. They had to constantly guard against the dangers that could be posed by a slip of the tongue, a wrong accent, recognition by a former acquaintance, looking "Jewish"—even by a circumcision. The story "In Constant Terror" introduces us to a young girl whose loving family, in desperation at the hopelessness of surviving the Warsaw ghetto, sends her out into the hostile Polish landscape. With only her wit and her Polish language skills to maintain her false front, she takes on the identity of peasant, working on the farms of Poland and Germany, barely catching her breath between moments when she is almost recognized.

One common aspect of life in disguise was the need to pose as a Christian. For young people who were raised in devout Jewish families—even when they were sheltered by people who knew they were Jewish, as in "Convert! Convert!" in the story "I Choose Life"—the masquerade was very difficult. It wasn't just that the hidden children didn't know much about Christianity and might be exposed this way. More than that, they lived with a kind of inner agony at the outer "betrayal" of their faith.

In contrast to these stories of children who braved existence on their own, the series "A Hidden Child in Greece" details one writer's experiences in a country where rescuers hid Jewish children within their own families. These rescuers, although complete strangers, not only took the children in but kept in touch with the parents, rescuers and parents together keeping up a web of pretense in order to stay a step ahead of the occupying Germans. The stories reconstruct the point of view of the young child who must act a part—and like an adult, not make waves—even while she little understands what is going on.

While the stories in this section focus on disguise, we must remember that many more Jews attempted to escape the Nazis by physically hiding. They hid in attics and cellars, in underground bunkers, in forests and haystacks, behind false doors, even in mattresses. Episodes involving these ways of hiding are in several stories throughout this book.

What comes out of all these stories, no matter what the method of hiding, is the enduring mark of having been a hidden child. That mark seems to spring from the writers' feelings of a lost childhood identity, an essential part of themselves which they can never get back.

A.B.

In Constant Terror

Cyna Glatstein
  b. Sochachev, Poland, 1928

The Escape from Warsaw Ghetto

When my family was in the Warsaw Ghetto in 1942, the Gestapo came and took my fifteen-year-old brother away.

My father realized that it was the beginning of the end.

The golden chain of Judaism which had existed for more than a millennium had to be continued.

"My two daughters, Hashem willing, might be able to do this."

Polish passports had been secured.

Now the escape. Through the sewers was abhorrent to me. Only the gates remained.

At the moment of the changing of the guard a group of us ran to the gates. An alarm was sounded; powerful lights made us highly visible and easy targets.

A few of us did make it.

We ran blindly. Only Hashem could guide us to the forest.

Fortunately, it was harvest time. In the forest we could subsist on berries, mushrooms, and fruit. To quench our thirst the morning dew had to do.

After many days and nights of wandering, I found myself on a farm.

A woman at the well said, "The good Lord sent you. We need help. Can you do farm work?" "Yes," I said, "I was raised on a farm. Our farm was destroyed; my parents were killed and I was left alone." She directed me to the barn. "It's milking time," she said.

How am I to milk a cow?

Nothing in my sheltered religious upbringing prepared me for this. With a pail and a stool I approached the cow. A kick landed me on a pile of straw. The farmer's wife ran in, helped me up and said, "I am sorry I didn't tell you to avoid the vicious bull."

Had I tried to milk the bull, all would have been lost.

An Incurable Problem

While I was growing up, I was always told that I was a beautiful child. My hair, my eyes, my skin, the timbre of my voice.

It was when I was hiding, working on a farm, that I was first made painfully conscious of my Jewish nose.

A group of young ruffians pulling at their noses pointed at me, dancing up and down yelling, "Jew, Jew, Jew."

I yelled back in Polish, "What kind of a joke do you think this is? You better get out of here right away or I'll get the police after you."

They ran away. I was still left with the problem of my nose. What could I do about it? If those urchins were aware of my nose, I had a problem.

Something had to be done. I wracked my brain but could not come up with an answer. I was only thirteen years old and had never had such an experience.

My flawless Polish had saved me on many occasions. Nobody could believe that a dirty Jew could speak "our beautiful Polish language" so flawlessly. But the problem remained. I had to do something about it.

Maybe, maybe if I wrapped a towel around my face, tilting the nose for the night, it might help.

When I got up in the morning, my face was swollen beyond recognition. Mrs. Hornovska called, "Lucinka, what happened to you? Was it a bee, a wasp that stung you?" She ran to the garden, came back with some leaves that the local people used for bites.

Two weeks later I was myself again, except for my fear.

The Inspector

Very quickly, I became an accomplished farmer. I milked the cows, fed the chickens, gathered the eggs, churned butter. In the morning I took the cows out to the pasture, at sundown I brought them back. When necessary, I ploughed the land.

The Germans set a quota on all the farm products. The quota had to be met on the threat of severe punishment. All this was done systematically with a capable person in charge, the inspector. She was responsible for the surrounding villages as well.

The inspector, I thought, was a typical German. Blond hair, blue eyes, very attractive and young.

Whenever we met, she seemed to look at me in a strange way. This caused me great anxiety. Did she suspect that I was Jewish? Would she betray me? And yet, I felt she was not my enemy.

One day she came into the barn while I was milking a cow, looked around, came close to me and whispered, "Leave the village for a few days," and silently left.

I didn't know what to do—where, how, or even when to go. But the warning was clear. I had to leave. After I finished my chores, I went. My feet carried me to the meadow where I always took the cows to pasture. I stretched out on the grass and, sobbing deeply, mercifully fell asleep.

In a dream, my beloved father came to me. "My child, go back to the village."

"Why?" I asked.

But he was no longer there.

At sunrise I went directly to the well to begin the day's chores. The farmer's wife was already there.

"Did you hear the shots last night? The Gestapo came and rounded up seven suspected Jews in the villages. They took the inspector."

I was grief-stricken. Was my turn next?

Christmas, 1942

Christmas is approaching. The air is festive. I must not be an outsider. I am Lucinka, a Polish girl, and I must do whatever any other young Polish girl would do. It's not easy, but Hashem will guide me.

Like all the other girls, I dress in my best. We are going to midnight mass. I must be careful. Any difference would mark me immediately.

The mass is over. I pass that hurdle satisfactorily, thanks to Hashem.

Christmas day is another stumbling block. We form groups and go from house to house singing Christmas carols.

Now follows the Christmas feast. We are all invited to the mayor's house. The Christmas tree is ablaze with colored lights. Food is plentiful, liquor more so. It is no surprise the party becomes uncontrolled. Every time my group takes a drink I have to do likewise. Pleading a headache, I go out for some air. I retch. When I feel myself again, I return to the party.

Why was I forced to drink?

Liquor loosens the tongue.

Then the game begins.

Believing me drunk, they shower me with questions.

Where were you born? Where was your farm? Where did you go to school? What church did you attend?

My answers satisfy them.

I am safe for the time being.

Once more Hashem was with me.

Janek

Janek had come to the Polish village where I was working, looking for work. Something about Janek made him different from other migrants.

I could not put my finger on it, but it was there.

Could I call it a rare kind of gentility?

Mrs. Hornovska, my farmer, did not need another worker, but the widow on the next farm probably did. Her workers did not stay long. She was difficult to work for.

She hired Janek. He proved to be a hard worker. He was industrious, polite, and quiet. Also, he did whatever the widow asked him to do. She was happy to have him.

The widow praised him—she used him as an example to other workers.

They were jealous—they felt he was different, they resented him.

I heard the widow shouting, "Leave him alone, leave him alone, louts."

One day while the widow was in town, Janek was in the field ploughing. I was weeding a patch of carrots. I saw a gang approaching Janek. There was something evil in the air. I prayed for Janek.

What did they want of him?

Clearly they were out to destroy him.

"Pull your pants down, pull your pants down."

"I can't, I can't."

"You must."

They pulled his pants down.

"We were right, we were right, you are a filthy Jew."

They dragged his nude body into the forest. There they hacked him to pieces and threw his remains into a pit so nobody would know what they had done.

The widow found his tattered clothing. Safely hidden in the lining of his jacket was a picture of a small family. She brought the picture to her friend, Mrs. Hornovska. When they left the room I turned the picture over. It said, "the Kleppfish family."

I found out after the war that this was a prominent family of prewar Warsaw. May Janek's soul rest in peace among the righteous.

The Epidemic

There was a dense forest adjoining the village where I had been working on a farm for over a year. In this forest, there was a group of partisans composed of Jews who had escaped the clutches of the Gestapo, along with Russian prisoners of war and some Polish patriots.

In order to survive, they raided the villages. They came during the night, and even during the day when the villagers cooperated with them, hoping the partisans would help with the crops.

They brought with them—lice. The result was a typhus fever epidemic in the villages. I did not escape the devastating effects of the epidemic. I became desperately ill with a raging fever. For days, I was delirious. Occasionally, I became lucid and was aware that I was being given water. Later again, I was delirious and babbling.

When I came to and opened my eyes, there was Helenka, the farmer's daughter. She said to me, "Lucinka, I thought you were one of us. You went to church with us and spoke Polish. But in your delirium, you didn't speak Polish.

I don't know what language you did speak, but it wasn't Polish. Are you hiding something? If you are, we are both in great danger."

"I will help you," she said. "When you are recovered, you must leave. In these times with workers so scarce you'll have no trouble getting a job."

One week later, my meager belongings were tied in a bundle and I was off. On my way, I suddenly remembered what I had been babbling in my delirium over and over again. In Yiddish I was saying, "I want to be buried in a Jewish cemetery."

No wonder that I repeated this over and over. It was with me all through the five years of my agony.

The Encounter

The Gestapo came to the farms of Poland and rounded up all able-bodied villagers for forced labor in Germany.

We were taken to Warsaw to be deloused and to have our papers checked and rechecked.

Why this checking again and again? The Gestapo, with the help of Polish informers, suspected that there were Jewish girls in the groups.

After the delousing we were marched to the barracks where we spent the night.

This gave the Gestapo ample time to check and recheck our papers.

In the morning we lined up for our rations—stale bread, a little marmalade, and chicory.

At the table, through the grapevine, I heard that the latest transport had been brought in from Sochachev, my home town. My heart froze. Despite this terrible shock, I had to act normal. That night I went through hell. I prayed like I had never prayed before.

The next morning after breakfast, we were lined up for inspection again.

The Gestapo marched in. *Achtung!*

From his memo, he read: "Jerusalska, Wojciech, Nasibirska, step forward!"

He raised his gun and shot them dead. The bodies were dragged away and the inspection continued.

After the inspection, we went to the barracks to do some personal chores.

It was time for the third ration of the day. Our group, workers from different towns in Poland, always ate together. I felt someone from the Sochachev transport staring at me. I knew who he was. He had been my classmate before the war. He looked almost the same as he had looked when we were ten years old and together in sixth grade. Now he was thirteen, a little changed, but with the same Polish upturned nose, the same blue eyes. I braced myself for the worst.

The worst happened.

Pointing at me he said, "*Ty jestes rabina corka*." (You are the rabbi's daughter.)

The group was horrified! "You are lying, she is Polish and we know it."

Looking him in the eye, I said, "Maybe you are a Jew. I am Polish."

His face was ashen. He stuttered, "I'm sorry, forgive me, forgive me, I made a mistake."

I never saw him after that.

Accused

I was on the train en route to Germany. I was not alone. I was once again with a group of Polish workers coming from Warsaw. The conditions on the train were bearable. They needed us for the war effort, so there were rations and coffee. Without food and drink we would have been useless. The soldiers who guarded us announced that our destination was Bremen.

Several times during the trip the train stopped to pick up SS officers.

Each time we were counted and our papers checked. We continued on our journey. There was an air raid in progress. "*Heraus, heraus,*" came the order. When the all clear sounded we continued on uninterrupted to Bremen.

Bremen was under attack. When the all clear sounded this time, we were marched to our barracks.

The classification began.

My papers indicated that I was a farm worker. I was assigned to a farm in Seuslitz on the Elbe; some were classified as miners; others were sent to ammunition factories and still others to—where, I never found out.

After the classification I was directed to the soup kitchen. I picked up my ration and started to the barracks. Suddenly I was surrounded by several young boys from my group. "You're Jewish, you're Jewish." I was petrified, horrified, paralyzed, numb. I felt like a caged animal.

Ironically, I was saved by an air raid—or was it by a miracle?

When the all clear sounded I realized not only was I alive, but I was unscathed.

I never saw my tormentors again. After that I was transferred to the farm in Seuslitz.

The Bike

It was harvest time. I was relieved from the burden of hauling the coal which had arrived by box cars and had to be distributed to the German households in preparation for the coming winter.

This chore was so arduous that I was certain it would break me physically.

I was glad when Mrs. Schultz told me that as of now I would once again work in the fields. The fields were four kilometers away. Bicycles were the means of transportation.

Mrs. Schultz had her bicycle and she gave me mine. I was also given a pitchfork and a shovel. My instructions were to follow her.

Why was I afraid to tell her I had never been on a bike?

Who knows what might have happened to me? So I was silent. Mrs. Schultz started off.

I placed the pitchfork and the shovel across the handlebars and tried to get on the bike. It was a hopeless situation. The bike went its own way and I hit a wall. I was dazed, but continue I must. Pushing the bike ahead of me I walked the four kilometers.

Mrs. Schultz asked, "Why did it take you so long? I have been waiting."

"I fell."

"Oh, I see the bruises on your face. I should have had the brakes checked."

The One-Eyed Monster

In 1944, I had been working for more than a year for Mrs. Schultz on a farm in Sachsenhaus.

Mrs. Schultz and her workers were excited and tense. Mrs. Schultz's husband, the Commandant, a high-ranking Gestapo officer, was due. He was on leave after a two-year absence. Most of the workers knew him and called him "the one-eyed monster" behind his back. Why? Because he wore a black patch on his left eye and was a cruel man.

He arrived in his resplendent uniform, covered in medals, with his beloved Schütze, a big German shepherd. Mrs. Schultz ran out to greet her husband and Schütze. Arm in arm, and carrying on an animated conversation, they walked into the kitchen. I was at the sink, washing dishes.

I was paralyzed with fear. Frau Erma called to me, "Lucinka, we need a dozen eggs for an omelette. I am planning a luncheon for some friends."

Could they hear the pounding of my heart? Hoping the Commandant wouldn't notice me, I turned away quickly to run for the eggs.

The luncheon was a great success. The Commandant regaled the guests. They laughed hilariously when he described how he had beaten and killed all the *Schweinjuden* inside and outside the Warsaw Ghetto. He was petting his beloved Schütze as he told the story.

On the last day of his visit, a few of us were helping Mrs. Schultz with the Commandant's luggage. Suddenly pointing at me, he shouted, "Erma, who is this girl?"

"She's Lucinka, my best worker."

"Where did you get her?"

"She came with a group of Polish workers. Her papers are in order."

"*Sie hat eine Jüdische Schnauze!*" (She has a Jewish nose.)

"Other people have long noses," Mrs. Schultz said.

"Be careful. Check and recheck, and let me know what you find out." He left.

Now, still another fear had been added to my already crushing burden . . .

Posing as a Christian

Dora Zuer Iwler
b. Chodoròw, Poland, 1923

More than anything, I wanted to live in order to tell the world that someone must stop the Nazi murderers.

I decided I had to escape. Inside the Jonowski camp, near Lvov, Poland, there was no way to get out because of the electrified fence surrounding us. But out in the fields where I worked, maybe I had a chance.

One day soon after that decision, I backed away from the other workers toward the high weeds, until I disappeared in them. The next day I made my way to Lvov. I posed as a Christian, taking my friend's sister's name—Sophie Lourecka. I didn't have papers to prove my Christian identity, but I managed to get a job anyway, as a janitor with an elderly couple. I convinced them that the Nazis had been taking Christian boys and girls from Poland to work in the ammunition factories, and I had escaped from there. I lived with this couple for a year and a half on Kopernika Street.

In May 1944, I was recognized by some former schoolmates who saw me sweeping the sidewalk outside the apartment building. One or all of them denounced me. In a few days, a Gestapo soldier and a plainclothesman came to the door and asked for "Miss Sophie." They demanded my documents, but I didn't have any to show.

I confessed to them right away that I was Jewish, hoping to avoid the beatings that I heard were done to all Jews when they were captured. They took me back to the apartment. The old couple asked me what was wrong.

"I'm Jewish," I admitted.

Shocked, the old man said, "Look what I have to go through in my old age."

I turned to the Nazis and asked for mercy on this old couple.

"If you believe in God," I said, "please don't kill them. They didn't know I was Jewish."

I found out later that their lives were spared.

My Nazi captors beat me in front of the elderly couple with a whip they found hanging on the wall. Then they took me out to the street and walking along, they asked, "Do you know any other Jews? If you turn anybody in, you will be saved."

"I'm alone," I said, "I don't know anyone here."

The plainclothesman burst out, "You dirty Jew! I'll kill you with my bare hands."

"I'm glad that you will have me on your conscience, instead of you on mine," I answered.

He slapped me very hard on my left ear. I couldn't hear for three days.

They took me to Lanscki jail, where I stayed for a week. Then I was sent back to the Jonowski camp. So that was that.

Six weeks after my return, the Russian army began advancing toward us. All the inmates were marched further into Poland. After walking about 80 or 90 kilometers, we stopped in a meadow. Determined to try to escape again, I looked around me for any possibility. With my friend Albina, I ran up a nearby hill. At the top there was a railroad track and a small station.

A train conductor came out and asked what was going on.

"Who are these people and where are they going?"

"We are Christians from Jonowski camp," I lied.

"Do you want to escape?"

"Yes!"

"Follow me."

By some miracle, the guards we passed didn't see us. The conductor took us to a Polish family in Rymanow who put us up for the night.

We were afraid to confide to anyone that we were Jews because there were collaborators everywhere. Albina and I knew that we had to leave this safe haven. Not knowing where else to go, we walked back through the fields we had escaped from the day before. We headed toward the Russian front, trying to get through the German occupied territory.

Tired and hungry, we went from town to town looking for work to support ourselves. Always we posed as Christians. Finally, we got a job in the fields outside the village of Bidynieglowice (near Yeslo).

In January 1945, I was liberated by the Russians. I hugged the first Russian soldier who approached me. He asked me if I was Jewish.

"No," I said, still afraid.

But I had my freedom to celebrate, and so did Albina.

I Choose Life

Libby Stern
b. Suceava, Romania, 1926

Convert! Convert!

I am in a small village, Andreyevka, in the Ukraine after leaving my fifth hiding place. The people here live in such a vacuum! They don't know what is going on with the Jews; they have no newspapers and no radios. It is 1942, yet all they know is that the entire male population over eighteen is fighting the Germans and that they have to wait till the war ends for them to come home.

I find work in a house managed by a matriarch, Hanelka, whose three sons and husband are at the Russian front and whose three teenage girls are at home. They own a herd of sheep and make a living by shearing and spinning the wool and knitting it into sweaters, socks, and gloves. My chores include spinning and knitting. I am treated well.

Hanelka explains that they belong to a Christian religion called Calvinism that her husband brought home in 1918 from Germany, where he was a World War I prisoner. Every night Hanelka reads to me and her children chapters from the Old Testament, and then refers to some passages of the New Testament and what Christ had to say about it. When Passover comes, Hanelka bakes unleavened bread for me and treats me like her own. I feel safe in this godforsaken place.

One day I get a visitor—the mayor of a nearby town, Pietor, a man about fifty years old who is tall and husky, with kind eyes and a soft voice. He wants to see me because he heard that I know German. He offers me a job to teach the children German and also to translate some papers from time to time.

"You know," he says, "the Germans will be here for many, many years to come and our children must be prepared. You will get room and board and also a salary. You'll live like a queen! And next week when the Romanian priest arrives here to baptize our children, he'll baptize you too. Then we'll issue you papers and you will be safe forever."

I don't know what to answer. So I tell him my German is not that good and besides, I don't want to be baptized because I don't believe in Christ; and so I cannot go along with his plan.

The mayor's face turns red. "You stupid *Yid*. Do you know what's going on out there? The Germans are killing the Jews all over the Ukraine. They burn your synagogues and shoot men, women, and children on the streets wherever they are. I offer you life and you choose death . . . "

Hanelka tries to say something but he shuts her up. "By tomorrow if I catch you hiding any Jews, I will personally arrest you and your children." He leaves angry.

That night, Hanelka tries to persuade me to change my mind. "What if you convert to Christianity? It's such a good religion. It teaches love, forgiveness, and generosity for all mankind."

Yes, Hanelka, I think, according to your Bible it is all that you say it is. But you have not read the history of the past thousand years. You know nothing about the Crusaders, the British expulsion, the French expulsion, the Spanish Inquisition, and the Russian pogroms, and you know nothing about what's going on now all over Europe.

The next day I leave for the ghetto of Shargorod. I am determined to join my people and share their destiny.

The mayor is wrong. I choose life, but on my own terms.

The Bridge

Shargorod Ghetto, where one-third of my hometown Jews had been deported, was only twenty miles away.

That year, spring came early to the Ukraine; the snow melted fast and flooded all the roads. I struggled through the roads until I made my way to the only bridge left standing over a swollen brook. In the distance, I saw a long line of peasants trying to cross. I inched my way to the bridge. I was the last one, and suddenly I realized that at the other end there were two German officers and two soldiers guarding the exit, not letting anyone get off the bridge. I tried to go back but already there were several German soldiers standing at my back. The place was surrounded and I was trapped.

I overheard two Ukrainian women talking.

One said, "I always take my identification card, and I've crossed this bridge a hundred times. Nobody ever stopped me or asked me for papers."

The other one answered, "Haven't you heard? Last night the Russian partisans blew up a train full of German soldiers going to the eastern front. So now they're checking papers and looking for spies."

I felt that this was really the last of my running. I had no papers, nobody knew me here, and what would I tell them—that I ran away from a death camp?

I counted fourteen persons in front of me. Many were searched for weapons but all had to show their ID cards. Soon only twelve were left. Maybe they'll hang me, or maybe they'll shoot me, or maybe they'll torture me to find out what I know. I felt I had to say *Vidui*, the last prayer, but my father had never taught it to me. Why would he teach a fifteen-year-old such a prayer? Nine more people to search . . . two were taken away to the left and handcuffed . . . . So, this is the way they will do it; first, handcuff me. Six more to go . . . a serene feeling came over me. I thought about how much I wanted to be reunited with my dead father and mother—I was tired of this life anyhow, and it didn't matter anymore. Four more to go . . . this time they took a young man to the side and handcuffed him . . . I saw the fright in his black eyes. Two more to go . . . I said the *Shema* and waited. A moment later the German officer approached me.

He looked at me with his icy blue eyes and in an angry tone shouted, "What are you waiting for? Keep moving!"

Lost Families

Sara Reichman
b. Yanova Dolina, Ukraine, 1942

When the Germans invaded the Ukraine in 1941, my father fled to Russia, but my mother, who was pregnant, stayed behind. She gave birth to me and went into hiding. When I was six months old my mother gave me to a Polish family, Pulit, for hiding, since she could not care for me under the conditions she lived in. It is with this family, a mother, a father, two sisters, and grandparents that I spent the war years and after. With them I moved from Poland to Holland and then Germany, where they were slave laborers. After the war the family returned to Poland, to a village near Opole in Silesia.

In May 1947, my mother's sister Leah, accompanied by a Polish Jewish officer, came to take me away from this family. It was only after a long search and many inquiries that my aunt had been able to trace me.

Although she presented herself as my mother, the family refused to give me back. But after being promised a monetary compensation, the family agreed to give me to my aunt.

My aunt and I went out to a field and, sitting on the green grass, she held me and hugged me and recited a children's poem to me. At night I was allowed to sleep with her.

But a few nights after my aunt arrived, my surrogate mother, Marianna Pulit, came in and snatched me out of my aunt's bed. This was the first time that I experienced a conflict between people. I felt anguished, that I was the cause for a disagreement and a fight. The family was not ready to give me away after all.

Finally, my aunt was able to persuade the Pulits to give me up, arguing that I was a Jewish child—and why should they have an interest in keeping me, after all? At the end of a week, my aunt and I left. I was told that I was going to visit relatives in town. I was given some clothes and big red round beads that I kept for many years.

My aunt and I lived in the city of Lodz, in a commune, preparing to go to Palestine. One night in bed, my aunt told me a story about a woman hiding in a cave who was killed. Later she told me that this woman was my mother. She had been spotted outside of her hiding place just a few months before the war ended and was shot to death. I felt a great letdown, a great sadness.

At the end of the summer my aunt and I crossed the border from Poland to Czechoslovakia and from there to Austria, to a Displaced Persons camp. There

I met my father, who had spent most of the war years in a prison camp in Russia. During the time in the DP camp, my father tried very hard to get close to me. He bought me a big doll which I kept for many years, and we took walks together. I learned to love him very much. After a year in the DP camp we went to Israel.

My father always told me that I owed my life to the Polish family who took me in.

Throughout the years, I have tried to recapture the harmonious feeling I experienced in my early childhood with the Pulit family. I had a father, a mother, siblings, and grandparents. I was loved. The unity of the family stayed intact, although they were slave laborers and we experienced hunger. My last year with them was tranquil. There were family religious celebrations, going to church on Sundays, my surrogate sister's wedding, green pastures with flowers.

In time, after I left the Pulits, I realized that I would no longer have the wholeness I had with them. My mother had been killed, as had other members of my family.

It is the theme of my life to recreate that wholeness.

Beyond Memory

Shulamit Bastacky
b. Vilna, Lithuania, 1941

On Yom Hashoah each year I kindle the memorial candles. I kindle them in memory not only of my grandparents, aunts, uncles, and cousins who did not survive the Holocaust. I kindle them also for a Roman Catholic nun, a righteous gentile who risked her life to save mine.

These memorials stir in me the image of a little girl who huddled by herself for more than three long years in a small, dim cellar. While my family and the nun are blessedly recalled now at middle age, they do not lead to any real recollection of the quiet, frightened, curly-headed little girl. She is the figure that won't come to mind, won't allow herself to be a part of me now. She crouches forever in the recesses of a deeper cellar, the cellar of my mind.

I was born in August 1941, in Vilna, the center of Jewish life in Lithuania, four weeks after the Germans entered the city. Our deadly game of hide and seek began that year and lasted until 1945. My mother and father, who also survived the war, have had to tell me the story of my survival. They did so in the barest of terms, for any detailed narrative was too painful for them. We rarely mention the past at home, even now in America in 1996.

I don't remember the nun, either. I know that she came as often as she could and brought me enough food to survive until she came the next time. I must have been overjoyed each time she appeared to interrupt the dark flow of hours. Now, I do not see her face; I cannot hear her voice; nor do I feel the touch of her hands. But somehow, even without memory, I know that she gave me more than food—she shared herself through a kind word, a show of affection.

I emerged from the cellar malnourished and sick when the Russian Army liberated Vilna. The nun had placed me on the bank of a river, where I was found by a Lithuanian man who then placed me in a Catholic orphanage where I was given a Lithuanian name. My family found me in the orphanage by recognizing a birthmark on my body. After our reunion, we traveled by train to central Poland where I went to a rehabilitation center sponsored by the Joint Distribution Organization, a facility for Jewish children. There I was physically and emotionally rehabilitated. They gave me quartzlight treatments for sun deprivation and more importantly, a safe place where I could be a normal child.

I often wonder why I don't remember. The answer I give myself is that my memory is blocked as a result of being deprived of family, of nurturing, and of the most basic human needs.

The feelings of a lost early childhood will remain with me the rest of my life. But my feelings of respect and gratitude for that nameless nun will remain with me, too.

A Hidden Child in Greece*

Yolanda Avram Willis
b. Salonika, Greece, 1934

Prologue: Memories Reclaimed

My stories start with my family's flight from our home town when Italy attacked Greece, but most of them focus on the period of the Jewish Persecution, from early 1943 through our liberation in October 1944. I was six at the war's start, eight when we went into hiding, and ten when we were liberated.

My immediate family—my parents, younger brother and I—first left our home city, Larisa, in central Greece, seeking safety from the Italian bombing of local military installations, beginning with the declaration of war in October 1940.

In April of 1941, immediately after Germany attacked Greece, we attempted to leave for Egypt via the island of Crete. My father used to listen to the BBC and thus anticipated the Jewish Persecution, given the inevitable German victory and occupation of Greece. Three days before our planned escape from Crete to Egypt, where the government and royal family had already fled to safety, the Nazis made a massive bomber, glider, and paratroop attack on Crete. It was the first airborne invasion in military history and took the British, who had a naval base there, completely by surprise. A Nazi-occupied island was the last place for us to be. So a few months after going to Crete we reversed our direction, heading back to the mainland and the Italian controlled zone.

When we reached Athens, in the fall of 1941, we expected to disappear into the relative anonymity of the capital. However, the famine of the winter of 1941–42 drove us back to much better-supplied Larisa which, like Athens, was occupied by the Italians.

Larisa had an ancient Jewish community, where my late grandfather, Moushon Avram, was legendary as a businessman, banker, philanthropist, and beloved president of his people. When the persecution in Salonika became unmistakable, early in 1943, we knew we had to leave Larisa again to avoid the unthinkable but inevitable hour when my father, as one of the leaders of the Jewish community, would be forced to register Jews and thus cooperate in their capture and deportation.

---

*Readers who are not familiar with events in Greece during World War II may wish to first read the Historical Note, beginning on p. 139.

We went to Athens with forged Christian identity papers and a detailed plan for hiding preventively, months before there were any anti-Jewish measures there. But then we were forced to move out of our comfortable Athens house, because the adults had occasionally been recognized by acquaintances who knew them as Jews from Larisa.

First, the immediate family hid all together in a flower farm outside of Athens. Later, in July or August of 1943, we dispersed for greater safety, in anticipation of the Italian surrender to Allied forces, as rumors of their secret negotiations leaked out. Several weeks later the Germans took command of all Italian-occupied zones of Greece, and the Jewish Persecution spread into Athens.

SS Colonel Jurgen Stroop, decorated for the liquidation and burning of the Warsaw Ghetto in May of 1943, had been promoted to SS Major General and reassigned to take personal command of registering the Jews of Greece in preparation for deportation. He worked in parallel with Dieter Wisliceny, Adolph Eichmann's personal deputy for the Final Solution in Greece. Less than twenty-four hours after arriving in Athens that October, Wisliceny summoned Chief Rabbi Eli Barzilai and ordered him to assemble and turn over the lists of Jews registered to the Athens community and to register all others who had moved elsewhere within the surrounding Attica region to escape the deportations from Northern Greece.

My memories of what happened at that time are confused because for almost five years, from 1940 to 1945, I knew nothing for sure. Certainty and clarity had vanished along with our home, my school, my playmates, our routine, our safety, and our country's freedom. My family stayed just one step ahead of capture, by devising elaborate plans of escape. At the core of the experience of those years was a fog of confusion, of always making new plans, and of guesswork, as we navigated on a quicksand terrain of ever-present and ever-changing dangers.

I know little of what I felt during those years, because most often I could afford to experience few of my true feelings. Many of the reasons I cite for our actions are probably my own unconscious inventions, created from scraps of information and the common human thirst for meaning. What I am certain of is that my parents and our rescuers showed seemingly miraculous and unfailing courage, foresight, and wisdom.

• • •

My stories include details gathered from many hours of interviews with our rescuers and their families, as well as several family friends and relatives, during a trip to Greece in 1994. It was the first time I wanted to know about those years, and the instigation had come a few months earlier from my daughter who persuaded me—and provided the needed emotional support—finally to face the past.

Pack the Suitcases, Karolla

It was barely light outside when Father told Mother, as he ran out of the door, "Pack the suitcases, Karolla," the refrain which would punctuate our lives for the next four years and precede many an evacuation and attempt to run away from danger.

Father returned right after breakfast with a horse-drawn cab, into which our suitcases were loaded. We all piled in, and soon we were at the big central square boarding the bus for Lamia. I carried a small bag and my doll. Father settled us and the luggage on the bus, and just as the bus started to pull away from the curb, he jumped off. Mother became hysterical and begged the driver to stop. A heated discussion between my parents followed on the sidewalk. Father won. Mother, sobbing, took her seat again, and the bus started off. Aunt Stella, Mother's youngest sister, was anxiously asking questions which Mother was ignoring. The baby was wailing in the maid's arms. I kept quiet, hugging my doll. I had turned six on October 2 and was full of the knowledge that I was now a big girl.

". . . Salvator has to stay in town." Mother dabbed her red rimmed eyes. "He promised to sleep in the ground floor of the Big House. There are two layers of reinforced concrete over that ceiling, it is as good as an air raid shelter . . . He feels he, as President, cannot leave the Jewish community during this crisis," Mother finally told Stella. It was Stella's turn to become hysterical. Mother, always Father's best advocate, made it sound perfectly natural that we would be tricked into traveling alone.

It was October 29, 1940. I heard the grown-ups say, "We are at war." I did not know what war meant. Over the next few weeks, war came to mean the terrifying wail of sirens, the packing of suitcases, the rushing off to some strange destination. . . . It was only much later that I understood why we fled Larisa, our home town. The day before, Mussolini had vowed to burn Larisa into a pile of cinders, when Greece refused the Italian ultimatum of surrender. The largest army camp in Greece was on Larisa's outskirts. Lamia, only a few hours away, was a town of no military significance.

Our bus was going through a long tunnel, when the driver suddenly put on the brakes, jerking us practically off our seats. It was very dark in that tunnel and for several minutes we did not know what had made him stop. It turned out to be an accident ahead of us. So we had to leave the bus, taking whatever we could carry, and head for the dim point of light ahead.

My feet were hurting as I trudged along with my little bag and doll. Looking down I realized that before leaving my seat, I had hastily put my Mary Janes on the wrong feet, sticking my right foot into the left shoe. I would not delay our group with this complaint. We were being urged to walk as fast as we could, in order to get away from the fumes of the "*gazozen*," the foul-smelling, oil-burning bus.

I went through the length of that tunnel wearing my mismatched shoes till we stopped clear of the accident. Then I could at last set my doll down, stop to slip my shoes off, rub my sore toes, and put the shoes back on correctly.

In Lamia we all crowded into a small hotel room, and Mother set up the little alcohol stove and supplies for the baby's milk and for cooking simple meals. My brother had diarrhea and was in a lot of pain, crying through the night, rocked by turns in Mother's and Stella's arms. Before dawn we were scared awake by the piercing wail of sirens. Loud knocks on the doors up and down the corridor ordered everyone to the air raid shelter around the corner. Blackout. . . . No one was to attract attention to our building by turning on the light. Mother bundled us up in the dark and dragged us out to follow the small crowd to the underground shelter. In the days that followed, we often reached that place only to hear the all clear, turn around and head back to our room again.

. . .

"Pack the suitcases, Karolla," echoed my father's words as Mother bundled us up again. As suddenly as we had left for Lamia, we were on our way again, riding in a hired black taxi with all our suitcases tied with thick rope on the roof. Lamia turned out to be on the path to the strategic Gorgopotamos Bridge the Italians were trying to destroy, to cut off Greek army transports resupplying the battle zone. We left on a pitch-black night. The driver kept his lights dim. Stella, nervous about the nightly bombings, noticed a bright pinpoint of light over our speeding cab. And then she thought the light was following us.

"It is a bomber tracking us!" Stella cried out, panic-stricken, pointing at the sky. Mother's reassurances that it was only an evening star were not making any impression on Stella. "Look, it is aiming to strafe our car!"

I guess it was then I decided never to act like a scaredy-cat—wartime or not—not to be like poor Aunt Stella. I was going to be like Dad, instead—fearless. That decision probably saved my life, but it also shut out much dimly felt terror. To this day worry comes in many disguises, seldom straightforward and direct.

The Dinner Invitation

The dinner invitation feels like a summons. Father says we must all go, Grandmother, my two aunts, the children and, under the guise of tending the baby, even the seventeen-year-old maid. He is not about to leave any of the women alone, surrounded by soldiers who have not seen a female in months. Besides, in our tent on this uninhabited, rocky island, there is the shipwrecked drunk Father had picked up off the coast of Crete, as our chartered fishing boat had begun to make its way from Crete back to the mainland. Though sleeping off his hangover, he is not to be trusted alone with the young peasant girl, Father whispers to Mother.

Using a borrowed flashlight, Mother sees that we get a makeshift sprucing up. She is especially careful with my two-year-old brother whom we still refer to as *Oh Behbis*, "The Baby Boy." He is a beautiful child, with huge brown eyes and a head full of luminous golden curls.

Aunt Allegra braids Grandmother's long silver hair and pins it into a low bun. Then she helps her mother into her old-fashioned black silk dress, fastened at the neck with her starfish diamond pin.

"None of us should speak Ladino tonight," Father reminds us. I understand why he does not want us to speak the Judeo-Spanish the grownups use at home.*

Aunt Allegra, my father's sister, underscores, "Please, stick to Greek during dinner, Mama."

I think to myself that this is because Grandmother sometimes gets confused. She is eighty. No telling what she'll say in front of those men, especially if her diabetes starts acting up again.

Mother and Aunt Stella, her youngest sister, are fixing their hair as if deliberately trying to look as plain as possible, but still appear well-groomed and aristocratic. Aunt Allegra, a few years older than the other two women and quite a bit taller, dampens her thick mop of dark brown wavy hair, trying to tame it down. She is the most "Jewish looking" person in our group.

I complete the entourage heading toward a temporary structure which serves as the officers' mess hall. I have my mother's very fair skin and my father's blue eyes. My hair is blond and softly waving, held on the top with a bow. Just before we leave our tent, Mother hands me a powder blue sweater she has knitted for me. It is a windy, starless night.

In the mess hall, the table is laid on a long narrow plank set on saw horses. In attendance are two uniformed soldiers. Grandmother, tall, slender and unmistakably patrician, is given the place of honor at one end of the table, seated next to her daughter, Allegra. Nothing reveals that this ramrod-straight, elegant old lady, who had raised six children, used to run a large household with two kitchens and four sets of dishes. In her basement she had conducted two businesses, selling cereal grains and raising silkworms, an age-old skill of Greek Jews.

The maid has taken a seat in a corner, tending the dozing baby, who is suffering from amoebic dysentery. He has been sick since we fled to the mountains of Crete during the German airborne invasion a few months ago.

Mother and Father are seated, with much ceremony, on either side of our host at the head of the table. I am between Mother and Aunt Stella.

Self-conscious about my table manners on this unaccustomed formal occasion, and generally disoriented and apprehensive about what we are doing here, I watch the people around the room.

---

*Since the migrations from the Iberian Peninsula, beginning with the expulsion from Spain in 1492, the dominant Jewish tradition in Greece has been the Sephardic tradition. Thus, the "Yiddish" of Greek Jewry is Ladino, based on medieval Spanish.

I look at my beautiful brown-eyed, black-haired Mother who is thirty-three. She is holding on to her dignity, a pleasant expression on her face.

It is understood, such occasions are handled by Father. So tonight, according to plan, his female charges are keeping their eyes properly downcast. Mother and Aunt Allegra are hiding their spunk and spirit under a mask of modesty and decorum. Aunt Stella is successfully hiding her fears tonight.

Waiting for the food to be served, I am thinking back at all the mixed signals we got since we came here. Only yesterday, as we were attempting to leave Crete, our boat was flagged down under gunfire. Our crew and boat were confiscated and sent to the other side of this uninhabited, godforsaken rock, taking most of our belongings and provisions. The duty officer examined our papers and kept them. He then motioned for us to climb to the top of that very steep cliff, jutting almost vertically from the water's edge. Two soldiers were ordered to bring down a stretcher for Grandmother.

Shortly after we reached the top, the *Kommandant* himself appeared. After a brief exchange with the officer who brought us up there, he barked some orders in German, a language none of us understood. We were thoroughly confused when the officers' tent, complete with double-decker bunks, was ordered to be vacated and turned over to us. By then it was almost nightfall, and Mother made a plea in French for a flashlight, gesturing toward the sick baby. Amazingly, the *Kommandant* knew French, and a large flashlight immediately materialized.

Our tent is made of parachute silk printed in camouflage colors; it is just tall enough for Father, who is close to six feet, to stand upright. The lower bunks were taken by Grandmother, Mother and the baby, and the drunk. Across from him Father, as an unarmed sentry, has kept for himself the bunk by the flap door.

In the dark, surrounded by the dry and dusty brush which covers the top of the island, the tent is full of ominous noises. Last night Mother kept flashing the light onto the doorway every time she heard a noise, every time the wind brushed a twig against the tent. She was certain they were coming to slaughter us or take one of the women. The others, too, wondered if *they* had discovered something wrong with our papers. Maybe they radioed back to Crete to check them out.

We are trapped on top of this rock, surrounded by water, with no means of escape. None of us understands what is going on, nor how we'll get out of here alive. . . .

And now, here we are tonight at the *Kommandant*'s dinner table.

Through the fog of my confusion and anxiety, I notice that the *Kommandant* and my parents are speaking in French. He is explaining to them that this rock. . . .

". . . is being used as a military observatory of the high seas . . . You are here in protective custody against the dangerous stormy Sea of Crete."

The tension around the table goes down a notch.

The second course is being served. Mother helps herself and then fills my plate.

The *Kommandant* is now holding forth about his Fatherland having no quarrel with Greece.

"The Germans are the preservers of the classical learning and tradition."

He says they are here to liberate us culturally, by reintroducing the glory of ancient Greece to our poor country which has fallen so far behind, after the four centuries of Turkish occupation. He talks about our history, about the "Big War". . . . The speech goes on and on . . .

"Germany will be your protector now!"

My head is swimming. This is all too preposterous even for me, a child of six. I strain to catch his drift.

". . . It is not Germany's fault. It is the Jews that caused this war. If we only had one of *them* here now . . ." he gestures with his hands in a strangling motion, his face flushed and mean.

Across the table Grandmother is audible now, talking in Ladino. Father is keeping our host busy, charming him. We hold our breath. The dinner drags on. Grandmother keeps talking to herself in "Spanish," seemingly in a world all her own. And then . . . nothing. I must have dozed off, exhausted with anxiety. Besides, it is past my bedtime.

The rest of the time on that rock is a blur. Some time later—was it days? weeks?—we are out of protective custody and finally permitted to sail back to occupied Athens.

I don't know how my father engineered our release.

Father's name was Salvator Avram, son of Moushon, which translates to Rescuer Abraham, son of Moses. The name turned out to be prophetic.

The Family Must Disperse

The decision to disperse the family was reached on a sleepless night, while my parents, my brother and I lay on pallets on the dirt floor in a small shack, several miles outside Athens. The four of us had been staying on a flower farm, driven deeper into hiding as the Jewish Persecution elsewhere in the Nazi and Bulgarian controlled northern cities moved into high gear. In this atmosphere of growing danger, my parents reached the desperate conclusion that two Christian families had to be found to take in my brother and me. This would increase the children's chances of survival. My parents also had to move once again, posing as a childless couple, and find new identity papers.

After I was gone, the search for a family to take my four-and-a-half-year-old brother continued. I was told I was the lucky one to go first, but at eight and a half, I had my doubts.

What I remember from that time is my sudden departure from the flower farm and arrival at my new home. I have a new identity. My name is Julia now.

I am supposed to have come from a distant town, because my parents could not feed me. My supposed "godparents," who own a bakery in Athens, have agreed to take me and rear me along with their six-year-old daughter, Eleni . . .*

• • •

It has been some weeks since I turned into "Julia." Out of gratitude, I try to act lucky and, as the weeks go by, begin to actually feel fortunate to be there. My godparents, Michael and Artemis, are a handsome, hard-working couple of humble origins, in their thirties. They are very good to me. We live in a neat two-story house, bright with sunshine. The bakery is around the corner, so little Eleni and I can visit it often.

One morning, while we are at home, there is a knock on the door, and I run to answer. It is my father, his face shaded by his customary gray Borsalino hat.

"*Nonos!* Godfather!" I call out. "Some man is here to see you."

That sudden appearance at the doorstep is soon followed by my parents and brother moving in with my godparents. This totally violates the plan to disperse. How was it that my family broke the cardinal rule against risking visits which could bring danger to me and my rescuers? I know that the chance of being followed is ever-present. I push back my questions, as I bask in this special good fortune, and give myself up to the reunion.

Later that day I learn that my luck is due to last night's terrible raid of their shack in the flower farm. Six armed Greeks and a uniformed German soldier had held them up.

The Extortion

"Give them the valuables, Xeni," urged my father, careful to use my mother's fake Christian name. Out came the money belt and jewelry hidden in a little flesh-colored pouch inside her bra. The holdup leader grabbed the offerings, while the other five men began to empty every sack and box and tin can of provisions and cart them out of the room.

The German soldier stood sentry with his gun pointed at my brother's head.

"How about the stuff in my little pillow?" asked the four-and-a-half-year-old boy, handing over the backup stash, the hidden treasure. His voice was tremulous, his brown eyes big, glued to the gun.

The ring leader snatched the small pillow from the boy's thin outstretched hands, tore apart the ticking, feathers clouding the air, as he hungrily extracted each gold coin and old piece of family jewelry, and hastily dropped them in his pockets.

When every scrap of food, clothing, and my father's merchandise had been

---

*The names of my "godparents" and others in their home and workplace have been changed to honor their firm request for anonymity.

carried out of the shack, my mother held out her hand to the ringleader. "Give me back a few drachmae, for transportation to the city tomorrow," she asked. He threw her some of her own money and slammed the door. When all six traitors and the German soldier had left, only an overripe tin of cheese remained. Even a sack of soiled laundry was gone.

In the bare shack, the three of them waited for daybreak.

At dawn, my parents took a jitney to Athens, suspecting that the robbers, after disposing of the loot, would denounce them as fugitives, possibly as Jews. What other reason would there be for this unlikely urban family to be living in a shack on a flower farm? But they had nowhere to go.

True to character, *Nonos* (Godfather) invited them to move into his home, where I was in hiding, till a more secure hideout could be found for them.

The Raid

Seven-thirty on a winter morning early in 1944, and *Nona* (Godmother) is already behind the counter at the bakery, her six-year-old daughter, Eleni, by her side. Her good neighbor, Mrs. Papas, is buying her allotment of bread for the day, while young Peter, the clerk, busies himself with his early morning chores. The place is fragrant with freshly baked bread, piled high in round loaves and long ones behind the counter.

Suddenly the Germans burst in the door, guns drawn. The Special Militia or Security Battalions, the *Tsoliathes*, serving as the Germans' escort, errand boys, and interpreters, add their own armed intimidation to the scene.

"Where are the Jews? Where is your husband?"

"My husband went for firewood."

Every corner of the bakery is ransacked. Up on the loft, mattresses on the floor reinforce the Germans' assumption that the family lives over the store and it is up there that they harbor Jews, as claimed by informants.

"When is your husband coming back?"

"I don't know when he'll be back. He's looking for firewood. You know, it's hard to get . . . " Godmother leaves unsaid the Nazis' systematic denuding of the Greek countryside in support of their war effort.

Godmother wraps the loaf of bread for Mrs. Papas in a bit of newspaper and quickly scribbles something on a piece of paper, as if handing out a receipt for the sale. The woman makes her getaway. When she is safely home she looks at the slip. "Tell Michael and George: Don't come back. Disappear!" Their phone number at work is scribbled under the note. No signature. So Godfather and "George," my father, are notified at the pasta factory, where they are both moonlighting to make ends meet.

Meantime at the bakery, the fourteen-year-old clerk wraps up some packages and leaves as if to make a delivery. Looking behind him and taking a circuitous route through the neighborhood, he finally reaches my godparents' home, around the corner from the bakery, and alerts Godfather's brother of the raid.

The Germans and their collaborators have settled in at the shop, setting a trap for my godfather and the "hidden Jews." The wait drags on till it is time to close the bakery for the mid-day siesta. It finally comes out that this particular baker and his family, unlike most others, don't live over their bakery. So Godmother and little Eleni, at gunpoint, are taken to their house, where a new search ensues. Both floors are turned upside down. But thanks to the clerk's warning, nothing suspicious turns up. No trace of me remains.

Fifty years later, visiting Godfather in Greece, I hear of this raid for the first time.

I ask Godfather, "How come they did not arrest *Nona?* They could have held her till you returned."

Beaming with the memory of his late wife, he answers: "Well, you know how your *Nona* was. So sweet. Of such a cheerful disposition. She made them comfortable, saw that they had something to eat. She kept saying calmly, 'There are no Jews. My husband went for firewood. I don't know when he'll be back.' So by four in the afternoon, they gave up and left."

Reciprocity

I am temporarily back with my parents, hiding in the suburb of Kallithea, after six months with the baker's family. All I am told is that the Germans are looking for my godfather and it is no longer safe for me to stay at his home.

I am running down a street flooded with sunlight. I fly toward the handsome man slowly approaching the house where we are staying. I call out loud "*Babaka! Babaka!!* Daddy! Daddy!!" Soon I am lifted high up in his arms. Good. The show worked out perfectly. It is really my godfather, but now the neighbors will think that this man is my father. This will explain what he is doing here when he stays in our cramped rented room. Leave it to the grapevine to fill in the blanks.

This new charade was carefully planned last night, when we learned that Godfather needed a hideout. My parents explained to me that a plausible cover story had to be quickly broadcast, before the neighbors started to wonder who this young and handsome man was, and why was he moving in with us.

In their succession of hiding places, my parents had always presented themselves as a childless couple, ever since they managed to disperse the family in 1943 in order to save our lives. When I suddenly needed to leave my hiding home at Godfather's, they made up a new story. I was introduced to the neighborhood as their niece. This explained the family resemblance and my temporary stay with them, for I was to leave them again, just as soon as a new Christian family could be found to take me. I was now supposed to be the daughter of my mother's sister, who was supposedly at the hospital for a cancer operation. So Godfather was to be presented as the sick sister's husband and my dad!

The problem was especially complicated because part of my parents' own cover was my father's rumored pathological jealousy, which was intended to explain why my beautiful mother, thirty-five and thirteen years his junior, was not allowed to mix freely with the neighbors. She stayed home and kept largely to herself. My father, by nature gregarious and friendly, normally the life of the party and an unforgettable storyteller, also needed a reason for keeping a low profile as he came and went to work throughout the Jewish Persecution. As part of his new disguise, he pretended to be quite gruff and reclusive, a polite man of few words, keeping a wary eye on his wife.

Now relishing this elaborate web of pretenses, I imagine how the neighbors will be even more sympathetic toward me, the supposed little niece. I visualize the head-shaking as they gossip. "Poor kid. It's lucky her mother's sister is so nice. As to her uncle, so glum and unfriendly . . . They say he is madly jealous of his young wife. The poor woman is not allowed to mix with the neighbors. So pretty, but childless . . . "

It makes me want to laugh out loud, knowing what a charming, sociable man my father is, and it is Mother who is the jealous one. I get a kick out of the clever story, leaked by the landlady! My parents are so smart and ingenious to explain away how I suddenly appeared after things got too dangerous at Godfather's. When I leave them again, they'll let it be known that the sick sister's health has miraculously improved.

My heart sings to see *Nonos* again. It is our turn to keep him safe. The *Tsoliathes* and occupation police are after him. For now, I am allowed to guess, it is because they think him a Communist. All the people suspected of acts of resistance have been declared Bolsheviks. What's a Bolshevik? He must have been denounced for selling bread without ration coupons to the resistance, I think to myself. But of course we must not ask questions. My parents say, better not to know too much.

The landlady has put an army cot in the kitchen for *Nonos*. My parents' only room is already cramped with an extra cot for me. It is only for a few days, till he finds a safer place to hide. It feels so good to be on the helping end.

The men leave the house early in the morning one at a time to go to work. I don't know where they go. Godfather cannot go to his bakery. They are back one at a time, before curfew. One night Godfather does not return. Father, my supposed "Uncle George," assures me Godfather is safe in a new hiding place.

I will miss *Nonos*, but I am glad he is in a safer home than our own hideout. We are left to leak out the explanation that he went to take care of my mythical sick mother who is supposed to be out of the hospital. Soon I also must be gone.

The SS Bloko

The Nazi raid on my godparents' bakery in early 1944 was only the beginning. *Nona* and little Eleni were raided a second time a few months later, in an infamous SS "Bloko," a roundup, whose purpose was to capture three much-wanted Athenian men. The first man was a member of the resistance. He was caught and shot dead. The second man had done nothing, but was mistaken for another person, someone who—being a patriot—had made some sympathetic statements about the resistance. He, the wrong man, was caught and thrown into a concentration camp. The third wanted man was *Nonos*, who had been in hiding away from his family since the first raid. It was for having hidden us that he was still a fugitive.

Nona, Eleni, and Panos, who had baptized her, were at home. Suddenly, the SS and quisling Special Militia burst into the house, bayonets at the ready.

They immediately demanded to know where was Michael, my godfather. Artemis told them she did not know where her husband was living. She had not heard from him in months. The Nazis shouted at her that her husband had gone underground to avoid his punishment for having sheltered Jews.

Panos, as the only man at the house, soon became the target of a merciless beating, since his answers and demeanor upon interrogation enraged the SS. He was, in fact, acting quite peculiarly. The Germans persisted in their interrogation until Artemis opened a cupboard and pulled out a sworn medical affidavit attesting that he was feeble-minded. With a final kick, they stopped the beating.

Then an SS officer held his revolver to six-year-old Eleni's head, cocked the gun and shouted at Artemis:

"We will kill your child if you don't tell us where your husband is!"

The woman crossed herself and said:

"There is nothing I can do! I swear, I do not know where he is. He told me he was going to get firewood for the bakery, months ago, and I believed him. But he disappeared, instead. He has abandoned us."

Then the Nazi officer moved his gun away from Eleni and held it to Artemis' head, threatening the child:

"I will kill your mother if you do not tell us where your father is."

Little Eleni crossed herself, as she had seen her mother do. Despite a secret encounter with her daddy the day before, she declared:

"I swear to God, I have not seen him."

Artemis was suddenly seized by a choking cough. She pulled out an X-ray and stated:

"See how bad my lungs are? I am dying of tuberculosis. My husband did not want to be with a sick woman. And even the child has bad glands. See how pale she is! He just abandoned us. He is not a fugitive from the law. He is just hiding from *us!*"

Another sworn medical affidavit attesting to her advanced illness clinched the matter . . .

Godfather explained:

There was a palace doctor, a good patriot, who used to attend the royal family before they left for Egypt during the German invasion. He gave people in trouble with the Nazis whatever medical certificates they needed to maintain their cover and escape capture. So that doctor had provided *Nona* with a dead woman's lung X-ray and had certified Panos, so his bizarre behavior could be construed as feeble-mindedness, thus rendering him useless for interrogations.

Word of the SS Bloko got out to Godfather immediately. The next day he sent a message:

"I have secured a place. All three of us can hide here."

He instructed his wife to leave right away, pretending to go to the market. She must bring nothing but the illegal radio, which Michael had promised to share with the new landlord. Everything else should be left behind, to avoid notice. There were bedding and kitchen necessities at the new place.

And so it was that my godparents stayed in hiding for the rest of the war, from Easter week till October 12, 1944, when Athens was finally liberated. Michael, Artemis, and Eleni went into hiding like thousands of Jews—like us, the Jews they saved. That is how a Christian girl became a Hidden Child like me—for me.

Another Hiding Place

My mother's worried face is visibly calmer when she gets back home. When Dad returns, they have a conference, whispering. He too seems relieved. Must be good news. Why is she holding me so tightly? Why are Dad's eyes shining wet?

Tomorrow I move to a new hiding home. A woman I do not know has agreed to take me. Silently I wonder, does she have children?

My new "Aunt" Vasso is a widow, I am told. There will be a grandmother and another "aunt," Theresa, there. My Christian name will still be Julia. I must be extra good, they are not used to kids. The old grandmother is very religious. Does she know about me, I wonder. I wonder about many things. How did my mother find this woman? Were they old friends? But, I realize, that's impossible—no one must be able to trace us through friends or relatives. She must be a stranger like Godfather, my first rescuer, was.

That night, my hair is given an extra thorough washing. I am pink with scrubbing. My clothes are packed. No room or thought of toys or kids' books. No family pictures. All burned with father's library, as too revealing, too cosmopolitan, too Jewish. I can still take my embroidery cardboard cards, needle and thread. They are babyish, I learned to use them when I was only six or seven, but they are easy to pack.

We meet my new Aunt Vasso at her shop on Athinas Street. The surrounding market area is full of beggars and emaciated people foraging for food near the produce stalls. How hungry they look. Vasso is wearing widow's mourning clothes, though she looks younger than Mother. She is very pretty, her smile is whimsical and bright, her eyes gentle. She kisses my cheeks, calling me Julia. Mother has disappeared. The charade is on for the customers and clerks. I am now the niece from an underfed family in the town of Farsalla. I, with my fat arms and thighs.

That night Vasso and I are staying at her friends' apartment in downtown Athens. No transportation to her suburb. Tomorrow I'll move to my new home. How will I be received by her family? My mother has explained that Vasso is the "head of the household." That means she is the boss. It will be all right.

In My "Cave"

I must concentrate on the chapter of the Gospel I am assigned to read.

Today I was caught with lipstick and cold cream filched from an older girl, a real niece, who is spending a few days at Vasso's. Somebody had told me about this trick of wetting your hands with thick soap suds. After they dry, the soap becomes invisible. You can impress people by later wetting your hands, and there! As if by magic, you make suds without using soap. I thought I could do the same with cold cream. While I was at it, I rubbed lots of lipstick on a hand-kerchief before sneaking the tube back to the big girl's dressing kit.

The old grandmother thought I must repent for the sin of stealing, so I must kneel at the icon stand, reading the Bible, till I finish a long chapter, days later. I can read the words, but the language is strange and I do not get much of what it says. All I know is that I am reading about Jesus.

My cheeks burn with shame to have been naughty and been caught. Didn't I have sense enough to know I can't make waves? I must be quiet and patient a bit longer. To the old grandmother, I am truly grateful. Still, I will not believe it was a sin I committed. God understands. Just shameful childishness. Did I forget? I'm already nine.

In the early afternoon the big girl invites me to go to the rooftop to help her hang out the laundry. I carry the clothespins and a small clothesbasket, trudging after her up the winding iron staircase. The sky is brilliant blue and cloudless. It merges far in the horizon with a patch of shimmering blue water. I can barely make out the distant shore. And all around us the flat rooftop terraces, some with clothes flapping in the gentle breeze. I suck in the air, the light, the freedom, the vastness, the sun. It must be weeks since I was last outdoors or in a bright space. For the rest of my life, an open vista would be like praying.

When the big girl leaves, I am back in "the cave" behind the shutters in the semi-dark rooms. Alone most of the time. Only the maid is eager to talk to me. She is telling me secrets about men and women. At the beginning, I'm very curious. The maid is fourteen. She is sometimes very lewd and frightens me with her stories on the facts of life. I'm scared we may be overheard. I do not want to know any more. Kneeling with the Bible is better. I can at least daydream in peace.

Every day, through the shutters, I see the children play on the sidewalk after school. I do not go to school. I read on the sly some very romantic magazines Aunt Theresa keeps around. She does not know. Her old mother thinks I read just the Gospel, the only available book. The magazines have grownup stories, but unlike the Bible, I understand the language; it is regular Greek.

Theresa plays solitaire a lot, sitting up on her bed with the shutters closed. They say she is recovering from a bad marriage and divorce. The only man I see is the very stiff, short, red-faced doctor who courts Theresa. He is very correct and always visits her with his two sisters. They wear long-sleeved dresses, no matter how hot. They belong to an extra strict Greek Orthodox "ethical-religious" group. They do not know about my being Jewish.

Today I skipped dinner. We had fava, a split pea dish drenched in olive oil. I saw the worms in the raw peas, before Theresa cooked them this morning. But I am full of the wonderful bread, thick with fresh butter, which I dunked in the sweet afternoon Turkish coffee. Here they never say, like my parents, that I am too young for coffee. It is truly delicious, if you avoid the dregs at the bottom of the little cup. They are thick as mud and choke you. Theresa reads our fortunes in the patterns the dregs make on the upended coffee cups. She comes out of her shell then and is almost fun. I miss Aunt Vasso. Most nights she stays in town. No transportation after her shop closes.

I miss . . . I must not think of this. I must keep my mind off things that make me cry. My face swells for all to see the next morning, even when I cry secretly under the covers, aching for my mother's arms.

Months have passed. Although Mother did come to see me, she was with me such a short time. Too dangerous to linger. Dad is O.K., she said. I have not seen him for five months. Sometimes I try to conjure up his face and can't. How can I forget my own father? I write a poem about my little brother and our reunion. All about how we will play without fighting when we get together again. There will be no more bickering over sharing my things.

I force myself to concentrate on how smart my parents are to save our lives; how clever are the stories they cook up; how impeccable their fake papers, how ingenious the disguises; how brave our rescuers. I fancy us all as members of a secret resistance. It is better than any hide and seek game, this silent outwitting of the Nazis. I fill my heart with pride and gratitude. I must not go near the longing and the loneliness, and the terror that I will never see my parents again. I am never scared. Almost. My parents depend on me to do my part, to be cooperative, not a bother to my rescuers. The worst thing I can do now is to be a burden. The grownups are going through so much. I must never be naughty again.

The Ring

A dozen years after the war, I came back to Greece to be married. That was when I saw my mother's engagement ring on her finger. We had been robbed or had sold our last possession to save ourselves so many times during the war, the Jewish Persecution, and the civil war afterward, that I had always assumed the ring was long gone.

Now its sparkle added a touch of elegance to my mother's appearance. She was determined to impress my American fiancé with my fine family background, the better to ensure I would be treated well in my new life far away.

Later my mother explained how she saved her engagement ring during the armed extortion at the flower farm, by quickly turning the large diamond under, so it looked like a thin platinum wedding band and was ignored by the bandits.

So I asked my mother, "Where was the ring all those years?"

"And how did you think you went to school all those years?" she asked back. She said she had not wanted me to feel bad, that's why she had kept it from me.

"After liberation," she explained, "there was a Jewish organization which made very low interest loans so that Jews who were financially ruined, like Father, could get on their feet again."

When that money ran out, Mother found another lending source. This time she needed collateral. So the ring went for the American College, an expensive secondary school for girls.

"It was the best school in all of Greece," Mother used to say proudly.

My father was the businessman; but never did he make a better investment than my mother made with her ring. That private education in Greece led to a Fulbright Scholarship to study in the United States, and to three graduate degrees "free of charge."

My father saved our lives again and again. More than anyone else, he was our primary rescuer. My mother gave me my future.

Now I have the ring, a trophy from my mother. A trophy for our victory, after all.

Messengers

It is three in the morning, April 1994. I am back in Athens. I have been listening to yesterday's taped interviews, sitting at the edge of the platform bed, in this square, pale gray room. The balcony doors are shuttered with wooden rolled-down blinds against the neighbors' windows across the narrow street. I have been too keyed up to fall asleep. The bedroom is still chilly, despite the small space heater turned up to its highest setting and beamed at me. The heater's red glow and a small bedside lamp provide the only light.

I decide to get under the covers for warmth. Now I am all bundled up in a sweatsuit and sweater, propped up on two pillows under a pale flowered quilt and small summer blanket. And yet my feet are still frozen. I jump up, turn on the overhead light, and reach in the built-in dresser for a pair of warm socks. The bare terrazzo floor is icy under my feet. Turning the room light off, I hurry back and start the tape from the beginning of the last interview with my god-father, the amazing man who saved my life during the Jewish Persecution in Greece fifty years ago.

Nonos' voice, at ninety-three, is still strong and always beautiful to my ears. I listen intently. His daughter Eleni's comments punctuate his account of the SS raid on their bakery and home. Humor and occasional chuckles color their voices as they recount how *Nona* outwitted the Nazis, warned us off, and avoided capture or worse . . . The distant traffic sounds are loud in the quiet residential neighborhood. The city was much quieter before so many Athenians bought private automobiles . . . But that was years ago, when I was growing up a few blocks away.

Deep sobs wrack my body. They are not of sadness, but of thanksgiving. I am overcome by deep gratitude and a sense of awe. I realize that today I have been listening to messengers of God, bringing a miracle of humanity and courage into my life—the life they saved.

The Greek word for messenger is *angelos*. It is also the root for the English "angel." In Greek tonight the word does not conjure up disembodied, winged cherubs flying in the heavens. For me at this moment, "angel" has little to do with a saintly person in a permanent state of grace. I think these people, at that time, listened to the best inside themselves and were able to outmatch the evil all around us.

And what of my parents? How did they find our rescuers who were neither close friends nor business associates, but often strangers? How did they reach those people's hearts? On this cold night, I believe that my parents' white-hot intensity and commitment to our survival found an echo in our rescuers. Perhaps my parents also carried a message.

They were all ordinary people, those grownups of my childhood, until the need arose—and after. But in those years of peril, they did become messengers, giving us not only our lives, but also faith in human goodness.

A Historical Note: Greece in World War II

Greece was plunged into World War II on October 28, 1940, when it refused Mussolini's ultimatum of surrender. The laconic reply was a single Greek word,

OXI (pronounced OH-he), "No." Surprisingly, small, underdeveloped and poorly armed Greece held back the far more mechanized Italian army for six months, while many more populous and industrialized countries were falling to Germany within weeks. The outcome of the Greek–Italian war was decided in April 1941, when Hitler finally came to Mussolini's aid by invading Greece through a corridor opened by Bulgaria. Within weeks, Greece was partitioned and occupied by three Axis powers: Germany, Italy, and Bulgaria.

Measures against the Jews began in German-occupied Salonika soon after the invasion, intensified in July of 1942, and soon spread to other Nazi-controlled parts of Greece. Deportations, which we always called in Greek "the Persecution," began early in 1943 from Salonika, followed by deportations from the Bulgarian controlled northeastern region.

Contrary to the German and Bulgarian occupation forces, however, the Italians used various subterfuges to avoid persecution of the Jews under their control, until their capitulation to the Allies in the fall of 1943. Italian diplomats came to the assistance of any Jew who could conceivably qualify for Italian identification papers, and in some cases Italian transport was provided to Jews out of the German zone and into the relative safety of the Italian controlled territories.

At the beginning of the war, the 80,000 Greek Jews were less than one percent of the population.* Approximately 86 to 89 percent of the Jews residing in Greece were murdered by the Nazis, most of them in Auschwitz. Official numbers consistently underestimate Jewish losses in Greece because parts of the country, such as Rhodes and other islands, were already under foreign occupation prior to World War II and are thus not included in the statistics. Furthermore, a significant number of Jews, though living as Greeks in Greece for generations, held foreign citizenship and, therefore, are not always counted with the Greek losses. The fate of over five thousand Jews is not known, perhaps lost to death within occupied Greece and to emigration between 1940 and 1947.

Jewish survivors in 1947 numbered 10,371 still living in Greece, plus approximately 1,000 to 1,500 who had managed to escape to Palestine during the Persecution. They included a small percentage of those deported who returned from the death and slave labor camps, but the vast majority had escaped deportation by hiding within Greece. Greek rescuers included most of the partisan units controlling the more unapproachable mountain villages; many Greek Orthodox churchmen, from simple parish priests to the Archbishop of All Greece; and countless civilians who showed remarkable decency toward their Jewish countrymen.

For 2,300 years Jews had lived largely in peaceful proximity to Gentiles in

---

*Statistics based on *In Memoriam: Hommage aux Victims Juives des Nazi en Gréce,* published by the Jewish Community of Salonika (1973), under the direction of Rabbi Michael Molho.

Greece, in the oldest Jewish settlements in Europe, reportedly dating back to the Babylonian exile from Palestine. Saul of Tarsus (St. Paul) preached in several synagogues established long before he came to Greece early in the Common Era.

Today there are only 5,000 to 6,000 Jews left, 3,500 residing in Athens, the other survivors having emigrated to Israel, the United States, and several countries in Africa and Latin America.

VI. The Sustaining Power of Family Love

Holocaust victims who survived the war commonly endured it alone, separated from family members who were killed or might be still alive in some other place. Some victims, however, managed to stay together with parts of their families, at least for a while. In these cases, parents and children, husbands and wives, sisters and brothers often were able to give each other physical support and spiritual strength.

A few stories in other sections of this book contain episodes about families suffering through Holocaust trials together, and about heroic acts by family members. The stories in this section, however, focus on specific, desperate, and courageous attempts of parents to save children, children to save parents, sisters to save sisters.

Several of these stories have a spiritual or psychological thrust, suggesting the power of parental love to sustain or save a child, even in absentia. In "The Promise," a dying mother exacts from her young daughter a promise to escape from their captors, risking her life in the wilderness. Fulfilling this pledge, the girl goes with the spiritual presence of her mother to find another, symbolic mother. In "A Dream of Milk," a girl near death is revived by a dream of her father. And in "In Praise of Manual Labor," parental teachings help to save a concentration camp prisoner.

Other stories are about courageous actions which save family members. In "A Mother's Courage," a woman improbably confronts Nazi soldiers and an Austrian police chief who have arrested her husband. In "Miracles," a husband and wife who are bent upon saving their daughter save themselves as well so that, in the end, their child will have a parent. "A Son in Deed" presents in sometimes wry, yet always sympathetic, terms a young man's efforts to sustain his father's life when they are together in a concentration camp.

The events in these stories stand for a deep Jewish commitment to the value of family unity, to bonds that no Nazi atrocity could finally break. The stories don't all have happy endings. But through their positive spirit they echo and counterbalance the underlying theme, throughout the book, of the writers' grief over the loss of their families.

A. B.

The Promise

Libby Stern
b. Suceava, Romania, 1926

We had been gone from home only eight weeks, but it seemed much longer.
After twelve days of marching through the fields of the Ukraine, we had been put in former military barracks by some Romanian officers who promised us that the orders to move us to a better location would arrive soon from the German command. And so we were sitting in these barracks in a godforsaken place in the middle of a vast field in Transnistria, toward the end of November 1941. We were over four hundred people—men, women, and children. Most of the old people had died on the march.

As the days turned into weeks and the orders never came, we realized that we were left here to die. My father had died last week, and my mother was sick with a high fever.

One day she called my name. She was so weak she could hardly speak.

"My child," she said, "you must promise me something. You must run away from here."

I put some snow on her hot forehead to cool the fever.

"Mother," I said, "how can I run? My feet are frostbitten. The snow is a meter deep. There's a snowstorm out there and the roads are all covered."

She didn't listen. "I am dying," she said. "But you're only fifteen. You still have a whole life and a future ahead of you. The new orders will never come. You must run away and save yourself. There are good people out there and someone will help you."

She continued: "And when the war ends, as all wars must, you should go to America. Your father and I have brothers and sisters there and you will not be alone. You must promise, so I can die in peace knowing that you will survive."

And so I promised. That night my mother died in her sleep. She died in peace.

I cannot remember the next three days. I was in shock, expecting to die too. But death didn't come. Eventually I got up from the corner where I was sitting and tried to see what was going on in the other compartments. In the beginning, it was crowded—over four hundred people in seven or eight rooms—but now there were only a few. A mother eating some dry bread and breastfeeding her baby, both looking weak and pale, probably their last meal; a newlywed couple, married a week before the deportation, lying on the floor with high fevers; a neighbor of mine, the only person over forty, who had lost his entire family, standing in the corner saying *Kaddish* all day long; a few boys in their teens; and in the last compartment, Miss Birnbaum, my former Hebrew teacher, age twenty-seven.

I went over to her. I hardly recognized her. She had cut her beautiful long braids and was pale and old looking.

"Miss Birnbaum," I said, "let's run away and save ourselves. This place is a death trap. Let's take a chance on the outside."

She looked at me with her gray sad eyes. "You foolish girl. Where will you go? Who will take you in? Who will hide you? I believe in fate," she continued. "If fate will have it that I survive, the new orders will come and we will get out of here. But if fate will have me die, I will run away and probably freeze to death or be shot."

"Look around you," I answered. "The new orders will never come. Everyone is dying. I must take a chance. I'm leaving. Anyway, I promised my mother and I have to keep my promise." I went back to my corner, packed my few belongings in my knapsack and walked out, not looking back even once.

It had stopped snowing, and the air was crisp. I walked for miles, looking for a sign of life. As I walked, I thought about how my life had changed in the last two months. One day we were sitting in the *sukkah* enjoying the holiday, the next we were deported from our town. The orders came at eight in the morning, and by noon we were supposed to report to the railroad station with two valises each and three days of food per person. We packed what we could— blankets, warm clothes. My father packed two valises of old holy books, saying that this was the food for his soul and he could not live without it. Then came the crowded trains, the crossing of the Dneister River, the march through the muddy fields of the Ukraine, the sleeping in the forests and, finally, our being resettled in the *Kazmazah*, those military barracks which were supposed to be a temporary shelter.

I was brought back to the present when I heard some voices and dogs barking on the top of a nearby hill. I climbed the hill with great effort, but when I came to the top there were no people, just some treetops blowing in the wind. The snow drifts covered the trunks and branches of the trees. I descended the hill, tired and exhausted, and decided to rest a while. I sat down on a tree stump. It started to snow again. I fell asleep and had a dream.

In my dream I was home, sleeping in my own warm bed. My mother came to wake me with a warm glass of milk, and I begged her to let me sleep a little longer.

Suddenly, I felt someone touch my shoulder. I woke up. There was no one there, but I was completely covered with snow. A few more minutes and I would have been part of the great white scenery.

I brushed the snow off my face and head, and took out a small Tanach my father once gave me. I opened it to Psalm 23 and read in Hebrew, "The Lord is my Shepherd . . . as I walk through the valley of the shadow of death, I shall fear no evil . . . " Somehow these words gave me the strength to continue walking.

At daybreak, I saw a dim light in the distance. I hurried toward that lonely little house in the middle of nowhere. The light came from the barn. Inside, an old peasant woman was milking her cow.

When she saw me she crossed herself and said, "My God, what kind of misfortune has befallen you?" I told her my story in the few Ukrainian words I had learned in my two months of wandering, and offered her my father's winter coat if she would keep me for a month.

She answered, "I will take your coat and I will keep you, but I am doing this for my son. He's fighting on the Russian front, hungry and cold like you, and I hope someone is helping him survive the way I will help you."

She wiped her tears and added, "Yes, my child, I will take you into my warm home. I will heal your frostbitten feet. I will teach you our language and I will teach you to spin wool. I will dress you in our kind of clothing, and you will become one of us, and no one will ever know who you are, and no one will ever hurt you."

A Mother's Courage

Edith Rechter Levy
b. Vienna, Austria, 1930

In the long, cold Vienna winter, it was often barely daylight when we got up for school. Nevertheless, I did not mind, for even as a first grader I was an avid learner and loved school. I was also an early riser, so I was always eager to start the day.

Yet this time when my mother came to wake me, I had difficulty opening my eyes. I remember rubbing them groggily and peering at the window. It was pitch-black outside, not a glimpse of dawn. I pointed this out to my mother:

"*Mutti*," I said, "are you sure it's already time to get up for school? It's still so dark outside!"

"Get dressed quickly," my mother replied in a soothing voice, and she started to help me dress. This was unusual and, sleepy or not, it caught my attention. Mom as a rule did not believe in pampering her children when it came to routine chores such as dressing for school. Becoming more alert, I noticed that Mom was somehow different, more subdued, less matter-of-fact than she usually was in the morning. I now saw some light filtering in from the side and base of the kitchen door, which was slightly ajar. My sleepy mind registered this as being normal. But then I heard voices, male voices, and this once more was out of the ordinary. I knew something was definitely amiss when I distinguished my father's voice for, as a rule, Father left for work long before we children were awakened.

I finished dressing as fast as I could. When I went into the kitchen, my older brother was already there, fully clad. My father and two Austrian policemen were engaged in what seemed a friendly conversation. The clock said 2:00 A.M.

My mother helped me with my coat and hat, and we all left together. Outside a storm was raging. The wind howled, the rain came down in sheets, drenching my face in seconds. One policeman took me by the hand and helped me along, shielding me with his body when one of the heavier wind gusts nearly lifted me off the ground. I felt a sense of security under the protection of this strong officer of the law, and I bravely tried to keep pace and march into the howling wind. The officer, however, had a less cheerful attitude.

"How cruel!" Addressing my father, he attempted to overshout the wind: "I wouldn't even force a dog out into this weather," he proclaimed angrily, "much less women and children!"

Our destination, it turned out, was the local police precinct. There the friendly policeman vanished. We were ushered into a dimly lit room. My first impression was a smell of heavy cigarette smoke mixed with moisture permeating the air, making everything appear as if in a dense fog. The room was crowded and noisy, with a dampness which emanated from the saturated clothes of the constantly new arrivals. I noticed a desk somewhere toward the center of the room and to our right, behind which a man in black Nazi uniform replete with swastika armband was sitting, speaking to the first person in line. Two more uniformed Nazis stood on the right and left side, in front of the same desk. Given my size, what was most visible at eye level and hence most frightening to me were the leather uppers of their spit-polish shiny black boots, reaching nearly to the top of my chest. A single light hung from the ceiling, directly over the desk.

As we entered the room, my father was immediately separated from us and led to a door at the rear left side of the room. An SS man reached for that door to admit my father. As it opened, a mass of male human bodies expanded into our room. They stood, crammed like sardines, in an area which appeared to be either a storage room or a windowless closet. Their arms tight alongside their bodies, some had bent their elbows in an attempt to gain some additional breathing space. The black-shirted Nazi raised his leg, intent at pushing this mass of people back into the closet with his boot. He accompanied his gesture with an outburst of vicious curses, the likes of which I had never heard in my sheltered life.

Before the door could be shut, however, several voices from the rear of that area shouted out that someone had fainted. The SS man stopped and lowered his boot. About six or seven men stepped or rather tumbled out, so as to try to allow access to the rear, but they were stopped by the SS man. As I observed with increasing horror, one lifeless body was finally pulled from between the legs of those still imprisoned in the closet. Then everyone, including my father, was pushed back in. Using his booted leg very efficiently, the Nazi managed to get everyone to recoil so that the door could be shut once more.

This frightening episode had captured my total attention thus far. I now realized that we had moved forward, were standing in front of the desk between the two SS men, and my mother was pleading with the person seated behind the desk.

"We are law-abiding citizens," she kept repeating. "We have never broken any law nor harmed anyone; please let us go."

My mother was normally blessed with a strong-willed, authoritarian personality. She certainly was not, to my knowledge, given to pleading. Her complete change of attitude heightened my fear to a panic. Surely, the worst was about to happen!

Yet my mother continued: "I have a sick child here," pointing at me. "She throws up all the time. We are good, law-abiding citizens. Please allow me to take my sick child home."

This statement was a half-truth at best. In reality I was a very healthy child, but was prone to vomit under stress or anxiety. The situation here now surpassed any childhood fear or panic I had every encountered. In the pit of my stomach, my whole insides were churning, demanding to be free. Oh, how I tried to hold back the upcoming flow; but to no avail. In an act of desperation and fright, I raised both hands toward my mouth. Too late. It all burst out, projectile style, and to my horror landed all over the spit-polished boots of the SS man to my right. I had seen similar boots in action at the closet door. Terror struck at the thought of what would happen to me now. I wretched some more, then started trembling.

The rest is somewhat vague. Perhaps I did indeed pass out, perhaps I have just blocked it all out of my memory. Apparently my mother, brother and myself were allowed to return home. My father stayed behind. All I remember is waking up the next morning in my own bed, with only my brother and myself in the apartment. My mother was gone, leaving a note for my brother. She would be back soon . . .

As it turned out, come morning my mother had composed herself and regained some of her strong-willed attitude. Although she was anything but tall, she was well-proportioned. Her pretty face, her beautiful auburn hair and milky white skin made people notice her. She wasn't afraid to speak her mind. This time she had gathered up our tax receipts, our *Sittenzeugnisse* (good-citizenship certificates), and other documents attesting to our exemplary citizenship, and had marched down to police headquarters where she demanded to see the police chief himself. Once in his office, she documented in detail what superb citizens we were and requested with authority that her husband be released at once.

The police chief, seated behind his desk, listened to her quietly and without interrupting. When my mother finally ran out of steam he beckoned her to join him at the window, located behind his desk.

"Come," he said, "and look."

The window gave onto a large courtyard, around the perimeter of which stood hundreds of people. The center of the courtyard was mostly clear, except for a few SS men taunting and having some fun with an old, bearded Jew.

There was sadness and resignation in his voice. "They have been there all night," he said, pointing at the people in the courtyard, "standing in the pouring rain and howling wind. Pregnant women, women holding children, children themselves. The young, the old and the sick, with no exception. Some were singled out to be beaten, some to be teased, others to do exercises beyond their ability. I don't know what you did to be allowed to go home. I know even less how you got permission to see me today. All I know is that at present I no longer have any authority to grant you anything whatsoever. Go home to your children and count your blessings. And when you leave my office, hold your head up high and walk with a strong, self-assured and steady gait as if you belong. For if they stop you and ask for identification, you might just wind up down there with them." And he pointed again to the courtyard.

My mother was shaken, but not yet willing to concede.

"I demand to know what will happen to my husband," she insisted. The police chief shrugged his shoulders in despair.

"I don't know," he replied. "All I know is that whatever is going to happen will happen this morning. So if your husband is going to be released, it will be before noon. Now please go, and remember what I told you about the way to walk."

My mother left thinking of her children, and following his advice on how to walk in the hallways. By twelve o'clock noon my father returned. Once more, I wanted to believe that it was all over. And of course once more, that wish was not to be granted.

Miracles

Rafael Levin
  b. Vilna, Lithuania, 1905
AND
Eta Levin Hecht
  b. Kovno, Lithuania, 1938

As soon as the Nazis occupied Kovno, Lithuania—it was in June 1941—they and the Lithuanians started to oppress Jews. From the beginning, Jews were ordered to wear two yellow Stars of David, one on the front and one on the back of their garments. Lithuanian partisans and Nazis entered Jewish homes and took clothes and jewelry, killed men and later women.

In early July, the Jews were ordered to put barbed wire around a suburb of Kovno called Slabotka. All Jews, about forty thousand of us, had to move into the Ghetto Slabotka, or "Kovno Ghetto." We got one little room in a house. We were four people: my mother, my wife Rachel, my four-year-old daughter Eta and myself.

We were not allowed to go out of the ghetto except for hard labor. We went to work in commandos under Nazi guards. The killing of Jews in the ghetto was a regular event. Survival was a matter of miracles.

MIRACLE ONE

October 28, 1941, at 6:00 A.M., the Nazis ordered all the Jews to line up, eight persons in a row in a big field, for the purpose of counting how many Jews were in the ghetto. Row by row we passed a Nazi officer who was sitting on a chair in the field. He ordered some rows to go to the left and some to the right. In our row were my mother on my right, Eta on my left, and Rachel. When our row approached the Nazi officer, he ordered us to go to the left. At this moment my heart told me to go to the right. I grabbed Eta's hand and pushed her and the others to the right.

It took a full day till the Nazis ordered us to return to our homes. The following day we found out that those who went to the left were killed. About ten thousand Jews were killed at this action, mostly the elderly, children, and the sick.

MIRACLE TWO

The Nazis came more and more often to search the houses for children and the elderly. One day we hardly managed to hide Eta in the bed, covering her with pillows and blankets. Nazis came in, searched around and walked out. They had not looked in the bed. This too was a miracle!

Eta: *When a search occurred, my parents would hide me inside the bedding, roll me up with the bedding and place me and the bed against the wall, parallel to the wall, so that it appeared to be a sofa. I had difficulty breathing, and yet I knew that I was not to move or the Nazis would find me.*

MIRACLE THREE

March 1943. I worked inside the ghetto while Rachel was sent to forced labor outside the ghetto in the city of Kovno. Suddenly, the ghetto was surrounded by an unusually large number of Nazi guards and Lithuanian partisans. Big trucks entered the ghetto. The Nazis, through loudspeakers, ordered the Jews to remain in their houses.

I noticed that the Nazis were grabbing children and old people and throwing them into the trucks. I took Eta, now aged five, into a tiny bin under the steps which led to the second floor. I asked my cousin Yacov Chaikin to cover the door to the bin with an old mattress. Nazis entered the house searching for children and old people and did not notice our hiding place! We hid here all day long. The following day the Nazis continued the search, and we stayed in hiding. About five thousand children and old people were killed in this action.

My father and I hid under a staircase which led to the second floor. We remained hidden for two days. It was cold and we did not have any food. I had a cough, which I would desperately try to suppress so as not to be heard. We could hear the Nazis climbing the stairs over our heads, and we could hear the shouting and the screams all around us.

After this, the Nazis declared our ghetto a concentration camp. The regime became even stricter.

MIRACLE FOUR

Now Rachel and I decided we had to find a place for Eta at a gentile's home. It was a tragic feeling to give her away without knowing about her future safety. The only hope was that maybe one of us, Rachel or I, would survive and have Eta back, and Eta would have a parent.

One day Rachel, at forced labor in the city of Kovno, managed to sneak out of her work place, took off her yellow star of David, and went to a priest. Maybe he could find a gentile who would like to take Eta and save her life. The priest promised to look for a family, but not before Christmas.

Time was critical; we felt something bad was going to happen in the ghetto.

Meanwhile, we started to train Eta. We taught her to say, if people asked her whether she had parents and who they were, that she does not know her parents, that she is an orphan, that her name is "Elenite" and that is all she knows. We trained her to sit still inside a potato sack, which was to be used for smuggling her out of the ghetto. Sensing the danger to her life, Eta trained herself to hide in times of crisis under the bed or in bed, covering herself with pillows and blankets. She never had a smile on her face in the ghetto.

I decided to try to contact a gentile school principal I knew. One day in March 1944, I managed, while working outside the ghetto, to ask a gentile lady to deliver a letter to this friend, Lazauskas. In my letter I asked him to come to my place of work the following day and meet me in the men's room. When he came, I asked him to keep Eta till after the war and then to contact my brother, Beinush, in Switzerland. Beinush would pay him for his expenses and take Eta to Switzerland.

His answer was, "You Jews deserve all the trouble you have now. But you, Rafael, you are an exception. I will take Eta to my house."

I was shaken but said, "I'm not going to discuss this with you now, but thank you for saving my daughter."

The following day we put Eta into the potato sack so it looked like Rachel was carrying tools. I had to stand behind a house in the ghetto, and as Rachel passed the house with her brigade, I ran up saying loudly, "You forgot the tools!" I gave her the bag in which Eta was lying.

The Nazi guards did not react (this, too, was a miracle!). Rachel carried Eta in the bag to her place of work. She managed to take the yellow stars off of Eta and went across the street to the lady who the day before had taken my letter to Lazauskas. This woman took Eta to Lazauskas. Lazauskas kept Eta from the middle of March to the middle of August 1944.

I had spent almost three years in the ghetto. During these years, I did not have toys; I could not play outdoors; I did not have companions my age to play with. The only companions I knew were hunger and fear. And when my mother carried me out of the ghetto, I did not know whether I would ever see her or my father again.

MIRACLE FIVE

In July 1944, the Germans decided to liquidate our Kovno concentration camp and send the Jews to Germany: the men to Dachau and the women to Stutthof in East Germany. We were pushed into cattle wagons. In each wagon there was a German guard. We were all standing because it was crowded. Suddenly, I noticed an opening in the wall of the wagon near the roof. I asked Rachel if she would like to jump out of the train.

"I will," I said. "Maybe Eta will be lucky and have a parent."

Rachel said that I should do it. So I asked a few Jews in the wagon to engage the Nazi guard in conversation so that he would not notice my jumping out. I climbed up to the opening, jumped from the moving train, fell on the ground and fainted.

A Lithuanian railway employee found me lying on the ground. He asked who I was. He said that he had looked in all my pockets and did not find any documents. It was then that I realized I had fainted.

I pretended that I was a gentile, a working man, and had gotten drunk. He didn't believe me and said he would take me to the German police office. I could not persuade him not to do it.

I had nothing to lose, so I started running through the fields toward the woods. In the fields I saw stacks of hay. I crept into one stack and covered myself with hay. After a while I heard a man talking in German. Germans were collecting the hay. They collected all except my stack of hay. Perhaps they had no more room for them.

MIRACLE SIX

During my wandering I entered a house in a village and asked for a drink of water. It was given to me. Then I asked if I could go to the stable and rest on the hay. This I was refused because they did not know me. I walked out of the house and saw a German walking around. I quickly went into the stable, climbed up under the roof and covered myself with hay.

Suddenly I heard somebody climbing up and poking around in the hay saying, "Cursed Jew . . . he got lost." I remained in the hay all day and all night. The following morning I walked away.

After this, the Russians occupied Lithuania and I became free. I went immediately to Kovno, about a 24-kilometer walk, to look for Eta. I came to Lazauskas. He told me he had to send Eta to his sister in a village because it was a danger to Eta to stay in Kovno. He walked with me, about 20 kilometers, to his sister's house and I found Eta. This was my happiest day!

Rachel was freed by the Russian army in January 1945. However, the Russians mobilized the rescued Jewish women and put them to work for the Russian army. Rachel worked as a cook. She sent a letter to Lazauskas asking if Eta and I were alive. Lazauskas brought the letter to me. I in turn sent Rachel a letter saying that "Beinush's brother" and Eta would be in Lodz, Poland. "Don't go to Kovno but wait until you can meet them in Lodz." June 16, 1945, Eta and I went to Lodz and met Rachel.

This was the greatest miracle of all—that the three of us survived and were reunited!

A Dream of Milk

Ilona Weiss
b. Kosino, Czechoslovakia, 1923

There were millions of lice all over. My sister Irene developed a high fever and diarrhea. I sold our bread and soup for some black powder to stop the diarrhea, and some aspirin and sugar water. I fed these things to Irene; I sponged her with cold water day and night to relieve her fever. I was afraid she was going to die. Finally, after a long time, her fever broke. She slowly recovered.

Then I became very ill. Irene was only twelve, still a child. She didn't know how to help me. She cried and cried. She kept on crying that I should not die, that I should not leave her alone at Bergen-Belsen.

At that time the Nazis no longer fed us. Irene would go out and eat little green leaves from plants. She didn't know what they were, but they kept her alive. I could eat nothing.

Typhus was raging in Bergen-Belsen, and I had it. Dead bodies were everywhere. The *Blockälteste* would have the dying people thrown out into the yard.

There was not even any water for Irene to sponge me down. I had a high fever and was delirious.

In my delirium, I thought that my dear father was with me. He brought me a bottle of milk and begged me to drink it.

He said to me, "Drink it, dear daughter."

"Thank you, dear daddy," I said. "It tastes so good."

Somehow I did feel better after that dream. Though I was still very sick, my fever broke.

Strange to say, Irene heard every word I spoke as I dreamed it.

In Praise of Manual Labor

Alexander Zwillich
b. Boryslaw, Poland, 1925

Next to luck, my parents deserve much credit for my survival of the Holocaust. My father, not the typical Polish Jew, neither a pious scholar nor a merchant, worked at a skilled job in the oil industry of my hometown, Boryslaw. It was he who taught me not to be ashamed nor afraid of manual labor.

My mother's special contribution to my survival was her perseverance. For in spite of the heavy odds against her, she managed to have me learn the skill that proved helpful in the time of great need. It was because of her insistence that instead of learning a trade, I went to the Technical School in Drohobycz, where, concurrently with mechanical engineering, I learned to do metalwork.

In 1941 the army of the Third Reich occupied our town, and my studies were interrupted. The Third Reich's task was to extract from us Jews all possible labor for as little cost as possible. This, of course, did not in any way keep them from fulfilling their main task of letting us die of overwork and of any other causes. We, the camp's inmates, on the other hand, tried to stay alive by any means.

In August 1944, after being in several other camps, I was transported to the concentration camp in Melk, a branch of the camp Mauthausen. There I had to do pick and shovel work on a defense construction project. This type of work was usually a killer, but it was summer and the weather mild. Also, by that time I had learned a very important survival art: how to appear working while conserving as much strength as possible. Whenever I could I applied this skill and did not tire myself. Also, I did not cause the Kapo to exert himself by having to administer punishment to me to prove himself to be a good overseer.

One day, a German civilian came over to where we were working and asked if any of us knew the locksmith trade (which encompassed work in a metal shop). Some people and I raised our hand. A few got the job, but not I, because the yellow triangle above my prisoner number made me unacceptable—I was a Jew.

I suspected that some of those who had volunteered and been selected did not have the slightest notion about what the job requirements were. They only saw a chance to get out of heavy work, a ruse for which no one blamed them. I myself was doing the same thing, except that the job was well within my capabilities and skills.

A few days later, my suspicion as to the suitability for the job of those who were selected was proven correct: most of them rejoined our group. The same civilian came over and again asked for locksmiths; I raised my hand again, but this time I was selected—Jew or not Jew.

This proved to be one of my most lucky days. For the rest of my stay in Melk I continued working at that job, a much easier kind of manual labor. The work was done inside a shop, a big help in trying to stay alive. We had heat in winter, which also kept us in good graces with the Kapo who often came under the pretext of making sure that we were working, but really to get warm by the stove. The stove did double duty: it provided heat and means on which occasionally we did some primitive food preparation of stuff we scrounged—in camp parlance, "organized." Also, the shop offered a chance to rest if we grew tired, provided we took precautions of being not too blatant about it.

While I worked in that shop, I got into the business of making identification bracelets and bartering them for food. These bracelets were more comfortable to wear than the officially issued ones. This came about after, by chance, I discovered a prisoner who was an engraver working for the camp guards and officers. He let me observe him a few times at work, and was kind enough to answer questions I asked. With this information I taught myself engraving, primitive at first, but gradually, with experience, better and better.

My work in the shop provided me with raw material: aluminum and scraps of other metals from which I made the bracelets. I also had access to other materials, such as wood for handles, and broken metal files (whether through accidents or on purpose) from which I fashioned gravers—the tools used in engraving.

Once, I made a bracelet for myself which was in the shape of a rectangular wrist watch. I made it possibly as a lark, or because I thought it would be good for "business," or both. Anyway, one time a guard saw the bracelet I was wearing and his greedy black soul took over. He pounced at my wrist, ready to confiscate the forbidden item—the watch. His expression of disappointment, when he discovered the watch to be a fake, added much to my resolve to hold on longer. Though my victory was small and inadvertent, it nevertheless tasted sweet and the taste lasted for several days. Even today, when I think about this incident, I still can taste that sweetness.

Following liberation, and to this day, I have kept the two original gravers and my identification bracelet.

Nowadays when I think of the Holocaust, I realize the debt of thanks I owe to my parents for all they taught me—especially to my father for the lesson that manual labor is not to be shunned, but rather to be praised.

A Son in Deed

Sam Gottesman

b. Irsava-Ilosva, Czechoslovakia (became Hungary), 1923

The Dilemma

The sun was setting behind us as we marched back to camp, all seventy-five of us *Häftlinge Kzetniks,* as we called ourselves. We were in the Silesian Mountain area. It was a warm July day. The work was going well for me. My German master at the building site was a genteel man, who never spoke a harsh word. Even though I was not a *Zimmerman,* he had patiently showed me how to construct the wooden form for the building foundation so it would not collapse when the cement was being poured. But now as we were marching back to the camp my thoughts turned again to what was more important—food.

The twenty-minute march allowed us the luxury of dreaming of anything our fancy could come up with for supper. And the *zulage*—will it be a wedge of Limburger (which I couldn't stand at the beginning but now found delicious)? Will it be a one-inch cut of wurst, or perhaps a pat of margarine and a spoonful of marmalade? And what about soup? Never mind what kind, but will it have some potatoes in it, or perhaps noodles? Will I be lucky enough to be somewhere in the line when the Kapo reaches toward the bottom of the canteen where all the good stuff settles? Or will he open up a new canteen just when it's my turn in the line, and all I'll get is a ladle of thin watery soup?

Once in the camp, we could relax while waiting until all inmates were present and accounted for. They were marching in from every direction, from four different working places. Meanwhile I tried to find out from inmates working inside the camp what's for supper.

Finally someone said, *Biscoten Suppe.* So what's *Biscoten* soup? We were familiar with potatoes, barley, cabbage, even sugar beets—but *Biscoten?*

The canteens with our suppers were brought forward. I strained to see what this *Biscoten* soup was all about. Finally at the head of the line, I put out my little tin bowl, which was my only property along with the spoon issued way back when we first arrived. I was given a ladle of a creamy golden yellow-colored mush, my *zulage* and the four slices of bread which was our daily ration.

Off I went with my mystery soup, but I couldn't wait to reach my barrack. I had to taste it right now.

Lo and behold! This tastes like tea biscuits soaked in water or milk. This was cake! Nothing like this ever happened before. Was it a mistake? Were these biscuits somehow nonedible for the German taste, but good enough for the slaves?

I didn't waste much time figuring this out. I went to my barrack and sat down on my bed, salivating over my bowl of soup. My father, who was with me, came in and sat down next to me.

I started slowly, ever so slowly taking it in spoon by spoon, not even swallowing right away, in order to enjoy this heavenly dish as long as I could. While I lingered over this, my mind started to race: how could I secure another bowl? The chance of getting a second portion was slim to none. Sometimes a boy could get killed for trying. But my brain would not stop.

Then an idea struck me. Perhaps, only perhaps—but I would have to sacrifice at least one spoonful of this mush for my plan to succeed. The decision was not an easy one. I could wind up with a bloody nose or head, but my senses would not let me rest.

Not mentioning a thing to my father, I nonchalantly walked out of the barrack, scooped up a handful of mud, mixed it with the spoonful of soup which I had purposely left in my bowl, smeared the mixture over my jacket, and walked toward the kitchen. I walked back and forth a couple of times. You don't dare go into the kitchen.

Just then the SS officer noticed me.

"*Du Schweinehunde*," he said, "*was machst du da?*" (You pig-dog, what are you doing here?)

I recited my practiced litany. "*Herr Oberführer*," I said, "I did get my supper. However, as I was walking up hill to my barrack the mud was very slippery. I fell and I spilled my supper and had nothing to eat." I showed him my jacket to convince him of my honesty.

I stood there frozen for a minute. Then I heard the SS officer shout to one of the men in the kitchen, "Give him another serving."

Swift as a breeze, there I was inside the kitchen, this time holding out my bowl as the man poured a generous portion of *Biscoten* soup. A miracle of miracles!

I walked back to my barrack holding on tightly to my fortune and taking a spoonful now and then. As I walked and tasted, it began to dawn on me. During all my scheming I hadn't thought about it. But now—oh, I was hungry all right, but so was everybody else in these camps.

Thus the dilemma—to eat or not to eat. My father was up there sitting on his bed, suspecting nothing of my adventure. Here I was holding a bowl of a delicacy, as well as nourishment. Do I share it or do I eat it all by myself? It was a struggle between my mind telling me one thing and my heart telling me something else.

My heart was stronger. Yes, I did share my extra ration with my father. Maybe this was what helped us both to survive the nightmare.

Getting Out of Hell

"Oh, my back, oh, my back," my father whispered to me. "My back is breaking, I can hardly stand it."

We were in line, five abreast, to be registered for transport out of Bergen-Belsen. It was February, around ten o'clock at night. The cold wind cut through our flimsy gray and white striped concentration camp uniforms, which hadn't been washed since heaven knows when, and were no protection from the elements.

"How's this?" I asked my father as I massaged his back, applying all the pressure I could muster, which wasn't much.

We had arrived in Bergen-Belsen only last night after a five-day trip on an open freight train from Wustegiersdorf in Silesia. No food during the whole trip except for a loaf of bread and about six ounces of granulated sugar for each of us.

Early this morning we were introduced to this indescribable hell. All we could see were half-dead skeletons dragging dead bodies that littered the camp grounds, stacking them like cordwood on lorries that took them somewhere.

Yes, we were tired, hungry, and miserable—but aren't we the lucky ones, to stand here this evening in a line of about five hundred inmates picked out from thousands, to be shipped out God only knows where to—for work.

As the night wore on, the line moved ever so slowly. While my massaging gave my father some relief, not until we would be registered and back into the barracks, where he hoped he could lie down, would he find rest and relief. If I could only jump the line somehow, get a few feet ahead of where we were, I could speed up the process. It would be hard, if not impossible.

Suddenly the air-raid siren came on, the lights went out throughout the camp, and the line came to a halt. The registration stopped, everybody was milling around and no guards were watching. I grabbed my dad's hand and guided him forward about eight to ten lines, without anybody noticing or objecting.

When the lights came on, we were not far from the head of the line. We got our numbers and names on the list and returned to our barracks.

Yes, indeed, we were lucky, as I observed next morning. Had we stayed in our previous place in line we wouldn't have gotten on the list at all. The SS had filled their quota long before our part of the line. The rest of the inmates were rejected.

Had we remained in Bergen-Belsen, chances are neither one of us would have survived.

The Staff of Life

The end was practically here. The only question was whose end would come first. I was so very tired, so very hungry. There wasn't much left of me to go on fighting to stay alive.

My dad was in the "hospital"—a barrack full of the already dead and the ones about to die—his legs swollen to three times their normal size, oozing pus.

The order came on a Sunday morning in early April. The whole camp was to evacuate back to Bergen-Belsen. We were warned that those who dared to step out of line would be shot. We were told that those who couldn't walk would be taken by truck to Bergen-Belsen.

While I wasn't fooled by the Germans' generous offer of transportation, neither was I capable of reaching Bergen-Belsen alive. I also had my father to consider. I figured that as soon as the transport left the camp, one of the SS would come in with a machine gun and finish off those of us who were left.

But the starvation, fatigue, and depression enveloped me like a heavy, wet, and stinking blanket. All I wanted was to lie down and sleep, just to rest in peace, even if it meant through death. I didn't care any more. I stepped out of line, come what may.

So there they go, around five hundred inmates marching out of the camp. Seventy-five or eighty that were left simply stood there on the *Appellplatz*. There was no direction of any kind, no dismissal and no lineup. We stood there in disarray afraid to move, not knowing what to expect.

After about a half hour, a few of the boys noticed the absence of the guards from the camp's four towers. Soon they dared to reconnoiter different parts of the barracks. Around the kitchen they discovered and broke into the warehouse. They struck gold—loaves of bread, a pile of carrots, even blankets!

Those of us who could still walk stampeded the warehouse. I came out with two loaves of bread under my arm, hanging on to them with my life.

I made a beeline for the hospital. I found my dad lying in one of the bunks. The place reeked from those who were incapable of getting up. The stench of human waste, bodies lying on the floor and in the bunks, some stretching out their arms asking for help, was unbearable. I insisted that Dad should summon superhuman effort to come out of this place, which he did. Slowly we walked into one of the empty barracks near the hospital, and slowly we started on the bread.

But to our amazement, we could barely nibble at it! It was as if we didn't even know how to eat. As if the hunger we had suffered from all this time just wasn't there any more, had lost its bite. We spent the night in the barrack with my two loaves under my arms, barely touched.

And so I had the staff of life in my hands, and we couldn't eat it.

The Psychologist

Violet Weinberger
b. Uzhorod, Czechoslovakia (became Ungvár, Hungary), 1928

In the concentration camps, my mother was our "psychologist." Time after time, she tried to cheer us up.

She told my sisters and me, "Girls, after we get home, I'll cook and bake for you like I used to."

"Don't give up," she said.

She seemed to carry an invisible torch of hope.

Even toward the end, when we were weak and sick, she still tried to boost our morale.

She would say, "Girls, after the war we will go to America."

Once I turned to her and said, "Mother, how can you say that? Look at us, look at yourself, we'll never get out of here alive."

My mother and my oldest sister Margaret died after the Russian Army liberated us. I was sure I was not to live, not to survive either—I would die, too.

As it happened, my other three sisters and I barely survived. We weighed sixty to sixty-five pounds—we had typhus, all of us, and were unable to walk.

So my mother's wish did not come true for her, but four of her daughters did make it to America.

I often wonder if my mother really believed that there was hope—or did she just want us not to give up? If she had survived, I would ask her this question.

VII. The Virtuous and the Vicious

The terms "virtuous" and "vicious" are used in a specific way here to refer to people who rescued victims of the Nazis or, on the other hand, turned them over to the enemy. The terms, however, are in some ways misleading. There were virtuous people in every country affected by the Holocaust: many men and women risked their lives to save Jewish lives. By now we have, indeed, learned a great deal about these individuals, known today as Righteous Gentiles. And there were vicious collaborators who—for money, Jewish property, or out of politics or hatred—betrayed Jews to their murderers. But for all those who may fit into these two categories, there were others who can't neatly be classified as virtuous or vicious—people who, as if in passing, helped or hindered Jews a bit along the way to life or death, sent them on with a dash of hope or a slash of despair. Furthermore, people from whom Jews sought help, or at least human kindness, often had mixed motives.

Thus, for the Jews, it was usually quite unclear who—among fellow Jews as well as gentiles—might help them, or even when somebody might help them. In addition, the attitude toward helping the Jews was radically different in different countries, and even sometimes in different areas of one country. The stories in this section imply this broad range of people and actions, from Righteous Gentiles to betrayers. Above all, the stories define some of the ambiguity involved in the issue.

Four stories convey the quiet, strong heroism of Righteous Gentiles who hid Jews: "The Kindness of Strangers," "A Saintly Person," "The Convent in Marseilles," and "Among the Righteous." The locales of these stories—Holland, the Ukraine, France, Italy, and Switzerland—show that good people were all over Europe, for the few Jews who were lucky enough to find them.

The more ambiguous themes of this section are presented initially in the first story, "A Narrow Escape." Here we see a child's point of view, confusedly working through the moral issues of just what is a betrayal, and why it is that one person gives only a little begrudged help while another risks all to rescue Jewish victims. The moral issue is subtly repeated in "The Killing Hunger," which again deals with a child's confusion over what people will do to or for each other. "The Volunteer Group," a story about a Jewish Kapo (overseer in the concentration camps), and "The Farmer Kowarski" echo this theme of ambiguity. The writers here reveal both their wonder at people who will act one way one time and another way another time, and their frustration over their inability to predict where a person stands.

On another level, some stories express the writers' sense of irony over people who defied the writers' low expectations. In "Captain Zimmer," "Mazel," and "A Surprise Package," the writers focus on men who—each in his own way—surprisingly turn out to be representatives of an essential humanity.

Looking back upon the events of the Holocaust, we can hardly replicate or imagine the complex pressures that might have influenced our own actions as bystanders, had we been there; it's difficult to know for sure where we would have stood among the virtuous and the vicious. What we must understand in hindsight, however, is that in the face of the Nazi determination and systematic program to eradicate the Jewish race, the Jews desperately needed every bit of help—and hope—they could chance upon.

A. B.

A Narrow Escape

Edith Rechter Levy
b. Vienna, Austria, 1930

How many Jewish lives for the price of a baby crib? This is unfortunately not as preposterous a question as it may seem. For we were denounced precisely for such a reason.

The year was late 1942. My mother, nine-month-old baby brother, my older brother, and I were living in semi-hiding in Brussels, in a house with two other Jewish families.

In the *sous-sol*, or half-basement, of a house across the street lived a young unmarried couple. In Catholic Belgium at the time this was a mortal sin. Therefore I must presume that they were poor, alone and ostracized. The woman was pregnant and probably in need of baby supplies. So she called the German authorities to come and collect some furniture stored on an upper floor in her building by a Jewish family which had either fled or was somewhere in hiding. The woman watched carefully as the Nazis carried out pieces of furniture. When she spied a crib she offered to tell, in exchange for the crib, where Jews could be found. She pointed to our building.

A truck was not an uncommon sight in this neighborhood. A truck full of Germans in uniform was, however, a different matter. One of the Jewish families in our building noticed the German uniforms and saw the girl point at our house. Worried, they slipped away as soon as the soldiers went inside to check the furniture, without alerting anyone else and before the Nazi leader stationed two soldiers in front of our entrance door to prevent anyone from leaving.

The husband of the second Jewish couple used to leave our building often, dressed in blue denim overalls. He was a husky young fellow who looked like one of the local workers. He was on his way home when he spotted the soldiers in front of the house.

Instead of running away, which would have drawn attention to him, he saluted the soldiers and entered the building. He went quietly upstairs, took his wife and daughter and locked them into a small loft, then left the building with the key, past the unsuspecting soldiers.

No one, however, alerted us. When the lieutenant barged into our room we were totally unprepared. My older brother and I were ill. My brother had eaten some contaminated food and had come down with a serious case of hepatitis, or jaundice, as it was called at the time. His skin, his fingernails, even the whites of his eyes were yellow. I was in the latter stages of scarlet fever, with certain complications. I had begun menstruation very early, at eleven. The scarlet fever caused me to bleed severely for weeks, and of course without the hygienic comforts available now.

At the beginning of my illness I had been visited a few times by a young Jewish physician. He gave my mother some foul-smelling disinfectant in a bottle, telling her to spread it on the floor in the corners of the room should the Nazis discover our whereabouts. The Germans were known to be morbidly afraid of contagious diseases, especially scarlet fever.

But no disinfectant was sprayed anywhere; the room did not smell of quarantine.

My baby brother had just managed to pull himself up on the door, and as it burst open, he fell and began to cry. The lieutenant picked him up, patted him and quieted him down.

The soldier asked my mother about the other Jewish families. She replied that she didn't know. "You Jews," he responded, "you never know anything." We all froze.

But my mother bluffed her way through it. She somehow convinced the lieutenant that we were known to be pro-Nazi (living under those conditions?), the proof being that my father had *volunteered* his services, and was paid for them. She proudly produced the stubs of the checks she had received from the German authorities.

Did the ploy work? Did he let us go because he suspected we had contagious diseases—or because he was not a killer? Or did he think that we were poor bait, and hoped that by waiting he would get the other families as well? We will never know. He calmed my mother (her hands were shaking as she showed him the stubs), saying that if she was telling the truth, we had nothing to fear. He said he would call to verify her statement and return within the half hour.

Immediately after the departure of the truck loaded with Jewish furniture for the glorious Reich, my mother packed up her sick children and the baby. We left the building, not knowing where to go.

As we reached the doorway into the street, a neighbor pulled us into her *porte cochere*, a large portal which allowed entrance to a horse-drawn carriage. Crying, my mother kissed her hand in gratitude. The woman, with a tone of despair, said, "I could not, I simply could not let them take you. But there is nothing I really can do for you. What is happening to you is a punishment from God, because you have killed Jesus Christ. And for that, for all eternity you will suffer and will have to roam the earth."

We remained with her only a few minutes, thinking of the lieutenant's promise to return. After a while, the woman sent a child out to reconnoiter. When he returned, saying that the coast was clear, we left quickly. We sat on a bench in a nearby square until nightfall, trembling with fear each time we heard a motor car go by.

I felt plain bewildered by the events of the day—the woman who revealed our hideout for a crib, the Jewish families who didn't stop to warn us, the German lieutenant who let us go, and now this neighbor. For here was a decent human being, willing to risk danger to herself and her loved ones in order to save other human beings, and yet a person who had been taught, and believed, such terribly wrong ideas! To confuse me even further, that same night we were taken in by a *German woman* living not too far from there, who was ultimately responsible for saving our lives.

As to the woman who denounced us, whether she enjoyed her ill-gotten crib with a clear conscience, I cannot begin to guess.

The Kindness of Strangers

Esther Haas
b. The Hague, Netherlands, 1919

My cousin Rachel and her husband David, who lived in Holland, were given the name of a "righteous gentile farmer" who was willing to risk helping Jews. They hid at his flower farm in the country, between The Hague and Amsterdam. The flower farms were relatively safe because they were spread far apart, and with no close neighbors, the addition of two people to the household could easily go undetected.

The good people at the farm allowed David and Rachel to move into a small bedroom in their house. The room—a plain, tiny room with an iron bed and a small chest—was their world for three years. All day long they sat in this room—quiet, afraid.

They had to remain still during the day because in those times, even in sparsely populated areas, people stopped by to have coffee. The mailman, the milkman, the fishmonger all stopped for coffee on their routes and deliveries.

At night, however, David and Rachel were allowed to sit with the farmer's family in their living quarters. Then they talked about other days, other times, before the Nazis came. Life took on a slow, steady rhythm—silence during the day and conversation during the long evenings.

Unexpectedly, Rachel got pregnant a few months into their confinement. The farmer and his wife were forced to make a difficult decision. Even though they wanted to let Rachel and David stay with them, a baby would make noise—noise that might arouse the suspicion of the few but regular visitors. The farm couple were afraid for themselves and for their refugees, yet they could not turn the young people out, nor could they accept the baby.

When the time came to deliver, Rachel signed into the hospital under an assumed name and delivered a beautiful baby girl into a world that was not safe for Jewish babies. She and the baby were undetected in the hospital. Upon her release David took Rachel home to the farmhouse and then went out with the baby.

He followed a country road until he came to a glade of trees, the beginning of woods. He placed the little girl under a tree. David hid behind the next tree and waited. He waited for someone to come by and hear the baby cry.

After what seemed like hours, a middle-aged flower farmer, his wagon loaded with the wares of his trade, stopped. He had heard the baby cry and decided to investigate. David stepped out from his hiding place and identified himself as the father of the little girl and as a Jew in hiding.

He begged the farmer, "Please take her home and give her lots of love until the war is over and I can get her back. I beg you to save my baby!"

The farmer and David exchanged information: names, addresses, locations, and promises to meet after the war. David promised to pay all expenses when he could.

This good stranger took the small bundle in his arms, climbed onto his wagon and slowly drove down the road.

David and his family were among the lucky ones. They survived and found the baby when she was three, after the war was over. Because of the kindness of strangers their lives were saved. With all the horror, all the terror, all the death, some of the good people came through.

A Saintly Person

Rubin Udler*
b. Braila, Romania, 1925

After killing tens of thousands of people, the Romanian and German forces that occupied Odessa in 1941 issued orders to move all Jews into the ghettos. This order was to be obeyed under the threat of summary execution. Many Jews, at the end of their hope, risked their own and their family's lives by hiding in their homes, or wherever they could. Our family—my parents, sister, and I—decided to hide in the apartment house where we lived at 73 Karl Marx Street.

On the second floor of the house, in a small two-room apartment across the staircase landing from us, lived a thirty-year-old Russian woman and her two small children. We knew her only as Tanya. Her previous house had been destroyed by German bombing. Her husband was a career officer in the Soviet Army. Tanya did not know of his whereabouts nor what may have befallen him.

We became friends. When Tanya had to go out, we watched over her children. My mother used to give items to her which she bartered for food. Tanya was our link with the outside because we did not dare leave our apartment.

Our trust of Tanya was in contrast to our fear of Pete, the twenty-year-old, lame son of the janitor. During the first days of the occupation he avoided the Romanians and the Germans. However, after it became apparent that the soldiers were going to stay a while, he began, at their urging, to guide them to the Jewish apartments whose inhabitants had been evacuated.

After seeing the soldiers pillage, Pete started to do the same. Soon he and his mother moved to a rich and handsome apartment where they began holding dances, complete with drinking and wenching.

Pete quickly became the lord of the court. He exacted blackmail from us, pretending it was for the Romanians who were roving through the courtyard, and also for himself as payment for the good deeds he did for us. Time after time, Pete and his mother came to our apartment, complained about the difficulties of their situation, and by-the-by hinted covetously about this or that item which they could see we had. Of course, we gave them what they wanted, and they swore that they always respected honest Jews like us.

---

*Translated from Russian by Alexander Zwillich.

At eleven o'clock one night, we heard, coming from the outside, loud German and Romanian voices as well as Pete's confused mixture of Russian and Ukrainian. He was repeating over and over that in this apartment building there were no more Jews. To impress the German and Romanian soldiers that he was telling the truth, he said, "There are no more kikes."

Of course, Pete had to say this, because his mother had said this to the Romanian authorities before, as part of her duty as the janitor, and he had to continue the lie. Had he brought the soldiers to where we were, he and his mother would have lost their privileges as well as the trust of the occupation forces, and could have been severely punished. Needless to say, he also didn't want to give up the loot he was getting from us.

The soldiers demanded anyway that Pete lead them to the Jewish apartments. We saw the lights from the soldiers' torches and heard them going from apartment to apartment, opening all doors and looking everywhere.

We became numb with fright. We thought that it was the end. My father, however, quickly came to his senses. He told us to take our knapsacks with us and to tidy up the beds in order to give the impression that the apartment had long since been abandoned. He knocked at Tanya's door. She immediately let us in. Her children were asleep.

The second room of Tanya's apartment was divided by a wall which was made of plywood covered with wallpaper; there was a door in the wall which was not noticeable. Behind this door was a small storage space, three to four meters in length and less than a meter in depth. A cupboard stood in front of the door. We hid inside this storage area with our knapsacks.

Tanya pushed the cupboard back into its previous location. My mother and sister stood in the corner and my father and I near the door of our hiding place. We thought that this arrangement would make my mother and sister less likely to be seen in the event, God forbid, we were discovered.

We did not dare to stir; we stopped breathing and stood stock-still, feeling more dead than alive.

After some time, there was loud knocking at the door and soldiers burst into the apartment. This awakened the children and they began to cry. Five or ten minutes passed, which to us seemed an eternity, during which the soldiers stomped around the apartment and looked into the kitchen and the toilet, all the while yelling that they were looking for Jews. Probably the agitation and crying of the awakened children and the sight of a scared, confused Tanya disarmed the soldiers. They abandoned their search of the apartment.

Tanya put the children back to bed and quieted them down. Afterward, she sat for a long time in darkness and watched the moving lights of the torches.

We remained for many hours in the storage space, without fresh air, standing all the time without being able to move. We felt resigned to the doom which we thought awaited us. Had the fascists found us, all of us would have been mutilated, torn to pieces then and there or later in the torture cellars of the police.

Some time afterward we were put into the ghetto. There, we often recollected Tanya, an ordinary Russian woman, emaciated, exhausted by deprivation and anxieties, who saved our lives. We remembered Pete, too—a cunning representative of the lowlife class of Odessan people.

In the spring of 1944, when my mother, sister, and I returned to Odessa, we did not find Tanya nor her children. Our former neighbors told us that Tanya had a very difficult time during the winter of 1941, and the following spring she and her children left, probably for her homeland. We never even found out Tanya's last name.

This story is the only tribute I can pay Tanya, a truly saintly person, for her brave deeds toward us.

The Convent in Marseilles

Hermine Markovitz
b. Volorice, Czechoslovakia, 1926

I was visiting my relatives in Belgium when the Germans took over my home town. My father wrote to my uncle asking him to keep me in Belgium. But in 1940 the Nazis took over there, too. My uncle and his family decided to try to escape, since he knew that all Jews were being taken away. We went to France by train.

The station at the border between France and Belgium was crowded. Everyone had to line up to get their identity papers cleared according to nationality, so I went to the Czech line while my relatives went to the Belgian line. I had with me a small parcel containing a few clothes, and around my neck a small sachet which my mother had made for me, which held about five hundred francs. When I went back to the spot where I thought I was supposed to meet my uncle, nobody was there. I waited. Finally, I sat down and cried. I didn't even speak French. I was fourteen years old.

Two kind families, the Tenenbaums and Sugarmans, came over and asked me why I was crying. They tried to page my uncle and searched throughout the station, but without success. They took me along with them when they boarded a train to Paris.

We learned that the Germans were approaching Paris also, so we left and went on toward the Pyrenees. At the stops along the way, we were fed by local peasants.

When the train arrived in the Pyrenees, we were given a meal. I was still with the Tenenbaums, and we all stayed in a room together. We had a small stove in the room which we used to heat light meals. We found that there were many other refugees in the area, including some Spanish victims of the revolution. We were all waiting for the war to be over.

After France agreed with the Nazis to be divided into two zones, the Tenenbaums decided to go to the nearest big city—Marseilles. None of us had any money left, but we felt that there would be other Jews there. We contacted the local Czech underground, which finally placed me in a convent.

My life in the convent started out comfortably and uneventfully. I even corresponded with my parents in Czechoslovakia. I was allowed to come and go from the convent, which also served as a rooming house for young girls. I went to visit the Tenenbaums and Sugarmans often. Since I couldn't go to school, I taught myself French by copying phrases from books.

The nuns were very good to me. They even knew that on Yom Kippur I would disappear for the day to fast, and prepared a special meal for my return. I knew it was Yom Kippur because the Tenenbaums and Sugarmans told me.

Then the Vichy government, in cooperation with the Nazis, ordered all foreign Jews to register with the authorities. Feeling that I had nothing to hide, nothing to be ashamed of and little to fear, I did as others were doing—I registered. I didn't tell anyone I was going to register or they probably would have stopped me.

One night I was awakened by one of the nuns, saying that the Gestapo had come for me. Sister St. Vincent talked to me with tears in her eyes, and I began to fear that I was in danger. I asked the Sister to remove all my parents' letters from my room so that the Gestapo would not know anything about my family.

I was taken to a detention camp in Aix-en-Provence with hundreds of other Jews who had been ousted from their homes. I could not understand why I was there. I had broken no laws, I had done nothing wrong. The gravity of the situation was incomprehensible to me. I cried continuously, and I could not eat.

One day, because of severe belly pain, I was given a medical examination. The doctor said that I had appendicitis and I needed to have surgery. I was taken to a Catholic hospital administered by nuns.

While I was recovering from the surgery, a nun from my convent and some people from the Czech underground came to see me. They kept telling me not to worry, that everything would be all right; but I had no idea what they meant.

The next day I was taken out through the laundry exit, because the front exit was guarded by the Gestapo. I was taken on a two-hour taxicab ride to the Czech underground headquarters in Marseilles. I was scared the entire time that I would be caught escaping and that my fate would be worse as a result. I did not know then that all those who were at the detention camp ended up in Auschwitz. So the operation saved my life in more ways than one.

The Czech underground returned me to the convent, where I lived in fear that the Gestapo would come back for me. I never again corresponded with my parents, so that the Nazis could not trace my parents or connect them with me. My parents wrote to me, but sadly, I did not answer them.

The Sisters, working with the Czech underground, arranged a new identity for me, changing my name from Katz to Casar. They took me to a different convent in the same town. I lived in constant terror.

One morning a German officer named Herr Müller arrived and extended his hand in greeting to the nun who served as the director. Instead of shaking it, she spat on it. I was terrified that it would mean instant arrest for all of us. Instead, he informed us that we would have to vacate our building and move across the street to the orphanage. I stayed in the orphanage until I was liberated.

After the war I wanted to go back to Czechoslovakia, but I was warned about the communists and that my parents and seven siblings probably wouldn't be there.

When I received a letter from my uncle in the United States, I fainted. They actually poured a pitcher of water on me to rouse me. The letter was written in Yiddish, and I had to get someone to translate it for me. It told me that my family had been taken to Auschwitz in April 1944.

My uncle asked me to come to the United States, but I was afraid, having even heard about the possibility that Nazis lived there. He finally convinced me that in America there was room for both Hitler and me. After three years of waiting for my papers under the Czech quota, I came to the United States.

Out of a family of eight children, only my sister Dora and I survived. I was reunited with my sister in 1970 when she emigrated from the U.S.S.R. to the United States.

Among the Righteous

Vladimir Lang

b. Osijek, Yugoslavia (now Croatia), 1925

The Germans had started to round up Italian Jews and were looking for us, too. It was apparent to our protectors and my parents that we could not survive being hidden on this farm outside Bologna.

I had come illegally from my home town, Osijek (now Croatia) in February 1942 to Ljubljana, which was occupied by Italy. Later the Italian government had sent me to the interior, to this village near Bologna. My parents came to join me in mid-1943 from the Dalmatian coast, which was also occupied by Italy.

The Canova family were the ones who were hiding us on their farm. They gave us shelter and plenty of food. They were good-hearted Italians, Catholics, and anti-fascists. Through friends of the Canovas, we heard of a possibility to cross into Switzerland. Some had already fled successfully, we heard.

So in late 1943, we took the train to Milan. Fortunately one did not need an official *laisser-passez* (permit) for traveling within Italy. Nevertheless, we all had some false papers. My document was a "postal identification card"—apparently considered a valid ID in Italy at that time. My new name was Pietro Nenni, born in Sicily. Much later I found that this was the name of the Socialist Party leader of Italy.

While we traveled to Milan, Mr. Canova was arrested and interrogated about our whereabouts. Someone must have notified the police that he was hiding us. Mr. Canova never admitted to that or gave our whereabouts, and after a week he was released unharmed.

In Milan, some people harbored us in a large apartment complex in a sublet furnished apartment where other Jewish families were waiting their turn to cross into Switzerland. We were not completely safe there and were advised not to hang out in the apartment during the day. It was winter by that time and we had to either walk around the city, or travel on the tram or bus. The "safest" activity was to walk in the large cemetery—Catholic, of course. We had never seen such large sculptures and monuments in a cemetery.

For me the big city was an adventure. I studied the map of the city and surroundings, looking to see more than I could by walking the streets—after all, I was only eighteen! I neglected to realize that my life depended on not being caught by the Germans or neofascists.

I have never found out who organized and paid for our escape: Red Cross from Yugoslavia, UJF, Italian Jews, or some other organization. In any case, one day I was told I would be given the chance to cross into Switzerland. I was to go first, and my parents would follow later.

I started out by train one evening in March 1944. I had only a backpack, my rucksack from the time I went to summer camps, with some clothes, false papers in my pocket, but a true document inside the backpack. At the railroad station in Como a man was waiting for me. He drove me in the dark to a mountain house. There, I met another young man, about my age, an Austrian Jew. The man who brought me to the mountain walked during the night with us further into the mountain toward the border. The other young man and I guessed that these people bribed the German border guards and knew at what precise time to approach the border. The man did not go with us into Swiss territory, but left us inside an abandoned, roofless hut that must have served as a resting place for shepherds. "When you see light," he said, "walk down the mountain and you will be in Switzerland." We followed his instructions, descended the mountain and were met by Swiss border police. They took us into a building, told us to completely undress and gave us some strong disinfectant soap for a shower. By the time we were out, our clothes and the backpacks were out of the "steam machine."

Later I heard how lucky we were that we were not caught by Germans or were not returned by the Swiss, as many others were. Being returned by the Swiss meant to be caught by Germans and deported to a concentration camp.

While I was being interviewed, given clothes and sent off to two different transit camps for processing—Chiasso and Bellinzona—my parents made the same trip. I received a postcard from them at my new home—a work camp in Hedingen, near Zurich.

It appears that, once the Germans were in retreat on the eastern front, the Allies in Italy and invasion looming, the Swiss gave asylum to anyone who crossed the border in flight from the Germans—even German soldiers!

There were at least a hundred people in the work camp I was in. They were mostly Jewish, from many different countries: Germany, Austria, Hungary, France, Poland, Yugoslavia. There were a dozen people in their twenties, and the rest were all ages. We lived in wooden barracks. Our main tasks were to cut down trees and to seed potatoes in order to feed, allegedly, the many refugees that Switzerland harbored. We worked about eight hours a day, were fed reasonably well and received some pocket money too. The Swiss police gave everyone an identity card.

My parents were only a few miles from my camp in another small town, Adliswil, in the next valley. With permission from the camp manager, I walked over the hill and met with them. That was a happy occasion—we were *free*. But it was the brave Italians who saved my family in the first place.

As a result of the initiative of my parents, who ultimately went to live in Jerusalem, Alfonso Canova received the Medal for the Righteous at Yad Vashem in 1965. Mr. Canova's name is inscribed on a plaque in the United States Holocaust Memorial Museum.

The Killing Hunger

Cyna Glatstein
b. Sochachev, Poland, 1928

In the Warsaw Ghetto in 1941, everyone was starving.

Killing hunger. Swollen bellies, bloated faces, empty eyes, walking corpses, many already dead and dragged away.

The American Rabbinical Association arranged for the Joint Distribution Committee to distribute packages for the rabbis and their families before the High Holidays that year. As a rabbi, my father was one of those to receive these packages.

Who was the one to go to the distribution center to pick up the package? I was the most logical one in my family. My older brother and sisters would have been picked up for forced labor, and the babies were with my mother.

The queue was long. We were very patient. Many of us were weakened by hunger and could not stand for any length of time. Some sat, others lay, and some collapsed.

At last, I was number two in line. The man ahead of me opened his package instantly, exclaiming, "Thank God!" He looked at the dried milk, rice, chocolate, and powdered eggs inside, and left.

Now it was my turn. Hugging this life-sustaining package, I ran off. Suddenly two clawlike hands grabbed my package. Before I knew what had happened, this skeleton was downing the whole package. String. Paper. Everything.

I became hysterical and ran home. My parents comforted me. They explained that this man was not evil. "We live in horrible times, and even decent people are driven to act in this inhumane manner."

My mother said, "With heaven's help we will manage. I still have my wedding ring for barter. We will usher in the New Year with dignity."

Captain Zimmer

Violet Weinberger
b. Uzhorod, Czechoslovakia (became Ungvár, Hungary), 1928

Awful as our lives were at Stutthof Concentration Camp, there was a tiny bright part. And that was Captain Zimmer.

Captain Zimmer was with us every day in the shop where we worked. He looked over the production.

Every day, a group of Nazis came to the shop to check the amount we produced. They stormed in and, before they checked our work, started beating us with a leather whip. They told the Captain that he should beat us too.

But he never did. He knew the approximate time that the Nazis would arrive. He stood at the windows watching and when the Nazis approached, he paced the floors, pretending that he was truly yelling and cracking his whip.

After the other Nazis left, Captain Zimmer laughed.

The Volunteer Group

Irene Berkowitz
b. Uzhorod, Czechoslovakia (became Ungvár, Hungary), 1920

My mother was starting to weaken. Because she thought that vegetables would help her, I went to the new group of arrivals at Stutthof Concentration Camp to ask if anyone had some vegetables they would trade for bread.

I got back late for roll call. A Jewish-German Kapo reported my late arrival to the German female officer, who took out her leather whip and gave me twenty-five lashes all over my body, including my face.

On a cold January evening some time later, the Germans came to the barracks in the middle of the night, announcing that they needed three hundred volunteers to work at the warehouses. Nobody wanted to go because it was so cold. But I remembered my father's advice that we should always volunteer for work, and felt that someone from my family should go, so I went out. My older sister, Margaret, called after me to come back because I would freeze out there.

Standing in line with the other volunteers, I looked back and realized that there were now more than the needed number of volunteers. Still hearing my sister's plea for me to return, I decided to go back to the barrack.

To my surprise, my family wasn't in the barrack—they were now among the group of volunteers!

The Jewish Kapo who had reported my tardiness that day had heard my sister calling me to come back, and told her not to call me, but that they too should join the volunteers. Now the Kapo took me by the hand and returned me to the volunteer group.

The next day, Stutthof was evacuated. Those who had not volunteered for the work detail were sent on a forced march. Many of them died in the bitter cold.

Did the Kapo know this would happen? Did she feel guilty about the beating? I wondered.

Mazel

Ray Naar
  b. Salonika, Greece, 1927

I think of him during the winter nights, when the wind and cold bring back memories of Bergen-Belsen. I close my eyes and think of him on his bed of straw, carefully rolling his tobacco in a piece of newspaper.

We called him "Mazel." It was not his real name, but he had the habit of saying the word whenever the going was rough: *Mazel,* which is the Hebrew equivalent of our English "luck."

No one knew anything of his past. Some claimed that he was Belgian, others that he was Ukrainian. When asked, he would say with a vague gesture, "I come from there."

We did not like him in the camp but tolerated him because he was so quiet and inoffensive. During the day, we saw him limping across the immense barrack, wearing wooden shoes, making an uneven sound as he walked. He wore a gentleman's morning coat, filthy with stains, buttoned up to his neck, and the dirtiest cap one could imagine, which he never removed from his head. This cap was the object of constant ridicule and much speculation as to its age and origin.

One day, a joker hid the cap and Mazel, in a state of helplessness, his eyes filled with tears, wandered around the barracks, begging that it be returned to him as he was unable to say his prayers without it. That day we remarked that he was bald.

Nobody was very handsome to look at in the camp but Mazel was of an outstanding ugliness. He was big, stooped, blind in one eye, looked haggard and starved.

At first we found him repugnant and drove him away whenever he approached us. He accepted all insults with invulnerable good humor, but with a hurt look upon his face which had the effect of making the rest of us feel ashamed.

No one had ever heard him complain. When conditions became atrocious and vexations unbearable, he would say with a gentle smile which rendered his face less hideous, "*Mazel!* Next year in Jerusalem."

Mazel had but one vice: smoking. As soon as he received his food ration he would make the rounds of the barracks exchanging whatever he could for a few cigarettes. Having acquired what he wanted, he returned to his bed of straw on the floor. His large body lowered itself onto the narrow space and seemed to shrink to fit. Then, proceeding very slowly, as if accomplishing a ritual, he opened the cigarettes, chopped the tobacco, mixed it with dry potato peels, and rolled it all in pieces of paper. It is at this occupation that I remember him best, with his cap pulled over his ears, his muscles rigid, rolling his tobacco in a slow and precise manner.

Early in the morning, despite the intense cold, he said his prayers. A shawl over his head, a strap around his arm, as in the Jewish Orthodox custom, with bent head, he chanted in a low voice. We gazed at him in astonishment for these practices were unknown to us. Oftentimes, I envied him. Was it faith that gave him an everlasting smile, an eternal optimism that made him mention *Mazel* every time we rebelled?

One winter evening, Mazel gave us a great surprise. It had been a very bad day. The weather was exceedingly cold and we had been drenched by a fine rain during a four-hour roll call. We had been punished for some insignificant offense and deprived of our daily ration of food. The lights in the camp were extinguished, as the Americans were bombing the neighboring city of Hanover. The rain had stopped and snow was falling. Through the windows of the barracks we could see the heavy flakes, dry and closely packed, as if they wanted to cover and bury the earth. We were hungry, unable to sleep, and felt the bitter loneliness and nostalgia common to prisoners. It was one of the moments of despair which come to the exiled, when nothing more matters, when one seems to have given up everything, even hope, and believes that the world has started and will end in the grayish darkness of a prison camp.

Suddenly, in the deep silence, a voice was heard. Clear, true and warm, it seemed to come from far off. It was an Italian song, "*Non ti scordar di me.*" Years have passed and each time I hear that song I am filled with the same feeling of calm and security. Should I live a hundred years, I shall never forget that voice. The singer continued to enthrall us for some time with his music; we felt our nerves relax and a wonderful feeling of peacefulness take possession of us. A sob was heard close by; behind me someone was crying.

From that day we all loved Mazel. His was the voice which had brought a glimpse of beauty, of hope and of peace once more into our life. He became one of us and no one again thought of mocking him. Oftentimes in the evenings, we asked him to sing for us, and his voice never failed to bring us comfort and, for a brief moment, forgetfulness.

One day, much later, near the end of our internment, a German guard appeared in the barrack and called for Ephraim Bragowsky. Thus we learned Mazel's name. For some time, Mazel had not had the strength to sing. Having given up his food for cigarettes over such a long period of time, he had become so weak that he spent entire days lying on his bed. He made an effort to smile and utter "*Mazel*" but his voice was low and his smile was sad. The German approached his bed and handed him two cans of sardines. "Here," he said, "someone has sent you these from Portugal."

Mazel was transfigured. He looked around at each one of us and two great tears rolled down his cheeks, while he repeated as a refrain, "They thought of me, they thought of me." Then, as if possessed, he pressed the cans close to his breast, thinking of all the cigarettes he could obtain in exchange for them, or thinking perhaps of a forgotten past, of a someone in Portugal who had thought of him.

Some young boys crowded around. There had been ten children in the camp; three had died. The others, emaciated and famished, regarded Mazel with envy.

Poor Mazel, so weak that he could hardly lift himself from his bed, gazed at them. Closing his eyes for a few seconds, he extended the cans toward the boys, saying "Take them, children."

Eight days later, he died. He slipped away gradually, without disturbing anyone. "He died of exhaustion," said the inmate doctor.

A great silence descended on the camp. Tears were in every eye.

The Farmer Kowalski

Moshe Baran
b. Horodok, Poland, 1920

A farmer named Kowalski brought my family out of Ghetto Krasny.

Kowalski traveled occasionally to the town of Krasny to sell produce and buy necessities. He did clandestine errands for the partisans, and was known to be reliable.

After I escaped from the ghetto and joined the partisans in the nearby forest, I approached Kowalski to find out the feasibility of rescuing my family.

Cautiously, I asked him whether he could deliver a message to my family in the ghetto.

"It's dangerous for outsiders to enter the ghetto," he said.

"I know it's dangerous—but is it possible?"

"It's possible if you know the right people and the timing is right."

"Do you know the right people?" I now inquired.

"I know one person who has access to the ghetto."

I hinted that he would be rewarded handsomely.

Impassive—as if he hadn't even heard my offer—he said, "Give me the names of your family and tell me which house they're in."

A few days later he told me he was going to town and would try to contact my family. Upon his return he told me that he had delivered the message.

"I told them to be ready to leave next time I contact them," was all he said.

Kowalski rescued my brother and sister in December 1942. On March 17, 1943, he rescued my mother—only. My father refused to leave because my other sister was recuperating from typhoid.

We paid him with cattle and other goods taken from farmers outside the area where the partisans operated.

On March 19, 1943, Ghetto Krasny was annihilated.

This same man, Kowalski, had earlier helped get weapons from Ghetto Krasny into the forest, enabling me and then my friends to join a group of partisans.

And it was Kowalski who, upon his return from another trip to Krasny, had told us about a group of young people from the ghetto who were due to arrive in the forest. They had weapons and were about to join a partisan group called Grischency, he had said.

Kowalski later told us that the men had arrived. But from then on, no one heard a word about them.

In mid-1946, at the railroad station in Minsk, as my family and I were on our way to be repatriated from Russia to Poland, I bumped into one of the former partisans from my own group.

Sharing memories, we talked about the different resistance groups that had operated in the area of Krasny.

"By the way," he said, "do you know what happened to the young Jewish boys who came from Krasny to join the Grischences?"

"I have no idea," I said. "They weren't heard of from the day they arrived."

"I'll tell you why," he said, looking strained. "After they arrived, they were shot and their weapons were distributed to local partisans."

Sensing my disbelief and pain, he continued. "I'll tell you where they were killed. Do you remember that big barn on the hill near the village? That's where."

"But why?" I asked.

"Because they were Jews, that's why! You were lucky—the farmer Kowalski, who helped you, was collaborating with the partisans and also with the Germans."

"How do you know?" I asked.

"Remember the last time the Germans blockaded the whole area in the spring of 1944?"

"Yes."

"Well, Kowalski retreated with the Germans. He sensed that the partisans suspected him."

I was stunned by the irony of it all. Kowalski, who had done so much—who had transported our weapons from the ghetto and brought my family out . . .

Kowalski was a double agent.

A Surprise Package

Ernest Light
  b. Uzhorod, Czechoslovakia (became Ungvár, Hungary), 1920

It was a cold, rainy night. Hungry and exhausted, we stood in line for hours while the Germans counted and recounted us, checking whether the number matched the number they counted when we left in the morning.

Finally we started back to camp. While stopping at a railroad crossing, I saw a German soldier with a gun over his shoulder approaching me. He was tall and looked well-fed, like all of them.

I wasn't scared. My mind just wasn't functioning.

Suddenly he slipped something into my hand. Surreptitiously, I glanced down at the package. It was a piece of bread.

Was I picked by chance that night? Did he do it every night, randomly choosing someone? One thing I do know—that piece of bread boosted my morale and strengthened my will to live. Despite all the inhumanity, there were human beings left in the world.

VIII. DESPERATE HEROISM

In the years since World War II, there has been a good deal of speculation as to why the Jews did not do more to resist the Nazis, why they passively accepted what befell them. There are rational, clear responses to this question. Basically, there was no way to resist, no hope of overcoming the numbers, weapons, and cruelty of the Germans and their allied oppressors. Anyone who tried to stand up to the Germans, let alone fight them, was immediately killed; in addition, if anyone escaped from a ghetto or camp, many others were killed as a punishment. Thus, by putting the responsibility for the murder of other innocent people on those who tried resistance or escape, the Germans devised a most effective preventive weapon.

In spite of this almost insurmountable difficulty, individual Jews as well as groups did carry out desperate, heroic acts of resistance throughout the war in all parts of Europe. From the ghettos to the slave labor camps and concentration camps, Jews managed to work underground, escape, accumulate weapons, sabotage German installations, attack German fighting units, even organize some major uprisings.

Three stories in this section are about the simple yet profound heroism of children. Often because they could get around relatively unnoticed, young girls and boys ventured out to secure food or to do other dangerous errands. The three stories in "Unsung Heroes" speak of these children.

Actual resistance fighters, for the most part, were single young men who did not have the responsibility of taking care of a family. Groups of these young men formed clandestine organizations, planning escapes from the ghettos even though this might very well cause punishment or death for other ghetto inhabitants. After escaping, they joined partisan bands in the forests, living in huts or underground, scrounging for food, attacking and sabotaging wherever they could. "Lithuanian Friends" and "Friend or Enemy?" detail the hardships and perils, the resolute strength of men who went this precarious route.

Even in the concentration camps, where conditions were most austere and death almost inevitable, organized resistance existed. "Resist in Everything!" is a gripping story about resistance brigades functioning with military precision under the noses of the Germans. The story takes place during a death march, one of many on which the Germans took prisoners when the liberators approached the camps in 1945. While it is in one way an epic about a young boy growing up, it is also about unquenchable, universal courage.

Like all the stories in this book, these are true stories containing true details, told by people who lived them. What makes these resistance stories stand out, however, is the spirit, the perverse optimism, that in a hopeless situation something can be done. Reading them, we are inspired with the passion that shines through them.

A.B.

Lithuanian Friends

Leon Brett
b. Skudvil, Lithuania, 1922

At the close of summer in 1942, a group was formed in the ghetto in Shavel, Lithuania, that dreamed of escape and resistance. It was only a dream. But our resistance group met regularly to hear ideas and options, and to plan.

Everyone in our group was to try to make contact with a friendly Lithuanian. Perhaps he could get us a gun. We knew if we were to run away and establish ourselves in the woods, we would need good clothes, an ax, a saw, a shovel, and also a gun.

So members of our resistance group who did not look Jewish would remove their yellow stars and go to their Lithuanian friends and plead for help. They did so at the risk of their lives.

But it did not work. We could not get even one gun.

We decided to confide in the Judenrat, the Jewish administrators of the ghetto. We told them of our plan. We wanted to establish a base outside the ghetto, to explore the possibilities. Perhaps we could get help from the outside world. Perhaps we could even save some Jews this way. They said that they would help us all they could. They would give us clothes. But they reminded us that should the Germans catch anybody in the ghetto with a gun, it could very well be the end of the ghetto.

As hard as all the members of our group tried, we were not able to get a gun.

One day, the Germans requested a new list—several hundred Jews were to be sent to a camp called Daugel. A member of our group became very excited. He had once been sent to Daugel for a short time. He said that Daugel was the most ideal place to escape from because the camp was in the middle of the woods.

Our group decided to ask the Judenrat to send about ten of us to Daugel. We also asked them to appoint a member of our group as administrator of the camp.

Daugel had a brick factory away from the populated area, in the woods. There was a big, dilapidated building. There were a lot of small rooms in the building, where the bricks were heated and dried.

The administrator the Judenrat appointed was good-looking with a nice personality, very smart. He spoke perfect German. Everybody liked him. He was perfect for the job.

He got the German *Lagerführer* to agree to let us have more water for washing. The extra water could only be gotten from a stream outside the camp. We would go with a barrel to get the extra water. But since that was outside the camp, a Ukrainian guard would always come along.

Our job consisted mainly of making forms or molds for the bricks out of wooden boards, filling them with clay, placing them in the drying rooms and then removing them when they were ready. In order to remove them from the drying rooms into the railroad cars, we formed a human chain all the way to the railroad cars. I was assigned to work in the chain. But my place was inside the drying rooms which were extremely dusty, irritating and inflaming to my eyes. I couldn't even open them, so our administrator got me different work.

I went to work for a local Lithuanian, Jurgis. Jurgis had a horse and wagon. His job was mainly to remove broken bricks from the premises, deliver supplies like wood to the mold makers, and deliver the finished molds to be filled with clay.

Jurgis was short, broad, and very strong. He was known for his strength and bad temper. He always fought with the other Lithuanians who worked in the camp. He would tease the Ukrainians, constantly cursing. Big Mouth Jurgis we called him. He was the kind of person who couldn't pass another human being without making some kind of comment, usually derogatory. They used to say that he could take on ten men and beat them. He could lift the wagon with one hand. Everybody was afraid of him and of his temper. Nobody liked him. Nobody dared make him angry.

I worked for him. When Jurgis brought the horse to a halt, I knew what to do and I did it. I sure did not want to make him angry. I watched myself. But as time went on I disliked him less, and perhaps for selfish reasons. A slice for me and a slice for you. He had food like there was no war. And when nobody was watching, he would take out a cloth bag, a little sack. There was a loaf of bread—a slice for me, a slice for you.

When I had worked for Urmanas the jeweler, he would refer to me as Zydas the Jew. But Jurgis called me by my name. He called me Leibas and I called him Jurgis.

One day while I was riding on the wagon with Jurgis, he holding the reins and I sitting in the back as usual, he said, "Today is your Sabbath, isn't it?"

"Yes," I replied.

"It's your day of rest, you shouldn't be doing any work."

"We are in a concentration camp, we have no choice."

"Why don't Jews touch money on the Sabbath?" he asked.

"I don't know why, we just shouldn't."

"But touching money, that's not work," he said.

"I don't know why," I replied, "we are just not allowed to."

He was silent for a while and then said, "I knew a Jewish family before the war. They had a shop. If I needed something on their Sabbath, they would tell me to go in by myself and take what I needed. I paid them the next day." He was silent for a longer time and then said, "You know what I used to do, Leibas? I used to steal when I was in the shop alone. I shouldn't have done that."

"One time or another we all do things that we shouldn't," I replied.

"They had four children. I liked them. The oldest one must have been about twelve. I shouldn't have done what I did. Do you think they hate me now?" he asked.

"No, they don't," I said. "They are all dead and perhaps in heaven. When you are dead and in heaven, you don't hate. It's when you are alive and on this earth that you hate."

After a pause Jurgis replied while turning to look at me, "I don't hate you, Leibas." It felt good that Jurgis did not hate me. At that moment, I wanted to live on this earth. I had tears in my eyes. In an ocean of hate, there was a drop of goodness.

His teasing the Ukrainian guards worried me. He would call them "Ruskies." For a Ukrainian to be called a Russian is an affront.

The Ukrainians were known for their cruelty. They once found some bread in the pocket of a man returning from work. They mercilessly beat him, left him lying there bleeding and wouldn't let anyone get close to him, not even the camp doctor. A few hours later, when *Kommandant* Heinrich came to do the roll call, our administrator told him what happened. Heinrich contemplated for a minute and said, "We Germans are a compassionate people, we don't want anybody to suffer." Then he pulled his gun from its holster, shot the bleeding man in the head, and the Jew did not suffer any more.

That's why Jurgis' teasing the Ukrainians worried me. He said he wasn't afraid of them. But I tried to tell him, "Sure, they couldn't do anything to you, but they might take it out on me." My reasoning helped, and he stopped doing it, which made me feel better.

Once when we were in a remote corner of the factory, he shared his food with me, as he often did—a slice for me and a slice for you. There was bread and there was butter, and the butter was as thick as the bread. I said, "There is a terrible war going on, everything is rationed. So where do you get all that food?"

"You can't buy anything for money," he answered. Then he told me that he learned from his father to make *somogon*. "Mine is the best moonshine around," he said. "Everybody wants to drink. I trade my *somogon* with farmers for food. There's a German warehouse for their army close by; I trade it with the guards for clothes, which I sell in town. But Heinrich, the one in charge of this camp, gets it from me for free. This is a priority job and I want him to keep me here. If you work here you cannot be sent to work in a war factory in Germany. I would rather take to the woods than go to Germany."

And then he said, "Leibas, you shouldn't be in a concentration camp. If you want to run away, I will help you." I felt like I had been struck by lightning from a clear blue sky.

At night I reported to my group what Jurgis had said. The opinion was to be cautious. Nobody wanted to trust him. Big Mouth Jurgis.

The next day he told me, "If you want a gun, I can give you one." Like lightning from a clear blue sky.

"What in the world would I do with a gun?" I said. Then I asked him, "How much money would you want for a gun?"

"Nothing," he said. He told me that he and his friend Geryba had found an abandoned supply of Russian long guns, hand guns, and ammunition. They had it hidden and wanted to give me a few.

At night I reported to my group again. We asked our administrator to send somebody else with me the next day to work for Jurgis. We must find out more, a second opinion.

Jurgis repeated the same to both of us. We asked him who was Geryba. He replied, "Tomorrow when we go to the stream for water, he'll be there. He wants to talk to you."

The next day he was there. He was a dignified man, the opposite of Jurgis. He talked very little, but came right to the point. He had a personality that you trusted at once. He repeated the same offer.

At night our group discussed the new development. Two strangers, Jurgis and Geryba: could we trust them?

A few days later, when the work day ended, Jurgis handed us a package. "That's for you," he said. We realized that we had a gun in our hands and we promptly hid it in one of the drying rooms in the brick plant. A couple of days later we smuggled it into the camp. At night we tried to learn how to use it.

Our administrator spoke to the people in the camp. If the Germans should find out that we had a gun, we would all be killed. We must not talk about it even to each other. We must not even think about it. Everybody understood. Several days later Jurgis brought us several more guns.

One day when we came to the stream, Geryba was there waiting for us. While Jurgis kept the attention of the Ukrainian guard, he talked to us. "There is a letter in Jurgis' wagon hidden in the hay. The letter is written in your language. It's from a group of young Jews who have been hiding out in villages since the war started. They were never even in a camp. Any Jew who wants to escape may come to them. They sent a messenger who can take us to them. The messenger is now in my house and is waiting for anybody who wants to escape."

Later, when we dropped off the water and the Ukrainian guard was not with us anymore, we probed into the hay, found the letter and read it. It was indeed written in Yiddish and told us the same thing. In the evening our group discussed the matter. I was the one who was going to escape.

We met as we usually did, around the small, low shoemaker's bench in the corner. This was perhaps the last time we would meet together. We had to discuss all the details. Most important, the plan to escape. I would discuss it the next day with Jurgis. We had to change the location of the hidden guns at the brick plant. It must not be known to me. If I were to get caught, I would not be able to betray the secret to the Gestapo, even under torture. Finding the guns would mean the end for everyone.

How would we communicate? We had to have a messenger, perhaps the same one who brought today's letter. I would write in Lithuanian. If the sun is shining, the fields are green, then all is well. If the skies are dark, the crop is bad, then all is not well. The going is rough. To show that the letter was indeed written by me, I would count eighteen words from the beginning. The eighteenth word would be a long one. In it I would conceal two small Hebrew letters which together would make up the word *chai,* meaning life. They would be obvious only to someone well versed in Hebrew.

Then there was the roll call to consider. Every day after work, we had to line up while the German *Lagerführer* counted to make sure that everybody was there. That nobody was missing. He had a cane, touching each person as he counted: *eins, zwei, drei.* This was one of our easier problems to solve. About five or six children from the ghetto had wound up in our camp. They had secret hiding places. One of them was always on the lookout. When a stranger entered our camp, they would dash for their hiding places. The plan was to take the oldest child, pin a yellow star on his back and chest and have him take my place at roll call.

The next day, I worked as usual with Jurgis. We quietly made plans for my escape. In the middle of the following night, I met with my group for the last time. They gave me strong boots and good clothes. We embraced and wished that we would meet again as free men. Then I left Camp Daugel, never to return to it or any other concentration camp.

I removed the yellow stars and went to the outhouse in the corner of the campground near the barbed wire fence. I watched the Ukrainian guard who regularly walked around the fence. When he was on the opposite side, near the gate, I carefully crawled through the fence. My main concern was not to get stuck in the barbed wire. If the guards found me there, I would be shot on the spot. I crawled on my stomach to the nearest tree and waited. Some shots were fired. The guard often fired shots as a warning not to attempt an escape. Or were they meant for me? I didn't know.

I crawled from tree to tree, moving further and further away. I knew I had to be very quiet. Any noise could alert the guards at the camp or the others at their quarters, only several hundred yards away. I finally made it to the swamp and the brush, to the spot that Jurgis had pointed out to me when we were in the wagon on the way to the stream for water. I hid in the small brush until morning, when Jurgis came. He brought me food.

He went to work at the brick plant as usual. I stayed in the brush all that endless day, plagued by swarming flies. After work Jurgis came back. We waited until dark and then started off over country roads for Geryba's house several miles away, in the middle of a small town.

We hardly talked while we were walking, but when we were getting close to Geryba's house, Jurgis said to me, "You'll be safer in the woods, Leibas. Lithuanians come to me for moonshine. When they get drunk, they brag how they killed all the Jews in the small towns around here, even the children. They brag how they went to other countries where there were a lot of Jews to be killed."

When we reached the town we first went through backyards trying not to be seen, but dogs were barking. We turned back and walked through the main street. I entered Geryba's house, but Jurgis left immediately. I never saw him again. Jurgis and Geryba did not betray me.

Neither did Praniukas. A Lithuanian lad of about eighteen, he was the messenger who was to take me to the Jewish partisans hiding in the villages. Nothing seemed to bother him.

He and Geryba discussed the best way to go. Praniukas wanted to take the main road and go during the day. Geryba was very nervous. The police station was across the street. He said we must leave at night. We compromised. We would go to sleep and leave before daybreak.

Praniukas asked my name. I told him, Leibas. He suggested I should call myself Ludvigas, a traditional Lithuanian name. That was to be my name until after the war.

Then we went to sleep. Praniukas slept. But I couldn't sleep. The change was too much for me. Yesterday I was in a concentration camp, a Jew who must be exterminated. But now I slept under the same blanket with a Lithuanian . . . and perhaps I was free.

Some time later Geryba woke us. He said we must leave in the dark. "The police station is across the street," he reminded us again. We got dressed. Praniukas suggested we should change clothes. I gave him mine, and he gave me his peasant sheepskin coat and cap.

We traveled through small villages. I was holding the reins and was dressed in Lithuanian peasant clothes. I felt rather safe.

In the villages, Praniukas would pause and chat with other peasants, mainly farm talk. I would merely tip my hat and say, "*Gera diena, ponas.*" "Good day, sir." Just enough not to draw attention, not to be conspicuous. So we kept on through small towns and villages, traveling in daylight. We went through a shtetl, a town like my home town, Skudvil. All shtetls are different and yet so much alike. The market place had homes on both sides. Jews used to live in those homes. But now those Jews were dead. Perhaps Jews were no concern of mine any more. I had a Lithuanian name, a Lithuanian coat, and a Lithuanian cap.

Two Lithuanians with rifles over their shoulders approached our wagon. They asked Praniukas, "Where did you get the Jew clothes?"

With a crying voice Praniukas pleaded, "Please, *Ponas*, don't take it away from me. I am poor and I never had a good coat, so I killed a Jew and took away his coat."

"What do you have in the wagon?"

"Please, *Ponas*, don't take it away from us. Our aunt is sick; she is dying. We are going for a doctor and doctors don't do anything for money these days."

The two Lithuanians searched in the hay. They found a jug of *somogon* and a bundle of food. They took it away and yelled, "You frogs, you liars. Get out of this town, and we better not catch you again."

In a matter of minutes, we were in the country, took the first side road and pulled into the first wooded spot we could find. Praniukas was pale and scared; so was I. He thanked God that we were still alive; so did I.

Eventually we came to our destination, to the group of Jewish partisans. Some of them had been hiding out all through the war in Lithuanian villages. It was an emotional meeting. They welcomed me with embraces. We were like one family.

As far as I know, ours was the only Jewish partisan group in Lithuania. Later, several Russian prisoners of war who escaped joined us. We were well armed with small guns, hand grenades and machine guns.

We walked only by night from place to place. We knew every path, every road in a radius of some thirty miles. Later in the war, we became more daring and would sometimes walk in the daylight.

Once we captured a small town, Kelme, in the middle of the day. After holding it for several hours, we suspected that a stronger force was coming to recapture it, so we withdrew.

We slept on hay in barns because you have a chance of moving out of barns fast if you are surrounded. You have no chance in a house. Sometimes we had to sleep in the woods or even in haystacks or wheat stacks. We wondered if we would ever get used to sleeping in a bed if we survived the war.

A lot of farmers opened their homes to us. We would come at night and stay for the day. When we came, we embraced, called each other brother. We parted in the same way. They would give us food and comfort.

The weeks and months went by in this way. Then the Germans began to retreat. The Russians were advancing. One day the front was right there, where we were. We could almost see the Russian positions. We decided to cross the battlefield, or no man's land, from the German side to the Russian side. We met a Russian patrol in the middle. We identified ourselves. *Jevreski Partizani,* Jewish Partisans. They took us to the Russian positions.

Rumor swept through the front that Jewish partisans had crossed over. Officers and soldiers came to look at us. Some of them had been fighting all the way from Moscow, and we were the first Jews they had come across. They were proud of us. Some of them cried.

After the war, I went back to the town where Jurgis lived. I stopped a middle aged man and asked him, "Pardon me sir, could you direct me to Jurgis' house? I do not know his last name. He was short, broad shouldered and swayed as he walked."

"You mean the moonshiner? Oh, he is dead," he answered.

"Are you sure? How did he die?" I asked.

"Somebody killed him. Who cares, nobody liked him," he answered. He walked away with a wave of his arm.

Unsung Heroes

Cyna Glatstein
b. Sochachev, Poland, 1928

At Risk—For Love

My baby brother was eleven months old. My mother could not nurse him. The war was too much for her. On the way from Sochachev to Warsaw in 1939, her milk dried up.

In Warsaw, we needed milk for the baby desperately.

The dairy was one block away.

I must get there.

I had to go without my parents' permission. They never would have allowed it because of the danger of air raids.

The baby and I were inseparable. We often played games together, laughed together, sang together, and I read simple tales to him.

While he was napping I could get away.

Down the six flights, across the street, and I was in line for milk.

Then came the sirens. In a panic, the people dispersed in all directions and I moved up to be first in line. Now I had the milk.

Clutching it, I ran.

A bomb dropped. In my flight I stumbled over a corpse.

Fires were raging everywhere. I heard screaming, moaning, crying, praying.

I kept running, with only one thought. I must get the milk to the baby. I saw my parents running toward me.

The family had gone down into the shelter when the sirens went on and found me missing.

Now, as I clutched the bottle of milk, we joined my siblings in the shelter.

When the all-clear sounded we labored up the six flights—step by step.

Watching the baby drink the milk gave all of us great joy.

My mother spoke softly and seriously to me. "We understand your deep love for your brother, but you should not have risked your life as you did. We would have managed somehow to feed him. Difficult times are ahead. He'll need you."

The difficulties were much worse than we had ever anticipated.

The Germans did not spare him.

For the rest of my life he is in my heart, in my thoughts, and in my dreams.

When my son was born I named him Isaac, after my brother.

Only then did my pain ease a little.

The Lookout

The Germans were occupying the country. Poland was in chaos.

Warsaw was no longer a safe haven for us. We returned to Sochachev. We hoped to salvage anything that was salvageable.

Nothing was. Houses were in ruins; all possessions were plundered by the Poles. The Torahs and Holy Books were torn and scattered all over.

We hoped to pick up our lives and go on. It was impossible.

Each day there were more decrees: to give up guns and ammunition, then radios, then valuables—all under the threat of execution.

All Jews over the age of ten were ordered to wear white arm bands with a blue Star of David on them.

The only constant in our lives was our deep commitment to Judaism.

Since our beloved synagogue had been destroyed, we continued our services privately, in our apartment on the third floor of a building, where a whole wall was missing. We covered the hole with boards and blankets. The people prayed as fast as possible because it was dangerous.

This privacy had to be protected. How? I was the lookout.

Since I was just over ten years old, I was not to wear an armband. I was alert and fast and small enough to be inconspicuous. It was my job to stand at the bottom of the steps and, if I saw possible danger, to run up and tell the people praying, so they could scatter.

The area was full of rubble. This time a German soldier appeared suddenly from behind the debris and surprised me. There was no time to warn the others.

I froze. Instinct took over. We were in a large area completely destroyed except, ironically, for the outhouse with its door.

I ran into the outhouse and slammed the door.

It seemed like an eternity, immeasurable time.

When I cautiously opened the door, I was struck and fell. Blood gushed from my head. The soldier left me without a glance.

My parents were alerted by some Jewish people who witnessed the incident. My parents came, picked me up and took me to the dispensary.

At the dispensary I was treated for the wound on my forehead.

I still have a scar from this wound.

The Unsung Heroes of Warsaw Ghetto

The Purest Light is born in Darkness.

Who were the Unsung Heroes of Warsaw Ghetto?

Fifty years later this is part of me—what the children did—these Unsung Heroes, ages seven, eight, nine . . . up to age twelve.

Back in Warsaw, in the Ghetto, I was one of them.

My parents would not let me go into Warsaw proper. They still thought they could protect me. Besides, I looked too Jewish. If caught, this would have meant torture and death.

But I did go as far as the mazes of tunnels and sewers permitted—into narrow passages with cobwebs, rats, and floating raw sewage.

There the smugglers were waiting. They could have been informers or police Gestapo disguised, but Hashem was always with me.

I was able to bring life-sustaining food to my siblings and parents.

Two of my dear playmates, Surele and Pesy, ages nine and eleven, could go into and out of Warsaw through the tunnels. They easily passed as non-Jews. Blond hair, blue eyes, short noses, and flawless Polish. They were successful many times, bringing back frozen potatoes, flour, cabbages, and stale bread.

I was waiting for them to return from their fourth forage.

I waited in vain. They never came back from the darkness of the tunnels.

Friend or Enemy?

David Katz
b. Sapinta, Romania, 1919

Proving Myself a Partisan

When I escaped from a German prison camp in Russia, the members of a Hungarian work battalion near Kiev hid me for a while. But the battalion, it turned out, was going to White Russia with a train of war supplies. The men who had hidden me told me not to worry—they would not abandon me. One of their wagons was to be loaded with hay for their horses. They would make a tunnel in the hay, and they would take me with them. They had heard that in White Russia some partisans were in the woods, operating against the German army. If I could find them, I would be a partisan too. I agreed.

In the evening, with a military cap on my head, we went to the train. I crawled into my tunnel of hay, and the train left. I was only able to come out at night. I was excited that I would have the privilege of fighting the Germans.

After four days and nights of traveling, we arrived at our destination. Somewhere not far from Slutsk, the train stopped. I waited for word that it was safe for me to leave. After a while a man came, gave me a sack of food and matches, and wished me good luck. I put the cap on my head and ran away.

Just around the corner, I threw the cap away and sped toward the woods. In the woods, I kept going, assuming that the further I got, the safer I would be. I walked until after midnight, when I felt tired and sleepy. I laid down and listened to the sounds of the woods at night. An owl beat its wings on the branches of a tree. When I awoke the next morning, the sun was shining brightly. I kept walking and thinking. Even if I did not find anybody, I would be able to live here for a long time. I saw all kinds of berries and many mushrooms.

Late at night again, when I was very tired, I saw a little house, very old, with grass growing on the roof; there were no doors or windows. Inside, I saw a bunk. I put my little sack beneath my head and lay down. At once, I was attacked by thousands of mice. Realizing that they wanted the bread from under my head, I hung up my sack. After that, the mice disappeared. I was about to fall asleep again when I heard something coming into the house. If it was not a person, it must be something else. In the dark, I could not see it. I thought that perhaps it was the devil. Very quietly, I reached in my pocket for a match. When I struck it, a beautiful deer jumped out. Then I knew that I was far from population, so I fell asleep.

Late in the afternoon the next day, I again began to think of where I would sleep. I wanted to gather some branches and lay down on them.

Then I heard a man commanding, "Stay! Stop!"

I stopped and turned around. There were two men and one woman. Only one of the men had a rifle. The other man and the woman were equipped with sticks.

I hollered, "Are you partisans? I too am a partisan." But introducing myself did not help me. They ordered me to put down my sack, in which I still had some bread. The man pointed the rifle at me while the other two searched me. Finding nothing but some matches, they ordered me to follow them. In the meantime, they finished my bread.

After three hours of walking, we came to a village of campers. I was told to go into one of the camps and was kept under guard. I was ordered to sit down. For a couple of hours, people came in, one at a time, and fired questions at me. I could see that they were told what questions to ask, because every person asked another question. They were not important questions. They asked me my name, how long I had been in the woods, who told me about the partisans. I wanted to tell them more, but as soon as I answered their question, they walked out. Since my guard was not hostile to me, I tried to talk to him. He told me not to talk, but to lie down and sleep.

The next morning, I was taken to another place for interrogation. I was asked to tell my entire autobiography. Here, I decided to tell the truth—how I was drafted into the Hungarian army at eighteen, taken prisoner by the Russians and then the Germans, and how I had escaped. I told them everything I had gone through up to the time I came here. The interrogator wrote down everything. As we finished, another interrogator came and started from the beginning, all over again. Then the third one began the same thing again. When we finished for the third time, it was after midnight. The guard told me to lie down and sleep. I slept for the rest of the night.

The next morning, a young Siberian fellow came in, unrolled a sheet of paper, and began to read me my sentence. As a German spy, I was convicted to death. The execution would be later today. With this, he walked out. This was an unbelievable and terrible shock. I did not expect to be killed here like a defenseless lamb.

Within a few minutes, two other guards came in. There was a long bench and a table where the interrogators had been writing. Now the two guards tied my hands and feet with rope. They threw me on the bench and tied me to the bench with another rope. I laid there, on display. In the meantime, men and women, young and old, came in to look at me. They spat on me, punched me, or kicked me. There was nothing I could do about it. I was already as good as dead.

Then suddenly, two young men came in and stopped at the entrance. One said to the other, in Jewish: "Listen, Nahum, if the Germans have such spies, then they are in trouble." I told him that I too was Jewish, and not a German spy. I would like to fight the Germans, and here I would be killed shortly. At once, they turned around and went out. I thought to myself—this time I have failed—no more hope.

It was not more than a half hour before a man came in with an order to the guards to free me. My guards untied the rope and the carrier of the order took me out. He told me that if I wanted to eat or sleep, I could go to anybody in the village. They were to give me food and shelter. But I was told not to leave the village, or I might be caught by the Germans.

I knew that here with the partisans I would be killed some day. They were going on dangerous missions to get the little food they had. They would not feed me just like that. This question bothered me for two weeks.

One day, I saw one of the Jewish boys who had saved my life. I asked him if he recognized me.

"No," he said. But when I told him I owed him my life, he remembered me.

I asked him where the other boy was. With tears in his eyes, he said that he was killed in action. In the brief silence, I could see that he wanted to go.

"What will they do with me here?" I quickly asked.

He told me that as an officer he was not able to tell everything, but still, he would tell me something.

"Your sentence is only suspended," he said. "Right now you are under surveillance. If you do or say anything wrong, your sentence will take effect, and you will be executed." He told me to listen and do as he said.

From that day forward, I was to go every day to headquarters and insist they give me service; tell them I want to serve the partisans.

"It is always better to die on your feet than to live on your knees," he said. "They might kick you out, hit you, or even threaten you, but you must ignore it all and keep going. One day they might need you, and then they will give you something to do. Then you will be halfway out of danger."

He asked that I handle everything wisely and not tell anyone of our conversation. After he left, I thought over what he told me and concluded that he was right.

I went to headquarters the same day. I asked the lady in command to give me something to do to help the partisans. She asked me who I was and if I had military training. She told me to go out and not to come back until I was called for. I thanked her and went out.

The next day when I went back, there was a young man at the desk. When I told him why I had come, he kicked me out, calling me a Pollack fascist. It did not bother me. I expected that. I kept going there for several days. One day, there was one of the interrogators who had questioned me in the beginning. He glanced at me and said, "Are you still alive?" He had heard that I was executed.

"Yes," I said. "I am alive and well. Ready to serve the cause of our victory."

He told me he was glad that I was well. They would take me into their service. Telling me to wait a while, he went out.

About half an hour later, he returned with another man.

"Let's go," the other man said.

We went deep into the forest, to an outpost. A muddy road led to a little bridge over a river. On both sides of the road were little villages of campers. The man who brought me there introduced me as a new soldier. Soon I received a very big, old, heavy rifle. I was told to guard the little bridge. I assumed that to guard the bridge was a test for me. The command sent people twice to smuggle arms over the bridge, and I caught them.

Shortly after that, on a beautiful morning, I stood guard duty on the little bridge. It was late fall of 1941, when the German army was advancing successfully everywhere. My sergeant approached me with another man who told me that he had come with an order from the commander. I was to give him the rifle and present myself to the commander. I gave him the rifle.

I sought out a Jewish man I knew. "I am being called to the commander and I don't know why. If I don't show up tomorrow," I said, "please say *kaddish* for me." Then I left.

Upon approaching the commander's house, I took a deep breath and went in. When the commander shook my hand, I felt relaxed. I knew that if he shook hands, he was not going to kill me.

I watched him carefully; he was walking nervously around the room, from the door to the window and back again. Suddenly he stopped at the table, opened a drawer, and took out a sheet of paper. He called me over to the table and asked, "Do you know what is on this paper?"

"Yes, it's a map." It was a local map, drawn by hand.

"Do you know where we are on the map?" he asked.

"I don't have any idea where we are," I replied.

He pointed to a place on the map.

"This circle," he said, "is our zone." He called it *partizanskaya zona*. The Germans would not come in that circle. They had made several attempts and had been destroyed.

Then he looked at me and said, "*Boyevoye Zadonie,*" which means combat mission. Pointing his finger on the map, he explained the mission.

He said, "You go eastward nine kilometers until you come to a main road. The road is patrolled by the Germans. Here, turn right one kilometer. There is a bridge, guarded by two Germans. One soldier on each side of the bridge. They have on their necks automatic guns, plus, on each side of the bridge, they have a machine gun with two boxes of ammunition."

"Now," he said, "the mission is those two machine guns with the four boxes of ammunition. You must bring them to me."

I said, "*Rad staratsia,*" which means, "I will do my best."

"Work out a plan as to how you are going to perform this mission. Whatever you need will be made available. You must know in your mind," he warned, "that you are going to attack the most powerful army in Europe. Well-trained and equipped. You are not well-trained and equipped. Everything must be done very quietly because only one hundred meters past the bridge, the whole German unit is stationed. If they hear any noises, you will never come back alive."

Then he said, "It is now eleven o'clock. At eighteen o'clock, I want you to present your plan."

I began to think how to do the impossible. No matter how I figured, the end was tragic. Finally I came upon an idea. The enemy must be fooled. I worked out the plan. Taking a few little stones in my hands, I went to the commandant to explain my plan by lining up the stones and changing the positions. The commandant approved of my plan.

The next morning, I left with my group of people. We had three pairs of horses and wagons. On each wagon were two men. After we came out of the forest, on the main way, we had to keep a distance of 40 to 50 meters from one wagon to the other. On the first wagon, I was dressed as a lady, with my husband. On the wagon I had several chickens in a cage. On the second wagon, two men were masked as very old. On the third wagon were two men with dirty and torn clothes.

As we approached the bridge, one German soldier stood there. My "husband" stopped and began to fix something on the wagon. In the meantime, I picked up a chicken and offered it to the soldier. He took the chicken and saw that it was a heavy one. He asked the price, and I told him a low price. As he was taking out his money to pay for the chicken, I told him to call his comrade too. He called the other soldier to come and buy a bargain. When the other soldier ran over to us, I pushed another chicken in his hands.

Meanwhile, the second wagon approached, and within one second, the four of us grabbed the two soldiers. We put four knives to their ribs and ordered them to cooperate or they would die. While we disarmed the two soldiers, the third wagon picked up the two machine guns and the ammunition. I ordered them to release the soldiers and we ran away. Before we made a kilometer back to the main road, where we were to turn into the forest, we heard the Germans shooting after us with machine guns and mortars. I ordered everybody to go into the woods and to keep moving as fast as possible.

We returned to our posts after noon, and I reported the success of our mission. The commandant shook my hand and wished me success with future missions.

Partisan Tricks

After the German army at Stalingrad was destroyed, the partisans in Russia were in good shape. The Russians sent in well-trained men who were prepared to organize and command the partisans on three levels: one for combat, another for politics, and the third for intelligence. The partisans became a regular army, with members infiltrating the Germans, serving in German uniforms, at high posts.

Once, around that time, we fought the Germans on a battlefield where about eighty of us were taken prisoner. The Germans did not treat us as prisoners of war, but as traitors. In one week, twelve of us were tortured to death, including several women.

One day, we heard unusual noises in the jail. The guard was ordering the prisoners to clean faster because the general was expected to arrive soon. A few hours later, they called out the names of several partisans, including the four from our cell. The Germans took us out to the jail courtyard and lined us up next to a girl. We had to stand with our heads down.

I saw the general and his officers marching around the jail yard. The guards and soldiers were running back and forth looking scared. The general was very strict and demanded reinforcements. More guards were called to watch the dangerous criminals.

I saw that the girl standing near us was full of emotion. With eyes in tears, she kept changing her lips from smiling to crying, and she was shaking. Feeling sorry for her, I touched her with my foot to attract her attention. Then I asked her what had happened.

She told me we are free. We could not communicate any more, so I thought to myself that the poor girl was confused. But she was not confused. She had recognized the general as one of the partisans.

He had sent a message to the jailers saying that he would take us to our trial. We were loaded onto four trucks with the additional guards. After we got out of town, we were ambushed by partisans. In the crossfire, the general and his staff, who were in the first Jeep, jumped out and raised their hands. After they did this, all the guards gave up. The prisoners took the guards' weapons, killed them, blew up their trucks, and ran away.

Then I understood the trick the general had played on the Germans. His name was Kulashnikov. He spoke perfect German.

Resist in Everything!

Steven Joseph Fenves
b. Subotica, Yugoslavia, 1931

SUNDAY, APRIL 8, 1945

The column marched slowly along the winding, hilly roads of Southeast Germany toward Buchenwald. The SS lieutenant walked in front, his large Alsatian tugging at the leash, the silver skulls on his "Death Head" collar-insignia flashing in the afternoon sun. The inmates followed in columns of five, emaciated bodies bent with fatigue, drawn faces soiled from the dust. Their striped uniforms or ill-fitting clothes with striped patches were filthy and tattered. The Russian POWs were in front, the Polish Jews next, and the Jews from Hungary and the Hungarian-occupied provinces of Romania, Czecho-slovakia, and Yugoslavia last. Every few rows on both sides marched elderly army guards carrying submachine guns. A truck brought up the rear, outfitted with a platform on which the relief guards slept. It towed an ancient field kitchen.

It was the eighth day of the evacuation march eastward from the satellite concentration camp at Nieder Orschel, which was attached to a Messerschmit airplane factory. At each morning and evening assembly after the lieutenant made a count and recorded it in his notebook, he gave orders, repeated by the interpreters in Russian, Polish, and Hungarian: "Anybody trying to escape, any stragglers, anybody talking will be shot outright."

The inmates in the first three rows looked a little different from the others: their faces less gaunt, their clothes slightly better fitting, their gait a bit more springy. They were the Kapos (overseers), orderlies, and interpreters. Among them marched a boy of thirteen, wearing a blue student's cap and brown overcoat.

The boy, Jóska,* was one of the two Hungarian interpreters. He was deep in thought as he marched.

The night before, Lev, the leader of the Polish Zionist resistance "brigade," had said that his group would escape tonight and had asked Jóska to join them. Jóska was torn between his desire to go and his concern that he might still be needed. He decided that if he escaped with them, he would continue on his own. What would he say to the first American soldier he would meet? . . .

---

*The Hungarian nickname for Joseph.

"Dirty business this is, at our age," a guard said, as two of them walked side by side next to Jóska's row, "and these filthy dogs have it better than us. They don't have to stand guard half the night and carry these damn guns."

"It's nothing," the other, a short old corporal, replied. "It's the least we can do for the victory of the Reich!"

"You are crazy!" Jóska blurted out loud in German, his self-discipline of the last year suddenly gone. He saw the barrel of the submachine gun flying toward him, threw his right arm over his head, and heard the crunch of bones breaking before he was enveloped by burning pain.

The column halted. The lieutenant approached, his dog sniffing Jóska's limp arm. The Kapos begged him to order a stop; he would only consent to five minutes. Vladia, the Russian interpreter, used the corporal's bayonet to cut down two branches. Shirts were ripped into strips, the medic tied the arm into a splint and fashioned a sling to support it. As much as he tried, Jóska could not suppress his crying. The medic gave him a drink from his makeshift canteen.

As the column reformed, Lev and Vladia moved over to support him.

"I forgot myself. How could I have been so stupid?" Jóska whispered, sobbing.

"Shhhh, brother, just walk and look ahead," Lev whispered.

The march resumed. Jóska estimated by the position of the sun that they had two more hours to go. He had to think, to fight off the burning pain . . .

He thought over the events starting with the last evening at Nieder Orschel, eight days ago. He had barely begun to eat his soup after the evening assembly when three soft whistles sounded the alarm. He knew what he had to do. Even though ravenously hungry, as always, he shoved his bowl over to his neighbor and ran into the hallway. He dodged inmates running to their assigned sentry posts at all doors and windows.

He was the last one to reach the Kapos' room. Jóska remembered looking around the room with amazement: he was always amazed when he entered it. He made a quick survey of the men crowding the small room.

The group of prisoner officials was organized by the SS with military precision. At the top were Karl, the head Kapo, a German Social Democrat imprisoned when the Nazis came to power, and Otto, the labor Kapo, a German Communist. They both wore the red triangle on their chests, marking them as political prisoners. The orderlies were next: Daniel, the camp orderly in charge of housekeeping, a gypsy; Sobotkin, the work orderly, a Czech political; the fat Czech cook; and the French medical student who was the camp medic. Then came the interpreters: Vladia, a Russian cavalry officer; Cantor Heimowitz, the Polish interpreter; and Alexander, the head Hungarian interpreter. Lev, a law student from Lvov, and Tibor, a textile engineer from Slovakia, completed the group.

These same men constituted the resistance organization that planned all actions of the inmates. The inmates were organized into three "brigades": the Russian POWs commanded by Vladia; the Polish Jews under Lev; and the Hungarian Jews under Tibor.

Jóska slipped to the floor, his back to the door. Although not yet fourteen, he was fully accepted as a member of the resistance organization. He had been made an interpreter because, coming from the part of Yugoslavia occupied by Hungary, he spoke Serbian, Hungarian, and German. Knowing Serbian, he understood Russian, Polish, Czech, and Slovak as well. He had arrived in Nieder Orschel in November of 1944 with a transport of Hungarian Jews. He had first worked in Daniel's housekeeping detail and later on the inspection station of the assembly line.

"They plan to move us out," Karl announced. "The orderlies taking the guards' dinner saw them pack."

The news was no surprise; for weeks they had been expecting the order to evacuate. From words overheard among the German workers and from stolen issues of the Erfurt newspaper, they had a rough idea of the Americans' advance. They took stock. They had an assortment of knives, axes, and clubs fashioned from scraps "organized" (the camp slang for stolen) from the factory, and a few Molotov cocktails, but not enough to stage a break.

Karl announced that on the march, everyone was free to escape. The cook distributed emergency rations he had prepared from stolen sugar, toasted grains, and leftover chicory grounds. They decided on the distribution of weapons. When everything was settled, they prayed. Cantor Heimowitz recited the blessings in Hebrew, then repeated them in Polish and German. Daniel, Vladia, Sobotkin, and the cook crossed themselves, Vladia in the Orthodox fashion, touching his shoulders, forehead and knee. They shook hands and left to pass the orders. Jóska was still awake at dawn when the whistles sounded and they were lined up, counted and marched out.

To most of the inmates, the first days of the march had been a relief from the murderous pace of the ten-hour work shifts, six and a half days a week, on the assembly line. Even though the camp was run by the Messerschmit company and not the SS, the food had been barely enough for subsistence, much less for the kind of work demanded. Sobotkin, who had access to many of the memoranda from Buchenwald, had reported the terms "extermination through work" referring to the inmates, and "a slight delay on the road to their final destination" referring to the Jews. The monotony of the twice-daily watery soup was only relieved by the cook's extraordinary skill of creating some taste and variety from the celery or beets "organized" by the housekeeping detail or from the guards' scraps.

At first, they had marched 25 to 30 kilometers a day, with two or three breaks. When the old field kitchen worked, there was some thin soup or ersatz coffee to accompany the daily ration of a quarter kilogram of dry, coarse bread. But in the last days the distance had been increased, the rations cut in half and, with the days getting warmer, thirst was beginning to hurt as much as the ever-present hunger. They had marched along fields plowed by farmers and woods turning green, passing bombed-out factories and railway stations. The villages seemed deserted, a few old women peering out from behind wooden shutters and lace curtains. The day before, they had crossed Erfurt, a major town, where most buildings were in ruins and the marching was tough on the broken cobblestones. Townspeople turned up side streets or ducked into doorways to avoid them. A guard hit a Russian inmate who had asked for food and water, and then shot him outside the town.

At night they had slept in open fields, huddled together against the chill, the guards patrolling the perimeter marked with lanterns and barbed wire. There were escape attempts every night. The guards shot many, but others got away. In the morning, they stood at attention while the dead were buried in a shallow trench. Several of the older, weakened men came at night to the Cantor or the Hungarian interpreter Alexander, saying that they would pretend to escape; they thought that being buried was more *männlich* (manly) than being shot on the road for failing to keep pace, and being left behind in the ditch. . . .

Had it not been for Lev and Vladia dragging him along, he would have lost pace and been shot too, Jóska thought. He was trembling when they were herded into a field after dusk. Daniel rolled up his coat for a headrest; Lev and Vladia eased Jóska down. The cook brought him his ration of bread and coffee. The medic gave him water and aspirin pills. Jóska managed a smile: it was he who had bought the pills with black market money in Nieder Orschel when, working Daniel's housekeeping detail, he had sneaked into the apothecary as the inmates loaded the camp cart, while Daniel diverted the guards' attention.

Karl sat down next to Jóska. The men of the resistance organization crawled over to plan the Polish group's escape and the next day. A metalworker from Warsaw was picked as the new commander of the remaining Polish Jews.

Lev and Karl shook hands, and Lev moved over to where Jóska was lying.

"Too bad this happened to you," Lev whispered, holding Jóska's left hand.

"I am sorry. Be careful. Shalom," Jóska replied.

"Shalom, *chaver*. Keep it up. We will meet again. *Khazak v'hamatz.** Next year in Jerusalem!"

"Herr Reinecken, can we talk?" Jóska asked, whispering, using Karl's last name and trying to use the most formal German he knew.

---

*"Be strong and brave"—Moses' admonition to Joshua in Deuteronomy xxxi, 23, the greeting of the Zionist organization.

"What is it, Seppl?"* Karl whispered back, sounding irritated.

"When we get up there, to Buchenwald, will we be separated? Will we—the Jews—be put back under 'green triangle' Kapos?"

"Who knows what will happen up there?" Karl's whispered words brought Jóska out of his thoughts. "In any case, you are trained. You know what you must do: 'Resist in Everything!'"

"Why do we resist? We'll all die, anyhow," Jóska whispered back. He had heard Karl's exhortation many times, but now, with his exhaustion and pain, it made no sense.

"Why?" Karl's shrill word brought a chorus of threats from the guards. "Why, you ask?" he repeated in a low whisper. "Because that's all we have, that's what makes us men."

The image of the "green triangles" was often on Jóska's mind. In his first months in Auschwitz, before Nieder Orschel, Jóska had lived under "green triangle" Kapos, criminals moved from German prisons into the concentration camps. These Kapos used every form of cruelty, brutality, and savagery on the inmates; they were allies of the SS in everything directed against the inmates.

Life under the "red triangles" was totally different. In front of the guards and German workers these "red triangle" Kapos yelled and bullied as hard as the criminals, but behind their backs they led the resistance and sabotage. The lieutenant was unable to break these Kapos' control over the men.

As he fell asleep, Jóska thought of Karl's words: he realized that behind all of the activities, even the ones that the Kapos made into games for him, was the relentless determination to act as men.

MONDAY, APRIL 9, 1945

The loud sound of a gunshot awakened Jóska. He looked around, bewildered. People were rising in panic. The guards formed a tight cordon outside the barbed wire, guns drawn. He saw the lieutenant walking away. Then he looked down. At his feet lay Karl. In the predawn light he could not see well; he knelt down and leaned over Karl. Blood was flowing from Karl's forehead, and he could smell gunpowder. Sobbing violently, he closed Karl's eyes, wiping the blood from his left hand on the grass.

"Form columns, fast," the lieutenant and the guards were yelling. The inmates, in a daze, obeyed. Jóska looked for a signal, from anybody.

"Up front!" Alexander yelled to him. Jóska ran to the first row, next to Otto; a Russian moved over to make room. The column stood at attention while a detail dug a shallow grave and placed Karl's body with five others in it.

---

*The German nickname for Joseph.

"*Yiskadal v'yiskadash sh'meh rabo . . .*" the Cantor's muted chant of the *Kaddish* could be barely heard from the middle of the column.

"*Y'heh sh'meh rabbo m'vorach, l'olam ul'olmeh olmayo: Yisborach,*" Jóska responded, mechanically.

The Russians stood with heads bowed, their mouths reciting a soundless prayer. The diggers threw dirt over the bodies, the sergeant put the shovels on the truck, and the column was off.

Otto and Jóska marched side by side, staring at the lieutenant's back. "My God, my dear God," the old communist moaned occasionally. Jóska understood that Otto was now in charge. He wished someone would tell him what would happen next.

After several hours of marching, they stopped for breakfast of ersatz coffee. There was no bread. The cook brought Jóska a cup of coffee and the medic gave him a few more aspirin pills. As they formed up, the ten remaining members of the organization took their positions in front.

"What now?" Vladia asked, quite loudly, as soon as they started.

"Shh, guard . . . ," others whispered. The old mustached guard who had hit him the day before walked up next to Jóska and cleared his throat, as if to say something. Jóska remembered the old corporal from before. Once, an old woman had accosted them on the street in Nieder Orschel. "Why are you a prisoner at your age?" she had asked Jóska. "He killed his father and mother," the corporal had said, before Jóska could reply. Now, Jóska spat loudly. The spittle landed just behind the Cantor's heel. The old corporal fell back.

The lieutenant was far ahead; it appeared safe to talk in whispers. They had long ago perfected their communication: Alexander and Daniel spoke in Romanian; the medic, Sobotkin, the Cantor and Alexander in French; Tibor, Alexander, and Jóska in Hungarian; and Otto, who had taught himself passable Russian in the camp, Vladia, the Cantor, Sobotkin, Tibor, Jóska and the cook in their Pan-Slavic mixture of Russian, Polish, Czech, Slovak, and Serbian. It was an effective scheme, requiring just an occasional translation.

They tried to piece together what had happened. Vladia had reported to Karl and a few others, late at night, that the new leader of the Polish Jews thought that there was an informer and that the lieutenant might know some of their plans. Later, several Hungarian Jews escaped. Just before dawn, Lev and eleven Zionists made their break. A guard shot one of them, the lieutenant another. Shortly after that, the lieutenant lined up all the guards and then walked back and forth between the sleeping men, searching; then he killed Karl. They didn't know why.

"What's done is done," Otto murmured. "Now we must organize. I want each of you to swear to obey me."

One by one, as he called their names, they did so. Jóska whispered "I swear" when his turn came.

In the back rows, the members of the Hungarian brigade tried to help stragglers from falling behind. When they failed, they walked on, heads lowered in
resignation, waiting for the shot that jerked them to attention.

The road was rising, winding its way between beech forests. There was little
traffic; a few army staff cars or trucks passed them. At small clearings farmers'
families watched them, the men pointing the sharp tines of their pitchforks at
them, the women holding on tightly to their children.

After the afternoon break, the organization was in front again.

"They are putting us up at the Berlstedt brick factory," Daniel said suddenly. Daniel and Sobotkin described the place where inmates made the bricks for
the Buchenwald factories and SS rest barracks. They had both worked there,
under terrible conditions.

The column swung off the road, two guards opened the gates in the barbed
wire fence of the deserted camp, and they marched onto the customary assembly
area. The inmates dispersed, rummaging for food. Some found a pile of rotting
potatoes and turnips, others gathered scrap wood, and soon groups were huddled
around small fires, roasting the potatoes. People snatched them out of the fire
barehanded and ate them half raw. With much shouting and threatening, the
guards had just herded them together when a staff car and three trucks pulled up.
Four SS officers and a Kapo got out of the car, and young SS guards jumped off
the trucks.

Assembly was resumed. With great precision, the SS officers counted the
inmates, the Kapo following them. The old army guards climbed into the trucks
and left; the new SS guards took their positions. The officers stood talking with
the lieutenant, their boots, belts, buckles, and insignia shining in the reflected
light of the guards' lanterns as the inmates lined up for food distribution.

Jóska noticed the Kapo repeatedly glancing toward them as he shuffled back to
the staff car and sat down on the running board. Jóska recognized the signal: he
had seen it in Auschwitz when someone wanted to attract another inmate's attention without the guards' notice. Making himself as inconspicuous as possible, he
crept up and crouched down a few feet in front of the Kapo without facing him.

"Do you understand Polish?" the gray-haired man whispered, not looking at
Jóska.

"Yes," Jóska whispered back, staring at the ground.

"Do you have an organization?"

"Yes."

"Send me one of them. Quick!"

"I am one. You can talk to me," Jóska said deliberately, glancing straight at
him for a second.

"All right, boy," the Kapo said, "now listen. Whether you can break out or not
with these new guards, that's for you to decide. But if you can't, stall! Transports are leaving Buchenwald by the trainload. Several a day. We don't know

where they're going. We have no control. . . . Get away, you stinking Jewish bastard," he blurted in German, getting up.

Jóska looked up, startled. An SS sergeant stood next to them.

"What's the matter, Kapo?" the sergeant asked.

"Nothing, Sir," the Kapo replied in an obsequious tone. "This little Jewish gas chamber fodder is begging for food."

"So we don't feed you enough, heh, you lousy Jewish dog," the sergeant yelled, aiming a kick at Jóska. But he had already jumped up and was running back, his arm in excruciating pain as it rattled.

His friends had saved his bread. Jóska ate it, with the last of his emergency rations. He walked around, signaling the organization. The staff car left, the rolls of barbed wire were laid out, and they were herded inside, the new guards patrolling the perimeter.

Lying next to the others, Jóska reported his conversation. With the guards on the periphery, they could speak in German. This was much faster than their multilingual code, as they all spoke it well, except Vladia and the medic, who spoke haltingly.

Sobotkin cleared his throat; he seldom said much, so now they all listened.

"I have it! We must play on their wretched orderliness and precision. Since we left Nieder Orschel, the lieutenant could do as he pleased, recording the count of the survivors in his book—but now we are back under Buchenwald control. The SS took an exact count up to the main camp, didn't they?" The others nodded, without understanding.

"So that's how many bodies the lieutenant has to deliver tomorrow, dead or alive, right?" Sobotkin asked again.

"Sure . . ." Alexander interrupted, excited, "and if the count in the morning comes up short, the lieutenant has to find anyone missing."

They decided that several would hide. Otto designated Daniel and Sobotkin, because they knew the camp, and Tibor. They picked a new commander to replace Tibor, and then they rehearsed the plan. The prisoners would force the guards to walk back and forth, revealing their position by their lanterns. Daniel, Sobotkin, and Tibor would slip through a gap left in the barbed wire and hide behind one of the buildings. At dawn Daniel would then lead them inside a brick kiln where they could wait until the Americans came. They broke into small groups. Jóska moved over to Sobotkin.

"Goodbye, little fighter," Sobotkin said, "and take care. After the war, come to study in Prague. There's a Yugoslav student hostel near my office—near the Castle."

"I would like that," Jóska whispered, shaking hands.

He crawled next to Tibor. They had spent many evenings talking about their families and what they would do after the war. Now they had nothing to say to each other.

Jóska, hobbling on one hand and his knees, went over to Daniel. "Good-bye. Please be careful," he whispered, worried that Daniel would do something reckless.

"I will," Daniel replied, "and you too. I hope you grow up as determined as you have been here. My son, he would be just a little younger than you. Thank you for telling me about the gypsies in Auschwitz." During the interrogation by the organization when he arrived in Nieder Orschel, Jóska had told them about the extermination of the gypsy women and children he had witnessed.

Jóska wanted to make a gesture to Daniel. "Here, take my knife," Jóska said, pulling it from the hidden pocket in his pants leg. It was pointed and very sharp, honed night after night from a stolen hacksaw blade, the handle and scabbard carved from a piece of broomstick, held together with aluminum wire and rivets. He had been very proud of it.

"Yes, I will," Daniel whispered. "It's better than my beaten-up kitchen knife. Let's trade."

Jóska embraced him and crawled away. As Otto ordered, he crawled among the Hungarian Jews, passing the instructions.

"After Otto starts, talk, murmur in small groups. Always at different places. Make the guards come toward you. Pass the word."

"What is going on? What are the plans?" everyone asked.

"You'll see in the morning. Talk. Keep them jumpy. Pass the word," Jóska replied and moved on.

He crawled back to Alexander and they began to talk.

"Won't that bratty kid ever go to sleep?" Otto yelled loudly in German. Jóska smiled: this was the signal. Sounds, conversations erupted everywhere. The SS, unaccustomed to guard duty, moved nervously, yelling and threatening, their positions clearly shown by the lanterns.

"Do you think they'll make it?" Jóska asked, watching the spot where the three were to crawl through.

"They'll make it, but will we?" Alexander replied. Jóska liked it that Alexander never talked down to him and always treated him as his grown-up assistant. "It doesn't matter anymore. We have tried; we've done everything we could; that's what's important."

"Tomorrow will tell," was all Jóska could say.

TUESDAY, APRIL 10, 1945

Jóska felt as though he had just fallen asleep when the guards' whistles sounded. Light was breaking over the hill. Jóska stumbled to his feet. The guards opened the latrine and washroom of the camp. "They want us to look good up there," a Russian mumbled. They were eager to wash their hands and faces after nine days on the road. Two of his friends helped Jóska. With a tiny rag and a small piece of soap, they washed his face and hands, and then the neck and shoulders under the sling; with their meager diet and the dirt embedded in their skin, any rubbing soon produced large open sores. The medic retied the sling. He was out of aspirin; Jóska would have to bear the throbbing pain.

Jóska joined Vladia and the two new brigade commanders who had replaced Lev and Tibor. The lieutenant passed them, the smoke from his morning cigarette making blue swirls under his visor. The small group dispersed.

"I am afraid . . ." Jóska whispered to Vladia.

"Fear, hell," Vladia replied brusquely. "Remember Lev Davidovich's words: 'Khazak v'hamatz.'"

"Yes, I'll try to be strong and brave," Jóska replied. He made a move to salute, but was stopped by the shooting pain in his right arm.

"Good luck," Vladia said as he returned the intended salute.

They lined up for a piece of bread and lukewarm gruel. Jóska looked for a signal. When the whistle for the assembly sounded, Alexander made a motion with his thumb, and the two of them fell in at the end of the column. Jóska's heart was pounding; the lieutenant counted, followed by the SS sergeant and, a few steps behind, Otto. Working methodically, the lieutenant reached the last row, did his figuring, then yelled:

"Six hundred seventy-two. That's three short, dammit!"

Jóska had counted too. "We started with eight hundred thirty-eight," he thought. "Take away six hundred seventy-two and the three he doesn't know about . . ." One hundred sixty-three men had escaped or died since they had left Nieder Orschel.

"Let's do it again, sergeant," screamed the lieutenant. "You check me."

"Shall I help, Sir?" Otto asked obsequiously.

"No, you won't, you bastard," the lieutenant spat out, his face red. "You criminals are involved in this. You stand where you belong, with the other animals!"

The second and third counts produced the same result. The lieutenant, nervous and sweating, ordered in all the guards, stationed a third of them around the standing prisoners, and sent the rest to search the camp. He kept pacing around the group, his growling dog tugging at the leash.

Time was moving imperceptibly. The shadows thrown by the men standing in front of Jóska seemed not to change.

The sun was high over the hill when the guards started drifting back, shaking their heads. Jóska was so excited that he was oblivious to the pain from his arm or the numbness in his legs.

The lieutenant gave orders; with the guards pushing and shoving, he made the inmates spread. They stood an arm's-length apart, each column four paces behind the other. He started down the first column, looking each inmate in the eyes, occasionally sending one up front. After the third, Jóska understood: the lieutenant was picking out the organization.

When the lieutenant got to him, Jóska returned his stare calmly. The lieutenant seemed to hesitate, his cold blue eyes in narrow slits; then, with a motion of his head, he indicated for Jóska to move. Jóska walked slowly, trying to pump blood into his stiff legs. He joined the cook, the medic, Vladia and the Cantor. Alexander and Otto followed. The lieutenant faced them, legs apart, his panting dog at his side.

"Now I see," he began, with a sarcastic tone that did not conceal his rage. "We are missing our crafty, degenerate orderly, our phony aristocrat account-ant, and that Jewish bastard who's always with our two Hungarian translators. What a coincidence! Can anybody explain this?" he yelled. There was silence, broken only by the dog's barking.

"I didn't expect an answer, yet," he said, "but there are ways." He yelled orders for the others to sit or lie down. There was not a sound, just as Jóska expected: the inmates did not respond, both to reinforce the belief that none of them besides the translators understood German and to show their solidarity.

"Shall we translate your orders, Sir?" Alexander asked, bowing to show his subservience.

"Like hell you will, you lying bastards," the lieutenant yelled. He rushed the inmates and pushed some to the ground, screaming until they settled down. Then he came back to face the seven of them, his face flushed.

"You will stand here, until you are ready to talk!" he bellowed. He ordered four guards to each end of the line, dispatching the others to search the camp again. He paced up and down, his revolver drawn, yanking on the dog's leash at each turn.

"NOW! NOW!" the words were screaming in Jóska's head. The Russians at one end and the toughest of the Hungarian Jews at the other could overpower the few guards. Jóska knew that the best trained "brigade" members' heavy throwing knives would be part way out of their sheaths, ready to be hurled with their much practiced accuracy, and that others would be prepared to sprint for the weapons to pick off the other guards. Vladia would go for the lieutenant. Jóska's job would be to kill the dog. "That was my assignment before my arm was broken; I wonder if I'm still responsible," he thought. He rubbed his legs together to feel for his knife, then realized he had Daniel's old, dull one. Jóska glanced sideways at Otto, who stood with head bowed, both hands gripping his walking stick. He decided he could only wait.

The spring sun was now beating down on their necks and shoulders. Jóska worried whether the older men could hold out.

Suddenly, the sound of distant artillery fire came from the West. The effect was electrifying: the standing prisoners drew themselves erect, and Jóska could hear those sitting or lying straightening themselves. The guards came running from all directions, looking in bewilderment at the lieutenant.

"Last chance! If you don't speak, I'll start killing you, one by one," he said.

"Haven't you enough blood on your hands?"

Jóska's first reaction was to smile at the Cantor's precisely enunciated words. Karl had joked several times that Cantor Heimowitz, Sobotkin and Jóska spoke purer high German than any of the German workers or guards.

"What . . . what did you say?" the lieutenant asked, incredulous, stepping up to Heimowitz and stabbing the cocked revolver to his chest.

"We don't mind dying and joining our millions of brethren," the Cantor continued, "but you, haven't you enough blood on your hands already, Herr Lieutenant?"

Jóska drew in his breath. Talking back to the lieutenant was audacious enough, but to address him by the traditional army rank and not his SS one could only mean death. Jóska got ready. He knew that if the lieutenant fired, Vladia would jump him before he could get off a second shot. Jóska decided that he would fall on the dog, trying to use his splint to break its neck.

Another thunder of artillery broke the silence. The lieutenant, whose eyes seemed to have hazed over after the Cantor spoke, shook his head as if to clear it, jabbed the Cantor hard in the chest with the muzzle of the revolver, and stepped back. Vladia and Alexander jumped simultaneously to hold the Cantor up.

"Up, up—fast, fast—we are moving out," the lieutenant screamed at the top of his voice, waving his revolver. "Quickly, quickly! Form columns—we're marching!"

"Are you all right?" Jóska whispered to the Cantor in the confusion.

"I'll live," the Cantor said, taking deep breaths, holding on to his chest.

"I'm not through with you yet," the lieutenant yelled. He organized a new marching order: the seven of them in front, two guards on either side, then the lieutenant, the sergeant, the rest of the inmates with the SS on both sides, and the truck in the rear. The gates were opened and they moved out. The sun was low on their backs. They must have stalled eight to ten hours, Jóska calculated from the sun's position.

After hours of marching, they found the road was getting steeper. At the top of a long bend Jóska looked behind.

"Slow down, there are stragglers," Jóska whispered as softly as he could. An SS hit him on the ear with a stinging backhand. He fell against the cook, but the fat arms caught him. A minute later came the sound of shots. The lieutenant turned and yelled orders to pile the bodies on the truck.

Dark was beginning to fall, and the sound of gunfire was heard again. The lieutenant stopped the column to let the sergeant distribute lanterns to the SS. Otto and Alexander begged him to allow a rest, but he dismissed them with a wave.

"They have done it, they have finally made walking corpses out of all of us," Jóska thought, as he saw Vladia supporting Otto and the medic and Alexander helping the Cantor. The cook was holding him up under his left shoulder as they shuffled up the steep road. He shuddered every time he heard another shot.

"In God's Holy Name, the men can't take this any longer," Alexander whispered in Hungarian. "Somebody tell them to sing."

Jóska knew what had to be done. The order was always given by Vladia, but he was now several steps ahead with Otto. He leaned down, as if to tie his shoe, and, as he rose, turned and yelled: "*Pesnja!*"

The SS guards looked at him, startled.

"*Soyuz nerushimlij respublik sovetskij . . .*" The column began to sing the Soviet anthem, its slow melody well suited to their shuffling pace.

The SS were nervous and apprehensive.

"What shall we do?" Jóska heard the SS sergeant ask behind his back. The lieutenant had heard them sing many times: on Friday nights and Sunday afternoons in the barracks, on the march to and from the factory and during the air raids when they were herded outside the factory.

"Let the goddamned bastards sing," he replied. "They won't be doing it much longer." Even his dog didn't growl any more at the singing.

"*Kol od balevav . . .*" The words of the *Hatikva,* the anthem of the Zionist Organization, were sung slowly to match their uphill gait. The singing had its effect: Otto released his grip on Vladia and walked ahead, leaning only on his walking stick; next, Cantor Heimowitz shook his arms loose and continued on his own, his head held high. Jóska, too, felt strong enough to stop leaning on the cook.

"Those goddamned shit-eating fucking bastards," the lieutenant swore, as if in pain. Jóska, pleased with the lieutenant's discomfort, felt like breaking into a skip-and-jump.

Russian, Yiddish, Polish, and Hebrew songs followed in succession. Although the majority of inmates were Hungarian Jews, Hungarian songs were never sung; they were all bitterly aware of the Hungarian fascist government's complicity in their deportation.

"The gallows, that's what you'll get!" the lieutenant yelled suddenly. "All seven of you, as soon as we're in the camp. The kid goes first, so the rest of you can watch, and the old stinking Jew goes last, so he can mumble his fucking prayers."

The others threw guarded glances at Jóska.

He was thinking about the lieutenant's words. Suddenly he realized that he was no longer afraid. After seeing so much death, after doing so many things punishable by death, after eleven months of living with fear every minute, it suddenly didn't matter anymore. He had become a man, who could give commands that the others obeyed. There was nothing the lieutenant could do to change that. From now on, he would live or die as a man.

To show his new resolve, he picked up his pace. The cook gave him a wink as he caught up with him.

Very suddenly the road leveled off, and they fell silent. Jóska could now orient himself in the dark from the others' frequent description of Buchenwald. The brick buildings on the right, extending far down the slope, were rest and recuperation areas for the SS. On the left was the camp, stretching down the side of the hill, surrounded by high barbed wire fence and watchtowers.

They passed through the wide gate with the cast-iron sign "JEDEM DAS SEINE" (To Each His Own). Jóska knew that they were in the reception or "quarantine" area, and that there were two gates before the main enclosure: the upper one to the gas chambers and crematorium, the lower to the delousing or "sanitation" area. Jóska looked at the chimney and sniffed the air. There was no smoke, and the air did not have the stench he still clearly remembered from Auschwitz.

"At least we won't burn," he announced loudly, first in Serbian, then in Hungarian, again aware of the change within himself, of his loss of fear.

They were ordered to march straight through the "sanitation" compound and onto the huge sloping assembly area. The lieutenant's plans for the seven of them were apparently not going to be executed right away.

A tall Kapo wearing the red beret of the resistance organization approached them in front of the first row of barracks. The column came to a halt.

"Otto, you old buzzard, you made it," he exclaimed as they embraced. "Where is Karl?"

"Killed, two days ago. We need food!"

"So do twenty thousand others."

"Don't give me that," Otto yelled. "We stood all day at Berlstedt and my men are starving."

"Let's see what we can do. Dimitrij!" the Kapo yelled. The Polish Kapo who had talked to Jóska the previous night came out of the nearest barrack, also wearing a red beret. He recognized Jóska and hugged him.

"You did it, little fighter! No more transports. There weren't any today, either, but I couldn't have known that last night." He turned to the group. "Now we just wait. The SS are still outside, but inside the fence the resistance organization is running the camp."

Otto pleaded for food.

"There is no more food. None. We just have to wait," the Pole replied.

Otto was asked to accompany the Buchenwald Kapos. He embraced the other six and left.

They were let into several barracks, two hundred men into each wooden structure. Jóska grabbed a bottom bunk, showed it to Alexander, and they crawled in.

"Did we or didn't we make it?" Jóska asked Alexander.

"That's a good question," Alexander replied.

Jóska drifted into sleep.

WEDNESDAY, APRIL 11, 1945

Jóska woke at dawn, his body accustomed to early rising. Everyone was sleeping. He shook Alexander's shoulder.

"Where are we? What's happening?" he asked, alarmed.

Alexander sat up, rubbing his eyes. His head hit the bunk overhead.

"I don't know," Alexander said, "but as long as nobody bothers us, let's go back to sleep," and he rolled over.

Jóska stared at the boards above him. His arm was throbbing and he felt exhausted and hungry. He thought back through the previous year. One incident came sharply to his mind. Last December, two Russian POWs had escaped. They were recaptured by farmers two days later and brought back to camp, their faces ashen, their hands tied behind their backs with barbed wire, the blood clotted in big clumps where the barbs had bitten into the flesh. They were paraded in front of the assembled inmates, the Russians and many of the Jews weeping. "Alexej Ivanovich and Mischka Petrovich, I swear by the name of St. George that I will avenge the two of you for this," Vladia had whispered, standing next to Jóska. The two walked up to the gallows and spat in the sergeant's face as he yanked out the board under their feet.

"I am ready for the gallows now," Jóska thought, remembering the lieutenant's threat last night.

He fell asleep again.

"Wake up, wake up," someone was shouting, shaking him. "The Americans are here!"

Jóska bounded up and, with the others streaming from the barracks, ran up the sloping street, toward the front gate.

"We made it, little fighter! We're free!" People were yelling at him, patting his back, shaking his left hand, embracing him.

He looked for Alexander, but didn't see him.

Jóska recognized Tauberstein, an elderly man from Galicia, running next to them.

"Where is Cantor Heimowitz?" Jóska asked, looking around.

"My dear boy, our beloved Cantor, may his blessed memory live forever in the eyes of the Almighty, is dead," the old man said, panting.

Jóska ran across the wide plaza toward the front fence. Thousands of men were crowding the fence and more were coming, shouting and waving. Jóska pushed his way through to the fence. Jeeps, trucks, and armored carriers were rolling by, the American soldiers waving to them.

Jóska thought of the many occasions when Cantor Heimowitz talked about the liberation service he would conduct. He looked around at the crowd pressing against the fence. There were many from the Nieder Orschel group nearby.

Old Tauberstein was pressing through the crowd. Jóska knew what his duty was now.

"Will you say the blessings, Herr Tauberstein?" he asked.

Tauberstein looked at Jóska, startled, as if in a daze. Then, very slowly, he straightened up, straining to remove his stoop, and began:

"*Boruch ato Adonai, Elochenu melech haolam, matir asurim.*

Boruch ato Adonai, Elochenu melech haolam, schechecheyonu, v'kimonu, v'higionu lazman haze."

"For the others too," Jóska asked. In halting Polish, Tauberman repeated:

"Blessed art thou, O Lord our God, who freest the slaves.

Blessed art thou, O Lord our God, who has kept us, sustained us and commanded us to observe this occasion."

Jóska turned toward the fence and yelled with all his strength: "Do you speak German? Does anyone understand German?"

An officer pulled his Jeep over and walked up to them. "What is it? What can I do for you?" he asked, his eyes scanning the inmates in disbelief.

"Take some paper and take down this name!" Jóska pleaded, holding onto the fence.

"What name? Why?" the officer asked, pulling a notebook and pencil from his breast pocket.

Jóska cleared his throat. "Franz Gelenk—on the morning of—well, three days ago . . ." he began, halting; then his voice steadied. "This man, SS Death Head commando Lieutenant Franz Gelenk, killed, in cold blood, the senior Kapo of the Nieder Orschel Concentration Camp—prisoner number Buchenwald one-five-seven-four—Herr Karl Reinecken—Secretary-General of the Social Democratic Party for the State of Württemberg."

"Is he responsible for other deaths?" the officer asked, writing busily.

Jóska thought of the Cantor, who had kept track of all of them and named them all, Jew and gentile, in his daily *Kaddish*. He tried to name as many as he could: Alexej Ivanovich and Mischa Petrovich; another Russian kicked to death for "insubordination"; the men selected at random and shot after the Luftwaffe found some defective wings; the young Polish Jew on the food detail, executed for having some German money on him; the old Hungarian Jew shot for being slow at a morning assembly; another old man mangled to death by the dog; his sixteen-year-old friend Paul, in the camp with his father, hanged when a piece of scrap metal was found on him; Paul's father, bolting with a scream from the assembly facing the gallows, shot in the back before he could throw himself on the electrified fence. . . . He thought of all the brave men in their shallow graves.

Soldiers had opened the heavy iron gates and people were streaming out. Jóska collapsed against the fence.

IX. Emergence into Light

A paradox: these are stories about the end of the war, about the liberation of prisoners and hidden people; yet they arouse deep sadness and empathy. The writers here express their exaltation at the moment of their liberators' arrival; yet as they are freed from the torments of their individual hells, they are haunted by these hells and at the same time flung into a trough of new troubles and anguish.

From the middle of 1944 through early 1945, Allied armies were closing in on the Germans and arriving at the concentration camps. The Soviets moved in from the east, while the British and Americans came from the west. In the Soviet Union, where the Germans had invaded, the Germans were caught by advancing Soviet troops and were retreating back toward Germany. In all areas, as the Germans understood that the war was lost, they and their collaborators brutally tried to finish the task of the Final Solution—to kill as many Jews as they could. They also attempted to hide the evidence of the Holocaust by evacuating and destroying the concentration camps. But since they still needed the slave labor that the prisoners supplied, they tried to move many camp inmates, by death marches and trains, into central Germany.

For the victims who had survived to the end of the war, then, the troubles posed by freedom took several forms. Survivors faced the practical problems of where to go and how to live. Thrust suddenly into the countryside, often in a foreign land, they had no homes—frequently no towns—left to go to. Their families were at best dispersed, more likely dead. They had no money and no means of subsistence. Alone, clothed in rags, without resources, lost in a landscape where local people were as anti-Semitic as ever—the survivors were faced with the task of picking up the pieces when there were no pieces to pick up.

As terrible as the physical problems were, the most traumatic aspects of liberation for survivors were often psychological. The wild emotional content of this period of time is expressed movingly in "The Golden Chain of Judaism." This series of stories about a young girl emerging from hiding recounts ups and downs of finding a place for oneself, and of life in the displaced persons camps. The stories prophecy both the Jews' profound elation over the survival of Judaism itself, and their inability to forget or outlive the horrors of what they endured.

The authors of "Flight to Freedom" and "The Last Hiding Place" detail their attempts to flee from retreating German troops in the Ukraine. Like "The Golden Chain of Judaism," these stories catch the reader up in the desperate need to find hiding places in these last periods of the war, the fear of being caught, and the incredible moment when the survivors see the Russians arrive.

This range of competing emotions, the joy and sorrow of liberation, was never more acute than for concentration camp survivors, who were usually in the worst physical and psychological condition. They were too exhausted to travel. Their starved digestive systems could not accept normal food, and some survivors died from the shock of eating. Typhus epidemics raged through the camps, and the liberating armies lacked the supplies, equipment, and personnel to even begin to deal with the survivors' illness. The last few stories in this section are about liberation from the camps. Here we meet in detail the sickness and suffering, the bitterness at the Germans and the distrust of liberators, the difficulties of being evacuated from the camps—and even a rare touch of humor.

Though it is full of the pain and difficulty of liberation, this section ends with an uplift. In "An Ending and a Beginning" and "The Tiny Flame," the writers describe their slow, painful, yet glorious awakening to the light of life, one through seeing a ballgame, the other through learning to trust the humanity of strangers.

A.B.

The Golden Chain of Judaism

Cyna Glatstein
b. Sochachev, Poland, 1928

Liberation

There was a great shortage of manpower in Germany since all the men were in the army.

Posing as a Polish farm girl, I worked on a farm in a German village on the Elbe. For two years I labored in the fields, milked the cows and fed the chickens.

By 1945 we were aware that the war was coming closer and closer.

We heard the war machine in action, but did not realize how close the conflict really was.

One morning while working in the barn I heard a shot, dogs snarling, voices yelling *lauf, lauf Hunde*.

I ran out to see what was happening.

I could not believe what I saw. Were these men human beings?

Emaciated, in tattered striped uniforms, barefoot, bent, shuffling. They looked like puppets. One heap on the ground was the poor soul who had been shot. He had stumbled. The corpse was kicked aside and the line straightened again.

Above all the din and uproar, I heard or did I imagine it, the words pitifully moaned, "*Wasser, Wasser.*"

I rushed back to the barn, grabbed a pail of water for this suffering human being. I was immediately arrested and dragged to the Gestapo prison. I was locked in with other criminals with no way to escape.

When they took me in, I knew it was the end for me. Would I be tortured before I was hanged or shot?

If that were to be, I would join my beloved family. On the other hand I wanted to live.

As the door was forced open I said what I thought was the last *Shema Israel*. But it was not.

The soldiers were Russians. I yelled, "*Ich been eine Jude, Jude, Jude, Ich been nicht eine Deutsche.*" (I am not a German.)

I was sobbing, I was hysterical. My head was bowed, fear gripped me, I was trembling.

What did fate have in store for me?

I felt arms around me.

Those were not enemies' arms.

I raised my head.

He was a Russian officer.

"What did you say, my child?"

Looking up I said, "I am Jewish."

I was crying, he was crying too, when he said,

"So am I."

Freedom to Feel

Through all those years while pretending to be Christian, I had to be constantly on guard. Even after liberation all my thoughts and energy were focused on protecting my life. The freedom to indulge in feelings only came much later.

When the Russians liberated us in 1945, the Russian officer said, "You are all free." He knew that as a young girl, I would be in great danger.

He told me to hide on the farm and that he would be back. Where to hide? There was a storehouse filled with hay from floor to ceiling; I hid in the hay.

Hunger and thirst finally drove me out.

It was dark, no moon or stars.

An eerie silence. Had the war ended?

Now into the forest . . . there I was not alone.

Many forced laborers, who had been taken to Germany to work, also escaped to the woods. That gave me courage. Some were headed to Poland. I was one of them.

We traveled on foot, days and nights.

Whenever we saw a burned-out farmhouse, we looked for food.

Sometimes we were lucky. We found potatoes, beets, carrots, and cabbage, which we shared.

The wells provided us with water.

At the German–Polish border we were joined by other groups of refugees and concentration camp survivors.

Do my eyes deceive me? Am I dreaming? Is it wishful thinking? Am I hallucinating? Dear Hashem, it's Ruchele, Ruchele! My sister called my name— "Cynele, Cynele"—running.

We fell into each other's arms. Neither of us spoke.

In spite of what she must have gone through, she was still the beautiful Ruchele. Her delicate features, her dark shoulder-length hair, her soft kind eyes full of sadness.

At last, we had a few tranquil moments and could begin to feel. We were bewildered. Emotions crashed inside us—one minute we were so joyful to have found each other, the next, aching with sorrow and fear for the fate of the rest of our family. The swings of emotion, so wide and wild, were too much for the human soul.

Yet Another Pogrom

After our liberation and reunion, my sister Ruchele needed much care.

I took her to the farm in Poland where I had worked before I was taken to Germany.

Pani Wroczynska, the farmer's wife, was a fine and sympathetic person. I felt that I could trust her. I guessed that she too had suffered. I would work as before, and my sister would help as soon as she was able.

By May 1945, things were going well. My sister and I felt secure enough to tell Pani Wroczynska that we were Jewish.

Pani Wroczynska did not seem surprised.

She may even have suspected it when I first came to her.

One night in early August we heard gun shots.

Pani Wroczynska came running into our room. "Children, run and hide in the fields, there was a massacre in nearby Kielce."

Next morning we found out that the A.K., The Polish Secret Police, had shot in cold blood forty Jews, remnants of the concentration camps who had at long last come home.

In history this is known as the Kielce Pogrom.

No, it wasn't over yet, in spite of liberation.

Once again we were on the run.

The Golden Chain of Judaism

Pani Wroczynska drove my sister Ruchele and me by wagon, avoiding Kielce where forty Jewish survivors were killed in the infamous Kielce Pogrom.

She gave us a few *zlotys* to pay for a *drosky* to take us to Lodz.

Why Lodz?

Warsaw was out of the question. There was no more Warsaw.

Before the war, Lodz was the second city in Poland, with a quarter of a million Jews. It was industrial as well as a city of Jewish learning.

When we came into Lodz, we asked the driver to direct us to the Jewish section. The driver knew Lodz well. He gave us explicit directions. We found ourselves in the market square.

Groups of people in striped uniforms, shaved heads, toothless—evidently survivors. Animated, gesticulating, all trying to tell their stories.

When they saw us, all this stopped abruptly. They surrounded us, stared at us, pointed at us.

"Who are you? What are you doing here?"

We were taken aback.

Don't they realize that we are also survivors?

Stammering, trembling, we said, "We are Jewish."

They laughed. "You're lying, you are *shikses.*"

"Where are your tattooed numbers? How come your heads are not shaved?"

"Look at you. Do you look like one of us in your peasant garb?"

"Did you come here to hide among us?"

"Have you done something against us?"

We were stunned and horrified. After five years of hell, to be accused of not being Jewish.

They seemed not to know how to handle this situation—better leave it to the rabbi.

When we heard the word rabbi, we felt as if the burden we had suffered for so long was miraculously lifted.

As we were approaching the rabbi's temporary quarters, we heard young voices chanting the Nigun of the Torah.

The Nigun brought back to us the childhood which we had lost.

The rabbi asked the accusers to leave. When we were alone he asked, "Who are you, my children?"

"We are *Yiddishe kinder,* Jewish girls."

"Where are you from?"

"We are from Sochachev."

"Sochachev is quite near. Have you been back?"

"Not yet."

"What are your names?"

"Ruchele and Cynele Wolman."

"Wolman? I knew a Rabbi Leib Wolman from Sochachev. We studied together in *Yeshivot.* He was a brilliant rabbi. Was he your *mishpocho* (a relative)?"

With lumps in our throats, we tearfully whispered, "He was our beloved father."

"*Baruch Hashem,* the Golden Chain of Judaism will with you continue."

These were also the last words our father said to us.

Sochachev, 1945

Why did my sister and I come back to Sochachev in 1945?

We came back to Sochachev with some hope of finding some survivors who, like us, had also returned.

Unfortunately, we found nobody and nothing.

The synagogue had been destroyed.

The Hebrew school a shell.

In the cemetery, the monuments desecrated.

Nature in all its glory had not changed. It was all as we remembered it.

The past for us was reduced to ashes.

Out of nowhere came our Polish music teacher.

She stopped short, stared at us, spat, crossed herself.

"My God, the rabbi's daughters. Why are you alive? I thought all the Jews are dead."

We left to return to Lodz.

The Dentist's Office

At the end of 1945 I was one of many Jewish survivors at Zeilsheim, Germany, where a Displaced Persons camp had been established by the United States Government and the American Joint Distribution Committee.

There was a dental clinic here manned by a single dentist, who himself was a survivor.

The dentist had to work under almost primitive conditions.

The people waiting for their turns sat on two long benches in one room.

On my right was a young woman playing an imaginary piano, moving her fingers deftly over the keys. It was not difficult to realize that she had been an accomplished artist.

Beyond her sat a man, his hands clasped over his head, muttering, "Don't take off my hat, don't take off my hat." Undoubtedly, he was a very religious man.

On my left, a fatherly looking man was swaying back and forth lamenting, "My children, Surele, Tobele, Estherle, Duvidl, where are you? Where are you?"

Dear God, why am I alive?

In the dentist's chair sat a man whose age I could not guess. He could have been young or he could have been old. His hair was just beginning to grow out. I was close enough to see his glaring eyes.

We all heard the dentist saying to him, "I am sorry there will be pain but I have nothing to help you. Please tell me when it hurts and we can stop for a few minutes."

The drilling began.

The man did not react to the pain. He seemed to enjoy it. He kept repeating, "Ah, ah, ah, good, good, more, more."

The dentist stopped drilling. "Didn't you feel any pain?"

"It was heaven compared with what the Germans did to me."

I couldn't bear to hear any more. I only wanted all this behind me. Like a streak of light, I was out the door.

Catharsis

In the Displaced Persons camp, we are waiting.

Waiting for what? There are rumors that some of us will be sent to Palestine, some to Canada, others to Australia, and those who have relatives or sponsors will be sent to the United States.

This waiting time must not be wasted.

Classes have been set up for girls at the Beit Jacov Seminary where religious subjects were taught.

No classes are mandatory.

If you choose to attend, you go. I attend.

Registration for the classes was high at first, but very soon many dropped out.

The hunger we had endured for all those devastating years had left its effect on our powers of concentration.

The loss of our dearest ones, being uprooted, the pain, the horrors, the constant anxiety and fear left deep scars.

I am sitting at the window studying. I am distracted by noise in the courtyard.

A group of young boys and girls are dancing to the music of an accordion. They wave, but I have homework to do.

Next time I look out, the group is dancing in a frenzied, hysterical, maniacal tempo.

The tempo increases, changes to a driving pounding storm of savage rhythm—the people whirling, moving faster and faster until all of them collapse on the ground.

Suddenly, as quickly as it started, it is over.

I understand exactly the why of what I have witnessed.

These young people had to forget the hell they had suffered. Hopefully, this catharsis has given them a chance to pick up the broken threads of their lives.

The Picnic

It was autumn. The trees had not yet lost their brown and gold leaves. The sky, an azure blue, was reflected in the water of the lake. In six years we had forgotten nature, but now we were seeing her in all her glory.

We had suddenly awakened from the hell of the killing years to a feeling of hope. I felt alive and young again, more like my true age of fifteen. For the first time, I felt that there might be a future for me and for all of us.

We decided to have a picnic. Some of the girls of Beth Yacov School decided to go to the forest, others boating.

There were two sisters in our group. Pesy decided to go to the forest and Rivy chose boating. I chose boating too.

That night I could not sleep because I was so excited. I was also uncomfortable. In the morning it was clear why I was uncomfortable. I was covered with a painful, itchy rash. I went immediately to see the camp nurse. She told me I had Rubella.

My heart sank, and I could hardly control my tears. Boating for me would have to wait for a more auspicious occasion. I watched my friends leave and was happy for them.

For me the afternoon dragged on. Then I was conscious that something was going on. People were running, shouting. Policemen came into the camp. What they told us turned our joy to horror.

A loaded freighter had rammed the little boat, throwing Rivy and the two other girls on the boat into the water. Investigation later showed that the freighter ran over the girls.

The whole camp sat *Shiva*. For the first time in five years they could express their grief through tears.

The only consolation for us, the living, was that these lovely young girls came to *Kavar Israel*, Jewish burial, something that six million Jews did not have nor will ever have.

May their souls rest in peace.

Under the Canopy

People are sensitive when there is evil in the air and people are sensitive when joy and happiness are in the air.

We at the Displaced Persons camp are sensitive to joy and happiness now. There is romance in the air.

Molly and Chaim Moshe are glowing. They are inseparable. We suspect they are in love. Are we really going to have an honest-to-goodness wedding? We must.

Now the planning. Among the many packages that arrive from the United States through the American Joint Distribution Committee, we find miraculously a perfect fit for Molly—a white dress trimmed with lace. For the veil, a short white curtain. Chaim Moshe must be a properly dressed groom. We go back to our *schmatas* and, believe it or not, find a tuxedo. It doesn't fit, but one of our group is a tailor.

Molly and Chaim Moshe announce the date—Sunday, September 29, 1945, at 7:30 P.M.

Now that they are finally properly attired, the next step is the *Mikvah*. We take Molly to the lake. By immersing herself she performs the necessary act of purification.

Through a joint effort we have all the necessary ingredients for a wedding feast—all, that is, except for a rabbi. We contact Camp Feldafing and are told that Rabbi Mordecai Glatstein will be available.

The wedding day arrives. The canopy is up, the rabbi is waiting. The beautiful sixteen-year-old bride is escorted by two *Beit Jacov* teachers. The groom is obviously nervous. The bride is now under the *chupa*. The ceremony is about to start. Suddenly the bride is crying and wailing, "I want my mother, I want my mother, I want my mother." We all cry, we all want our mothers.

The rabbi, also a survivor, understands, and calms us down. "Today we make a new beginning. Let us continue with the marriage ceremony." When Chaim Moshe successfully crushes the glass, it is a catharsis for all of us.

The rabbi raises his hand. We become quiet. "My fellow survivors. It is indeed a happy and historic moment in our lives, a new beginning. Let us in unison recite this *Brucha*."

"Blessed are Thou, O Lord our God, King of the Universe, who has kept us alive, sustained us and brought us to this moment."

We all sing and dance, rejoicing in the bride's and groom's happiness.

A Beautiful Love Story

When Rabbi Glatstein came to perform the wedding ceremony at the DP camp, he talked to all of us. He advised us to look forward to the future and to make the best of it. "We must go forward. There is no looking back," he said.

We were very impressed. The rabbi was also a survivor. And in addition, he was young and handsome.

I had the feeling the rabbi was staring at me. After he left, I kept thinking of him.

Two months later, he returned in his uniform, looking even more handsome, with a delegation representing the American Joint Distribution Committee. Rabbi Glatstein served as Associate Director for Religious Affairs in the American Zone.

I was chosen to greet the delegation. My greeting in Yiddish was so funny that everybody laughed. This laughter relaxed us all. Rabbi Glatstein explained the purpose of the delegation: Jewish life was to be reestablished to the fullest. We began classes in Torah studies, rituals, and holidays.

The rabbi asked my name.

"Cyna Wolman."

"Wolman?" he asked. "I remember a famous Rabbi Wolman in Sochachev."

I said, "He was my beloved father, of blessed memory."

A week later, I was surprised that someone in Munich wanted to talk to Cyna Wolman. Who could be calling me?

It was Rabbi Glatstein asking if he could come to visit me. I was pleased. "Of course," I said. "Please come whenever it is convenient for you." This was a Sunday; he would come on Tuesday.

I was excited and nervous. What would we be talking about? Monday was a very long day. Did I dare to think that he was serious?

Now it was Tuesday and I was waiting.

He came handing me a gift and said, "I want to speak very seriously with you. From the first moment that I saw you, I knew that I loved you and wanted to marry you. I know there will be lots of competition. You are very young, you are beautiful, and you are the daughter of the late Rabbi Wolman, of blessed memory. I am willing to wait. I am sensitive to your youth, to your need for maturing. I hope you will not forget me when you are planning your new life."

I continued all my studies—secular as well as religious—but in my mind was always Rabbi Glatstein and what he had said to me.

Communications between us did not stop. Either by phone or by mail or by personal visits which did not interfere with my studies. This continued for two years.

Once again, the rabbi came to see me. This time he said, "It's now two years that I've been waiting for your answer. Will you marry me?"

I said, "I love you and nothing would give me more happiness than to spend my life with you. Yes, I want to be your wife."

After forty-five years, the bond has continued stronger than ever and, Hashem willing, will continue forever.

Flight to Freedom

Rubin Udler*
  b. Braila, Romania, 1925

The Escape

For two days, we heard loud thundering noises. At night we saw on the horizon sporadic glows, as from fires. It was March 1944, and we were convinced that what we heard and saw were artillery salvos from the long-awaited Soviet front line. Now, we had to save ourselves from the dangers of that nearing front line.

The inmates of the ghetto met to decide what to do. We were in Transnistria, Southwestern Ukraine, in an area occupied by Romanians. We had to escape from the ghetto because Vlasov's[†] soldiers, Kalmucks[‡] from the German Army, and the SS, who were withdrawing behind the retreating Romanians, were brutally killing the Jews.

Some people wanted to return to where they had lived before the ghetto, in the hope of finding their relatives. The older people thought of waiting for the Soviet troops to arrive, joining them in the fight against the fascists, and thus avenging the deaths of their parents, brothers, sisters, and children. Others were undecided. All the proposed plans were very risky. However, all of us craved to be liberated.

My parents, sister, and I decided to go westward, away from the advancing front. Hurriedly, we packed into our knapsacks bread, homemade rusks, fatback, and some clothing. Before going to sleep, we all said goodbye and wished each other good luck.

In the darkness of night, we escaped the ghetto. All the native inhabitants of the area were still asleep. The going was difficult because of mud and snow. Each of us used one hand to carry a thick walking stick, and in the other hand a sack. We proceeded in single file, my father in the lead, followed by my mother, my sister and at the end by me. We walked in silence.

Daybreak found us in a valley far from the village we had left. The March sky was gloomy; gray clouds hung low. Snow lay on the slopes bordering the valley

---

*Translated from Russian by Alexander Zwillich.
†A former Soviet general who together with his division deserted to the Third Reich.
‡A Mongol people of the Soviet Union who chose service in the German army rather than POW camp.

236

through which we were going. In places we saw rabbit tracks. It was cold; my father constantly tried to quicken the pace to keep warm and to put more distance between us and the ghetto. All was quiet. We did not see animals or birds.

After some hours passed, my mother became tired and asked my father to stop. Shortly after this we saw a straw rick. We went to the leeward side of it and there began to remove straw until we made a sort of cave. We crawled into the space, covered ourselves with straw and lay down exhausted. My mother gave each of us a piece of bread and a slice of fatback, both of which we swallowed in an instant. Afterward we dozed fitfully, though it was warm lying in the straw.

Later in the morning we resumed our exodus. The weather was not fit even for dogs to be outside. Maybe because of this, no one saw us.

With the approach of twilight we hoped to reach some shelter for the night. The skies continued to be gray; the cold wind seemed to blow from every direction. Again we were lucky. On the slope of a hill we saw an abandoned sheepfold and near it a shepherd's hut. We found sunflower stalks, brought them inside the hut and kindled a small fire. As long as the fire burned, and we sat near it, we were more than warm enough. We ate and then lay down close to each other to keep warm. Sleep, however, did not come though we were very tired. All kinds of anxieties went through our minds. The least noise invoked scary images. One of us, I believe my sister Fira, spoke of wolves that were found in this area. We thought about the possibility of an attack and about the fact that our only weapons were our walking sticks. Then we realized the improbability of anything like this happening, and decided to forget the entire thing. After a while we dozed off.

In the morning, stiff from the cold, we continued on our way. Not a soul was around. Snow mixed with rain began to fall. We stopped at a well, where we drank and washed our hands and faces, ate some bread and rested a little. We continued our flight, driven by fright and the inclement weather.

The second night we spent in a straw rick.

The next day, the weather improved so that we could see the sun. We left the valley and came to an open field. Around eight or nine o'clock in the morning, we saw a two-story building approximately five hundred meters away. It looked like a hospital or a school. The building was in the center of a large parcel of land, enclosed by a high steel fence and tall poplars. In front of the building stood about forty uniformed men in two rows, facing the way we were walking. An officer stood in front of them, speaking to the men.

We stopped, thinking that it was the end of us all. My father was the first to regain his senses. He ordered us to continue walking as before, not to run, not to make any noise nor behave in any unusual way. We followed him moving like automatons, one foot before the other.

It appeared that only God's miracle could save us and remove the inevitable danger from us. Then we heard, in a half-whisper, but from the depth of my father's soul, the Hebrew words of the Prayer on a Journey: "May it be the will from before You, Eternal, our God, and God of our fathers . . . and that we stride toward peace and guide us toward peace, and let us reach our intended destination, in life, happiness and peace; rescue us from the grasp of every enemy and lurking ambush, bandits . . . let us obtain grace, kindness and compassion in Your eyes and in the eyes of all who look at us . . ."

The miracle happened! The soldiers must have seen us, but possibly mistook us for peasants on the way to the hamlet, for vagrant gypsies, or I do not know what. We walked on.

In about thirty minutes, we reached the outskirts of a hamlet. We avoided the road through the hamlet and instead took the path that ran behind the houses, past their gardens. Near one of them we saw a woman who surveyed us intently and with curiosity. We had no way out of the situation. My father approached and told the woman who we were and where we came from, and asked for help.

She quickly looked us over; made sure no one was observing what went on; opened the garden gate and told us to follow her without delay. That was our rescue! God sent this woman and her husband to us and directed our steps toward their house.

The hamlet was Vovhovo, a part of the Karataev-Village-Soviet, Andreyevo-Ivanovsky district, region of Odessa. Sergei Petrovich Mezinovsky was the name of the man who hid us. The faded page of my diary of that time includes this entry near the above name: "P. I. Lapchinsky." Possibly, it is the name of the woman who took us in—our rescuer. Regrettably, however, I am not sure whether it is so.

Our Slavery Ends

Several days before my parents, sister and I escaped from the ghetto in South-western Ukraine and arrived at the hamlet of Vovhovo, a detachment of retreating German troops had taken up quarters there. The few soldiers occupied two public buildings in the middle of the hamlet. They took their nasty mood out on the local populace. A policeman and two Germans went door-to-door, listed the number of cows and calves owned, and ordered that they be brought the next morning to the center of the hamlet. From there, the animals were to be driven westward. These were convincing signs that soon they were going to leave the hamlet. This, however, was not the end of the Germans' demands. They forced the proprietress of the house where we were hiding to give them a dozen eggs, bread, and a large piece of fatback. From others they took hens and piglets. They beat many people unmercifully.

After hearing our sad history, the farmer Sergei Petrovich and his wife, who had taken us into their house, offered to help us. We ate together. My mother and my sister Fira took off their worn-out jackets and dresses, changed into clean peasant blouses and skirts, and covered their heads with kerchiefs in the manner of Ukrainian peasants. Only their eyes were visible. From then on, my mother and sister were to claim to be relatives of the woman of the house, having arrived from a neighboring region after being displaced from their village. They stayed in the house.

Sergei Petrovich, my father, and I had to hide. At first, we crawled into a pit, dug in the garden like a well, deep enough to stand in. It was covered above with wooden boards and slabs, and on them lay corn stalks alternately with straw. The chinks between the decking permitted air to enter, so we could breathe. Above that stood a conical haystack. Nearby was a chained dog.

From time to time, the wife of Sergei Petrovich approached the pit and told us what was happening in the hamlet.

At night we came out of the pit and went into the kitchen, so that we could warm ourselves and eat. From sitting in the pit for a long time, we ached all over. We walked briskly around the kitchen and were massaged to restore our circulation.

We were afraid to stay long in the house. Unexpected guests could come at any time. Sergei Petrovich and his wife decided that he and my father should go back into the pit. When only two of them were there, there would be more room for them to lie down. They took something to cover themselves with, because the night was cold.

I had to crawl into the hen house, which was attached to the side of the main house. It was a low—possibly one meter high—adobe brick lean-to. The entrance was through a narrow opening in the side. To crawl into it was possible only for the hens or a thin teenager. Though I was only skin and bones, I had trouble squeezing through the entrance.

Once inside, I leaned against the front wall of the hen house that joined the wall of the house. After my eyes became accustomed to the semi-darkness, I could discern the perches on which roosted the sleeping hens and roosters, poles used to take the eggs, and two vessels—one made from a hollowed out log and the second one made of tin—and some brooms.

It was warm in the hen house, and I fell asleep in a crouched position. In the morning I was awakened by voices. Some Germans and a Ukrainian policeman were rounding up the men of the hamlet. They looked for them in the house, in the attic, in the cellar, in the cattle shed. They searched in stacks and ricks that they pierced with bayonets and pitchforks.

I placed the brooms I found in the hen house in front of me, faced the wall, remained as if glued to it and held my breath. One German, while speaking to someone, thrust his head into the hen house and frightened the birds. They began to cackle loudly and flap their wings, causing feathers and dust to fly at him. He recoiled, probably thinking that a man could not hide there. Sergei Petrovich and my father were not found.

Suddenly I heard yells. The Germans were beating someone, and women were moaning. I could only imagine what happened to the victim. As the hue and cry slowly subsided, I decided to go out, to find out if anything had happened to my people. However, the wife of Sergei Petrovich spoke so that I could hear her, saying that the Germans had left. They had beat black and blue a lad whom they found hidden in the attic of the neighboring house. They were preparing to hang him as a warning for the rest of the people.

Soon after this, Sergei Petrovich's wife took her cow to the center of the hamlet, where the police took it from her after checking it off the list. She returned crying. The monsters had really hanged the neighbor's only son. The woman was a soldier's widow.

In a feverish hurry, the Germans organized to drive the herd and the men they had collected out of the hamlet. This was entrusted to the policemen and the soldiers of Vlasov, a former Soviet General who had deserted to the Third Reich. No one knew where the men were being taken. They could have been shot behind the hamlet, put in front when the Russian troops advanced, put to work digging trenches and antitank ditches, or sent to the deep rear to work in camps. The women, children, and old men who remained in the hamlet were deeply depressed.

The bursts of artillery shells could be heard very near. Sergei Petrovich and his wife thought it was too risky for us to remain in our hiding places. He had another hiding place outside the hamlet. After dark, we slipped past the gardens and followed his lead toward it.

The sole street of the hamlet, straight and wide, led over the level part of the hill. Behind the gardens began the slope that in places was overgrown with bushes.

When the snow melted in the spring, and when it rained hard, the valley served as a stream bed. The flowing rainwater had eroded pits in one side of the bed, four or five meters wide and one meter deep. A coppice grew on the opposite side of the hill.

Sergei Petrovich selected one of these pits. We dropped down into the pit feet first and lay on our bellies. Each of us had to force his entry into the pit. Once inside, we covered the pit entrance by piling on clods of earth found nearby. We could not be seen from the outside. We had sufficient air to breathe, but the earth was very damp and to move in the narrow cavity was almost impossible.

We lay there for a long time. It was totally dark when we saw at the edge of our pit, between the clods of earth, silhouettes of boots. We heard German being spoken. We heard sharp orders, hoof beats, squeaking of wheels, and the sound of digging picks and shovels. We also heard Russian curses. The noise lasted for over three hours. Afterward all was quiet.

We were nearly frozen; we shivered so badly because of the cold that we could not utter two words. Our teeth were chattering from being cold and from being frightened. It was incredibly difficult for us to move our fingers or toes, or turn our necks.

Sergei Petrovich spoke to us with difficulty, in a whisper. If we remained lying there, by morning we would be frozen stiff. Or if we managed to come through the night unharmed, in the morning it would be too bright for us to be able to reach the house safely. We decided to get out of the pit and reconnoiter. With great effort Sergei Petrovich was the first to get out; then he helped me, and both of us helped my father crawl out. Carefully we pulled ourselves over the rim of the ditch and cautiously looked around. We did not see or hear anything. We began to beat our hands against our chests and our feet against each other to restore their circulation. To remain there longer was impossible. We jumped out of the ditch and quickly, quietly, in a single file followed Sergei Petrovich. Near the top of the slope, we saw an outline of a cannon about 150 meters away, and near it a stack of boxes with ammunition; a sentry paced forward and back.

We did not stop, nor did we run, but hurriedly walked past. I walked last in the file. After we passed the cannon and the sentry, I looked back. The sentry stood, did not move, and looked in our direction.

Shaken, we continued to walk up the hill. Although exposed to the view of the Germans and Vlasov's soldiers, we passed the gardens of the hamlet and safely reached Sergei Petrovich's garden, listened, and entered the house. We embraced our loved ones and remained in silence, in the dark, for a long time. Our suffering had been almost beyond human endurance. We felt as if we had returned from the dead.

Recently, I thought again about what we went through that night. We really had lived on the verge of death. The Germans, while looking for a place to position their cannons, stood very near where we were hiding and from our footprints could have guessed that someone was in the pits. A test shot into our hiding place would have been fatal. The sentry, who undoubtedly saw us, could have, with a burst of machine-gun fire, killed us all. But he apparently was not sure who we were nor how many of us there were. He possibly thought that we were scouts—part of a group, and others were near, to the right, left, in front or back; that we were partisans, and our comrades were in the woods, following us. He may have calculated that we were armed and at any moment would press the trigger; in the end, he may simply have cared to save his own skin.

We had little time to warm ourselves and eat before we had to crawl into the pit in the garden again. My father and Sergei Petrovich, lying tightly side by side, one against the other, slept. I was overcome by pictures of the recently passed days.

Suddenly, I heard muffled Russian voices and knocking at the window of the house. I awoke Sergei Petrovich and my father. We listened. A door slammed and again it was quiet. After some time the woman of the house came out to the garden and asked us to come inside. There we found five or six young men armed with automatic rifles. On the table were potatoes boiled in their jackets, bread, onions, and a kettle with boiling water. The newcomers ate hastily. When we entered, they stopped for a moment and looked at us with piercing eyes. They were Russian scouts. One of them unfolded a map at the edge of the table and began to question Sergei Petrovich and his wife about the Germans, fortifications, roads, and police. When my father told them who we were, they looked at us with astonishment. Soon they left the house. After this, we remained there and did not return to the pit in the garden.

Shortly, in wide formation, the Red Army troops entered the hamlet. They came through the gardens and the street, in the direction from which we had come only four days ago. This was the infantry. They moved quickly forward, crouching, their automatic rifles at the ready. They looked with concentration, straining. Their unshaven faces and flashing eyes have stayed in my memory all my life. They were our liberators!

The long-awaited end of our utterly dark slavery had arrived. A slavery that lasted eight hundred ninety-six days, a time of suffering and humiliation, loss of life of relatives and friends, loss of belief in humanity, in decency, in people's honor. We personally experienced all the abominations of fascism, nationalism and boundless anti-Semitism.

We were happy at the survival of our immediate family and simultaneously deeply saddened by the loss of grandparents, aunts, uncles, and cousins—our extended family. Why had they been savagely murdered? Only because they were Jews. My mother was inconsolable.

The joy and sorrow overcame us on this significant day, March 30, 1944.

The Last Hiding Place

Libby Stern
b. Suceava, Romania, 1926

I was living in the ghetto of Shargorod in the Ukraine, where thousands of Romanian Jews had been deported in the autumn of 1941. The Ukrainian Jews had been ordered to take us in, or they would be deported too. So a town of about three thousand Jews became a town of six thousand in an area of a few square miles.

I lived in a large house at the edge of town, sharing a room with two other girls. The other rooms were occupied by several families and the owner, an eighty-five-year-old man.

Feter Chaim, as we called him, loved to tell us stories, especially about the Russian Revolution and how he had escaped being killed by Pilsudski and his armies in 1918. The story went that, as Pilsudski approached the town, *Feter* Chaim took a bottle of water and a loaf of bread and hid in a cave not far from his house for four days, until the gang retreated. This story somehow stuck in my mind, for I had been in hiding many times.

One day when I met *Feter* Chaim on the street, I asked him to show me the caves. We walked for about an hour to an embankment. He said the caves were underneath this road but the lowest place of entry was further down. We descended a steep hill and there we found the place of many caves. He showed me where he had hidden. It was a cave within a cave, a perfect hiding place.

In March of 1944, rumors began to circulate that the Germans were retreating and that the *Sonderkommando* (a special detail used only to enforce the Final Solution) were burning ghettos and killing all the Jews they could find.

Soon I heard cannons and gunshots nearby. I knew the Germans would pass through our town, because we were near the main highway. Remembering the old man's story, I decided to hide once again. I told my two roommates about my plan but they refused to come with me, saying that they were going to stay with some relatives in the center of town. I was determined to go to the caves. I took a few pieces of bread and a bottle of water, and off I went.

It took me several hours to find the lowest part of the embankment. When I finally got down there I saw smoke in the distance. I approached the area and to my dismay saw soldiers sitting around a fire. The retreating German army had decided to camp there. The smoke came from a field kitchen that the army put up to feed its soldiers.

Nobody saw me, and I ran home as fast as I could. When I opened the door, I found the house empty. Everyone had left to hide somewhere in town with friends or relatives. I decided to stay in the house because I knew very few people elsewhere. I spent the night full of fear and anxiety, anticipating the worst.

The next morning, as I looked out the window from which I could see the main road, I saw the German army retreating . . . thousands of them. The line kept on going and going—foot soldiers, motorcycles, trucks, cars, and horses. I thought, "Now that the army is retreating, can the *Sonderkomando* be far behind? They'll be here soon, burning and killing us all, as they did in so many other ghettos in the Ukraine."

Suddenly, the line stopped. The entire army turned around. They were coming back!

And then it happened: I saw them throw their guns down and put their hands behind their necks. They were surrounded! One entire German division was trapped by two Russian armies—the partisans on one side and the Ukrainian army on the other side. The Master Race had collapsed like a house of cards.

I had no need to hide!

I stood near the window crying. I wept because there was no one left from my family to share this moment, the long awaited day—to witness the monster being destroyed.

One Day War, the Next Day Not

Irene Berkowitz
b. Uzhorod, Czechoslovakia (became Ungvár, Hungary), 1920

My mother often talked about plans for after liberation. She talked about her sister Helen who lived in the United States. My mother planned to go there and open a restaurant.

We were sitting and talking one night at Stutthof Concentration Camp—my mother, sisters, and I. The temperature was near freezing. We were starving and thirsty. Icicles had formed on the inside of the roof. They were low enough for us to reach, so we broke them off and sucked on them to moisten our mouths.

We were walking skeletons—I weighed about sixty-five pounds.

So I asked my mother, "Do you think that we can survive in this physical condition?"

She replied, "Children, I remember World War I. The war went on for years and then one day it was over."

As we talked, we heard airplanes and loud noises in the distance.

It was 1945 and the Russians were approaching.

Soon after this night, the Germans rounded us up for the last death march, telling us to form rows of five. Those too tired to walk were told to stay behind and they would be taken by wagon. My mother's feet were very swollen, so she chose to stay. My sister, a doctor, stayed with her. That was the last time we saw them.

Later we found out that those left behind that night went to a Russian hospital. There was a typhus epidemic and with no medication available, my mother and sister died there.

The Germans marched us for several hours until it was too dark to see. They pushed us into a field where we tripped over people. In the morning we saw that the field contained thousands of people dead and dying of typhus.

The Russian Army had the area surrounded, so the Germans were not able to take us further. So that was the end of the war—April 17, 1945.

Left on our own, sick as we were, thirteen of us found an abandoned house where we stayed for a few days without food before some Russians found us. I thought my sister Roshi was dead, but when I put a few drops of vodka that the officer gave me on her lips, she coughed.

A Russian woman wanted to give us some soup, but a Jewish officer said it was too rich in fat and it would make us sicker. They gave us canned milk and we found canned sardines, but we had no opener.

At first we could only crawl on all fours. After a few days we dragged ourselves into a nearby town. Some Russian medics recognized how sick we were and took us to the hospital. While in the waiting room we learned that our heads would be shaved and that there was no medication to treat people. We sneaked out, going we knew not where.

So this was our fate after liberation. Just as my mother had said, "One day there was war, the next day not." But our mother was wrong about one thing: our suffering didn't end the day the war was over.

The Long Road after Liberation

Jack Sittsamer
b. Mielec, Poland, 1924

Going back and forth to work every day on the train, we could see the flowers starting to grow and the trees blooming. People spoke about how good it would be to be liberated.

When we came back to camp on May 4th, just like every other day, we got our portion of soup and went to sleep. The next morning, there was no 5:00 A.M. reveille. I heard people saying "Look out, look out the windows." I looked out and there were no guards or machine guns; the guard towers were empty. There weren't any guards at the main gate, either.

Even so, everybody stayed inside because we suspected that the Germans were up to something. Finally at about 10:00 A.M., a jeep and four American soldiers pulled inside the camp and informed us that we were free. Liberated!

Few people left that day. The majority were too weak to walk. The second day, more people left. They felt stronger because they were fed better. Finally, on the third day, I left with a friend from Mielec.

We didn't go through the main gate; we tuneled underneath the double fence to the outside. I didn't believe I could safely leave through the gate.

The nearest city was Linz, Austria, about twenty miles away. We hitchhiked, we walked, we rested. This short distance took us three days.

In Linz, we walked around still wearing our concentration camp clothes. Suddenly, sirens sounded. An Austrian woman opened her door and told us to come inside. There was a curfew; no one was allowed out after 5:00 P.M.

It was a Mrs. Weber who took us in. She called her neighbors over, one of whom was a barber. He took us out to the backyard, shaved our long hair off and burned our clothes. Then we took our first hot shower with real soap in many, many years.

Mrs. Weber gave us new underwear and nice clothes. These things had belonged to her two sons who died while fighting in the German army.

She showed us the bedroom where we would sleep. It had two beds in it, but we slept on the floor because we weren't used to sleeping in a bed. In three months, she nursed me back from my weight of seventy-five pounds to about eighty-five pounds.

Feeling stronger, I decided to travel, to try to locate my brother. In Italy, I found someone who told me that there was a man in Germany who had been in the same camp as my brother. I left Italy and found this man, who had survived Pustkow camp, only to be told that my brother did not survive.

I had known long before this that my father, mother, and the rest of my family also did not survive.

In June 1949, I sailed to America.

On the Way to Health

Ilona Weiss
b. Kosino, Czechoslovakia, 1923

A Marvelous Feeling

On Sunday noon, April 15, 1945, we heard the loudspeaker announcing "Greetings, everybody. The British Armed Forces have just liberated Camp Bergen-Belsen."

The healthy girls went on a rampage. They went into the warehouses. They took bicycles, sewing machines, typewriters. My sister Edie, who was well, went into a barrack where Nazis had lived. In their hurry to leave they had left behind suitcases packed with silk pajamas, cashmere sweaters, dresses, crocodile leather shoes and belts, a mink coat and many other beautiful things.

Most of all, we wanted food. Finally on Monday evening we got some porridge cooked with potatoes. We ate very carefully and slowly. Later the British brought us some condensed sweet milk. I drank at least a half gallon a day.

They gave us some cigarettes which we sold for potatoes. But there was no wood, so we cut the mink coat to pieces, made a fire with it and cooked the potatoes.

A former Kapo would deliver our food in a big pot. With his filthy, bare hand, he would take the meat and potatoes out of the container. The girls didn't want to eat what was left.

He had the nerve to say to us, "Eat, you stupid Hungarians." We told the Canadians, who kicked him in the butt and told him that if he dared come close to the barrack, they would put him in jail.

"*Musserem!*" he shouted at us on his way out, still hoping for the last word. But we were rid of him.

So we had food and whatever else we could find. All in all, it was a marvelous feeling—no Kapos, no Nazis, no greedy people calling us names.

But the death rate was incredible even after liberation. Most died, after typhus, of heart failure.

Fried Chicken

Ironically, it was now that my sister Edie got sick. Before the liberation, the SS women made her drag dead bodies to the burial pit, and she got infected with typhus.

Edie wouldn't eat. Then one day, she told me she smelled fried chicken. She said she would eat that.

I said, "You must be dreaming." But I agreed to go and look.

I washed my hair, put on the pretty cashmere dress and crocodile leather shoes that the Nazis had left, and went in search of fried chicken.

I walked a block or two to the cook house. I went into the kitchen. Nobody was there, but there was some fried chicken. I found a half empty can of chocolate syrup and placed the chicken in it.

Then I heard somebody coming. I was sure they would take the chicken away from me and would even give me a beating.

I saw a door. I ran in. To my astonishment, it was a men's room. It was full of drunken soldiers celebrating V-E Day.

I didn't dare look left or right. Spotting a window, I darted toward it, crying.

How they laughed, those drunken soldiers! Only one kind young man understood how embarrassed I was; he helped me get out through the window. It was years until I forgave those other young Brits.

My sister Edie was so happy I got her the chicken.

She asked me, "Did you have any problems getting it?"

"I had no problems at all," I said.

The Hospital

The ambulances came several days after liberation. We had to totally undress before they took us to the hospital. It had been a German military hospital.

When we arrived, the hospital was already filled. We wound up in the attic. We had no mattresses, just straw mats on the floor, and a pillow and a blanket. At night, we would take off the pillow cases and make ourselves nightgowns from them.

We didn't have any medication or X-ray equipment. The Germans had taken everything with them when they evacuated the place. We had German nurses and a German doctor.

I had only one roommate. She seemed to be in good physical condition, although she slept most of the time, almost as if she were unconscious. When she woke one day, she asked for chicken soup. So I told my sister to sell my clothes. She sold them to a farmer, bought a chicken and some vegetables and made chicken soup. In the evening, she brought the soup and fed it to my roommate. The next day, my roommate died. I didn't even know her name.

After this, I got four other roommates. Two of the girls were Jewish, one was Serbian, and one was German. We spoke with respect to the German doctor, but the German girl was very disrespectful. And the Serbian girl would not let him near her. She would scream, "Go away, Nazi; don't touch me, Nazi!"

In the afternoon, all of my roommates would go out. One day the German nurse brought several Canadian officers to my room to visit. They asked about Bergen-Belsen and I told them about the camp. When they left, they gave me some candy. I offered the nurse some.

She said, "Was that candy bar worth making up such horrible lies?" She was very angry with me.

I wondered. Could she really not know about the camps?

I spent two years in that hospital.

An Ending and a Beginning

Ernest Light
b. Uzhorod, Czechoslovakia (became Ungvár, Hungary), 1920

Around April 26, 1945, orders came to pack up our belongings—a mess kit and a spoon. The following morning those who had enough strength to walk were marched from Muhldorf Concentration Camp, near Dachau, to the near-by railroad station. We were loaded into cattle cars, for a trip of unknown destination. Most of us—there must have been about a thousand men—were emaciated and half-dead. Somehow the crowding was not a problem as in previous train trips. For the next two or three days we were moving back and forth, without knowing or caring about our destination or our fate.

At one railroad stop the American Air Force mistook our train for a German military transport, and turned their machine guns on us. Two men in my car were killed, as were men in other cars, and many were injured. Once the attack halted we managed to open the cars. We ran out to an open field. When they saw our striped uniforms and emaciated bodies, the shelling stopped. The following day, the Germans realized there was no place to take us. We were surrounded by American troops. Suddenly the car doors were opened. The guards disappeared and we were left on our own.

So that was the end of our captivity.

A group of about eight of us, who still had some strength left, took the first road we saw. We walked until we reached a farmhouse. The people gave us food to get rid of us.

Unfortunately, we had nobody to warn us not to overeat. Not that warning would have helped. It was impossible to resist the urge to eat after such a long time of starvation. The eyes just wanted to swallow everything. None of us thought of the consequences.

We ended up in an abandoned German military barracks. Most of us were bloated and very sick. Many died, and there was nobody to help us.

A few days later, in the evening, we heard shooting nearby. I thought, "The Germans are returning and this will be the end for us." After a short time, the shooting stopped. In the morning we found out that the shooting came from American forces celebrating V-E Day.

The following day doctors, medics, and nurses came to our barracks. We were taken to a nearby sanatorium in Weileim, run by Sisters. Little by little, we gained back our strength.

The first day I felt better, I went for a walk. I headed for the center of the town. I saw a ballfield close by. American soldiers were playing a strange game with a small ball. I saw one man crouching with a mask on his face, throwing a ball toward the man in front of him, this man throwing the ball toward the man with the mask. The man standing in front of this man had a bat in his hand. Suddenly, the man hit the ball, all the men in the field with gloves on kept running, hollering, and throwing the ball.

This was my introduction to baseball. I never could have imagined that one day I would become an avid fan of this game.

So that was a beginning.

The Tiny Flame

Malka Baran
b. Warsaw, Poland, 1927

The only sound I hear is the steady, somewhat rhythmic rattle of the wheels on the cobblestone road. The only other vehicle I see is the one we are following, a gray, open truck, identical to ours: two benches on each side filled with grayish-green uniformed soldiers, tired, silent, their bodies moving back and forth, ever so heavily, drowsily, some dozing to the monotonous hum of the engines.

The streets we are passing are deserted, quiet as though tired, heavy with things unexpressed, burdened perhaps with the screams, explosions, havoc and fear of not so long ago—some of the buildings are in ruins—others seem to be inhabited, but the naked, gaping windows show nothing of their inner life.

Under the gray indifferent skies we drive on, going somewhere in Poland, to yet another unknown place.

It is 1945—perhaps. Dates are difficult for me to remember. My friend and I are traveling with a lieutenant of the Russian army and his soldiers. We are eighteen years old, and recently liberated by the Soviets from our concentration camp. He, the officer, brought a note written by Isidor A., that said simply, "Follow this man, trust him, he will bring you safely to me."

The wheels continue their steady rattle.

We trusted Isidor. He was a benefactor, bringing food, a towel, a shirt—whatever he could salvage. Isidor was a Jew and we were the first Jewish prisoners he met. His wish was to adopt me, the youngest in our group, and take me to Leningrad after the war, where his wife and daughter waited for him.

"Follow this man," he wrote, and we trusted him. I am glad that Roza decided to come along. She is active, strong, a decision-maker. I am passive, life still flows over me, but not through me. I'm still numb.

The soldiers are dozing—the gray sky becomes grayer. Evening approaches and we are still travelling. How strange, it never occurred to us to ask how far we are going, how long the journey.

We are passing an empty, abandoned village, not a soul nearby, not a house standing . . . the trucks stop. The lieutenant gives orders, the soldiers jump down and begin to prepare. There is a barn without a door. Someone makes a fire and soon the smell of cooked food reaches us. Roza looks at me; we are the only ones left on the truck. Suddenly we realize that they are settling here for the night.

"We are staying on this truck," she says to me. A sense of fear, of foreboding, envelops us. The lieutenant walks toward us. "Come down and have some soup," he extends the invitation. Roza thanks him politely.

"We will stay here," she says.

"Please come, it's warmer near the fire," he tries again, kindly. She asks him to allow us to stay. He walks away.

The soldiers sit on the ground around the fire. Someone plays the accordion, others begin to sing. It drizzles. Huddled together, we watch the scene. Somehow the sad melodies, the fire, the aroma of soup make me forget where we are, the abandoned, forsaken, open land with a barn without a door.

The officer brings two bowls of hot soup and two blankets. "Eat, warm up, please," he says. We thank him. The soup is good; the blankets helpful. The sounds of the accordion cease. The soldiers clean up and enter the barn.

The lieutenant tries again. "Look, there is a place I prepared for you, near the entrance, come, it is too cold, you cannot stay here all night." We are cold, wet, and frightened. "We will lie down near the opening, but don't dare to fall asleep," Roza says to me.

We come down wrapped in the blankets and enter the dark barn. Soldiers line the walls. It is quiet, they seem to be asleep. Silently we lie down on the army blankets prepared for us, near the open space where a door used to be. We hold hands, listening to the sounds of breathing and soft snoring.

"Don't fall asleep," my friend whispers. It is quiet and dark. We drift off into a deep sleep.

Something drops on me, my heart stands still, then pounds. I feel Roza's body freeze as well. We wait . . . breathless, nothing . . . dark and quiet . . . nothing, the pounding of my heart eases. I listen and strain to see . . . nothing . . . quiet . . . dark. I drift off and sleep overtakes me.

Bright morning. The barn is empty. We look at the down blanket covering us, and at each other. A joy fills me, a warmth, more than the blanket can provide.

"Come, have breakfast," says our lieutenant. "Then we'll be on our way again. Was the blanket warm?" he asks. "The man on duty found it nearby and covered you," he adds.

We come out into the sun. The cook motions us to sit down with the others and gives us food and a smile.

A thousand colored balloons seem to float in the air and deep within me, a tiny flame of belief in human kindness, dead for so long, begins to flicker again.

X. The Aftermath: Remembering

In the first story in this section, "The Aftermath," the writer responds to a question: "What was the worst part of the Holocaust?" Her answer: what came afterward. This writer was a hidden child rather than a concentration camp prisoner, and thus some other survivors might respond differently to the question. But none would be likely to disagree with the issue to which she points: after liberation, survivors had to find ways to live on through the years with their personal memories of suffering and loss.

Two stories, "The Aftermath" and "The Barber," tell of lifelong yearning for a lost parent. The writer of "It Shall Not Be Forgotten Nor Forgiven!" deals with memory by chronicling in detail the deaths of each of his family members. With a somewhat broader range, the writer of "Kaleidoscope" evokes fragments of scenes he remembers from Salonika, Greece—scenes peopled with many named and unnameable individuals.

The sense of loss called up in these stories is tempered in this section by bittersweet, even uplifting sequels to liberation, such as in "The Sewing Basket" and "Children from the Camps Going to England." And in "The Chief of the Gestapo" and "Herr Schluemper," survivors act out what must have been a recurring fantasy of all Nazi victims both during and after the war. The cruel German officers who get what they deserve come to represent all evil perpetrators of the Holocaust who we wish would be punished.

Despite this positive note, this section finally underscores the pain that energizes the survivors' ongoing need to speak as witnesses in the aftermath of the war. "To Bear Witness about the Holocaust" and "It Shall Not Be Forgotten Nor Forgiven!" tell of these writers' determination to keep the memory of the spilled blood alive. Surely it is in a real sense the individual survivors' inability to forget that informs our collective memory of Holocaust history.

A.B.

The Aftermath

Edith Rechter Levy
b. Vienna, Austria, 1930

Wide-eyed and innocent, a student once asked me what I considered to be the worst part of the Holocaust. I smiled. Is it possible to answer such a question? How to choose, to single out one horror greater than another?

That day, I had no answer for the student. But the question kept haunting me. I now believe that I know the answer.

I survived the war by hiding—a hidden child. The idea was to live with the cunning of a hunted animal, and with courage well beyond my years. But mixed among the terrors of this dark world lay the hope of the innocent. If I could escape the clutches of the hunter long enough, this horrible nightmare would eventually end, and things would return to normal, to the way they were. This hope, this faith kept me going.

Eventually liberation did come. Since my father had been deported in early 1942, my main concern now was for him. I lived for his return.

Though undernourished and sick, I walked miles, day after day, to check the lists of names of those who had been liberated from the camps.

The lists were posted at three synagogues in Brussels, each one situated at a different end of the city and at a great distance from the other ones. The most cumbersome to reach was the large *Holländische Shul,* near the *Palais de Justice,* which necessitated a considerable climb up steep streets. But this *shul* had the most complete lists, and I believed with absolute faith that it was only a matter of time until my father's name would appear among the returnees. I waited and walked, walked and waited, coming home more and more exhausted, but unwilling to give up my search and my hope.

I dreamed about my father's return. I knew that we would have to be very careful not to offer too much or too rich food, which could kill him, as had been the case with other released camp inmates.

Little by little, the lists began to dwindle, the names became more and more sparse, trickling down to a mere few. My visits became less frequent, first because of exhaustion, but also because not many new names appeared, and so the same names remained posted for a longer time.

Fear of the unthinkable slowly began to creep into my soul when suddenly one day, there was a post card in our mailbox.

Did hope play a cruel trick? It looked to me to be in my father's handwriting, though somewhat shaky. It stated simply: "Father is in Hospital St. Pierre."

I didn't care. I didn't care what shape he was in. He was back! I had no doubt that I could bring him back to health, no matter how long it took! It had all been worthwhile, all the suffering, all the hunger, all the fear! Finally things could return to normal. I began crying hysterically, I ran up the stairs to our apartment. I knocked on the door and Mother opened it. I was sobbing uncontrollably, unable to speak.

"What happened? What is the matter?" my mother wanted to know. All I could utter was "Daddy, Daddy," as I handed her the post card.

Mother didn't say anything for a while. She let me cry, waiting for me to compose myself, allowing me to catch my breath. Then she said, ever so gently, "Calm yourself, dear, this is not *your* father, it's Jacob's dad."

That was the moment when my soul was torn apart with one agonizing thrust, as surely as if some demon had reached into my breast and physically removed part of my being, leaving behind a tattered, empty *neshumah*. I cannot describe the pain of that instant.

This was the beginning of my recurring nightmares—this moment when I knew that life could never truly be complete again. And this then is the legacy, the aftermath which has no end.

The worst part of the Holocaust is what comes afterward. It is the realization that one must continue living for the rest of one's life with part of one's soul amputated.

The Barber

Malka Baran
b. Warsaw, Poland, 1927

POLAND, EARLY 1930S
He was a barber, and we were neighbors.

His little shop was next door and I often sat on the three steps which led to his door.

He cut my father's hair and my brother's hair, and maybe mine too. I don't remember.

MANHATTAN, 1980S
My husband and I are watching the second part of the documentary *Shoah*, a painful experience.

I see what I saw then . . . I hear what I heard during those horror-filled years . . . my eyes glued to the screen . . . my heart pounding.

Then I see him! He is cutting a client's hair and answering the interviewer's questions: haltingly, reluctantly.

Yes, he was a barber in Treblinka.

Could he talk about it a little?

He shakes his head, "No, I can't."

"No, no," his head shakes repeatedly.

The interviewer presses on . . . gently.

"It is important—please."

He talks with pain . . . stopping . . . sobbing.

Yes, he cut the women's hair, before they entered the showers. Yes, they were naked.

"Anyone you knew?" asks the interviewer.

He nods . . . cannot speak, the pain is excruciating . . . visible.

"My wife . . . others . . ."

"Did you tell them where they were going?"

Sobs . . . He tries to stifle them . . .

"No," he whispers.

I sob with him . . . the barber, our neighbor . . . he cut *her* hair there in Treblinka . . . my mother's.

Kaleidoscope: Salonika, Greece, 1945

Ray Naar
b. Salonika, Greece, 1927

I remember things that I have seen . . .

I remember them, marching five abreast while I was watching from a side street. Isaac, the plumber, was in the front row, big, wide, and very tough. Next to him was the banker, short, skinny, dressed in black, holding his head high and brandishing an umbrella. I did not know the other three but they looked scared. Germans on horseback were herding them to their death.

I remember young children (I was one of them) taking candies and cigarettes to wounded Italian prisoners of war in a hospital, in Salonika. They (the prisoners) looked very surprised.

I remember a very dark evening when beaten soldiers returned from the front lines, tired, bloody, disheveled and with their heads bent. They walked slowly, a step ahead of their pursuers and were throwing their equipment behind bushes, in the fields, in the gardens. We picked up many things; they made interesting toys.

I remember a very thin woman, begging on a sidewalk, holding two very thin children; a big car drove by and splattered them with mud.

I remember a little shoe-shine boy in tattered clothes. He looked starved and tears streamed down his cheeks. He was watching a German soldier emptying his canteen in a garbage pail.

I remember the cattle cars tearing through the night, from Athens to Belgrade, through bombed-out cities and deserted fields, hurrying to get nowhere. The peasants, at dusk, would look at the disappearing shadows and cross themselves.

I remember Marika, homely, shy and very lonely. When it was found that she was pregnant, her father kicked her out because she had dishonored his name; he was a very strict man. When the war ended, her father was tried and shot for betraying patriots to the Gestapo. Marika ended in a whorehouse.

I remember the fellow who used to clean the latrines in the concentration camp of Bergen-Belsen. He was old and dirty, saliva ran from both sides of his mouth and he was always afraid. His name was Julien R. Many years ago he had been President of the Supreme Court of France. He was a Jew.

I remember Jako. He was my friend and six feet five inches tall. He was not very bright but very strong and afraid of nothing. He spat in the devil's eyes and in the faces of the German guards. He died in Israel. Rather than be taken alive, he pulled the pin off a grenade and blew himself and twelve Arabs to kingdom come. He was also a Jew.

I remember the priest who visited my father in the hospital every day for six months, talked with him, sang with him songs from the old country. He prayed when my father died. The priest was a Christian.

I remember the picture in *Life Magazine* of a priest sending soldiers to kill men and women in the name of God. That priest was also a Christian.

I remember . . . faces . . . sounds . . . Athens . . . sky, feelings, sweetness . . . never again . . . grayness, Germany, nothing. . . . God help . . . there is no God . . . gentle faces, hard faces . . . forgotten names . . . never again . . . rain, rain, rain . . . gentle faces, dead faces, I love you. I remember. . . . I remember. . . .

The Sewing Basket

Marga Randall
b. Lemförde, Germany, 1930

We stood in the middle of the cobblestone street in front of my grandparents' house. The windows were not shiny glass any more, with those lovely lace curtains. They were all boarded up. It was getting dark. I clutched my doll and my sewing basket close to me.

We had survived Kristallnacht in this village of Schermbeck, in the Rhineland, North Germany. We stood there, my mother, my Aunt Paula, my grandparents, and I. We were about to walk away from our home, where generations of my family had lived.

As we were leaving, my Christian friend, Irmgard, leaned out of her second story window and asked, "*Wo geht ihr hin?*" (Where are you going?) I told her I was not sure, but we would go to a big city and stay with my aunt's family. I couldn't even tell her when I would return. She had been a loyal and sweet friend to me and now I had to leave her. Impulsively I tossed my sewing basket to her. She caught it and began to cry.

We walked toward the train station silently. It was a long sad journey. My grandmother was ill, my Aunt Paula weak from worry and stress. As for me, at eight and one-half, I just felt secure because I had my mother there to hold my hand.

At the train station we boarded the train to Berlin. Special documents in hand allowing us to travel, we found our seats and the train slowly pulled away.

I loved this place. The village, the church bells so crystal-clear with few street noises to interfere. Horses' hooves, clickety-clack on the cobblestone streets, accompanied by pots and pans rattling in the distance. How excited I would get! But when the horse-drawn wagon appeared around the corner, I would stay close to the front door. The gypsies were coming through Schermbeck on their way to the countryside where they would camp overnight. I loved the lake where the ducks chattered, the swans honked and the frogs made their unique sound.

Our family welcomed us in Berlin. Through air raids, food shortages, and curfews, we managed to stay together until my mother, sister, and I were permitted to leave Germany in 1941.

Meanwhile, in Schermbeck during the war, my friend Irmgard kept under her bed a wooden suitcase built by her father. She stored all of her precious possessions in it. She carried it to the bunker out of the village during the deadly air raids. In the wooden suitcase was my sewing basket.

After the war, Irmgard married and had a family. In her dining room china closet sat a curious little sewing basket. If her children asked if they could play with it, the answer was always "No." When they were old enough to understand, Irmgard told them the story of a little Jewish girl who lived next door, her very good friend, who was made to leave her home one night because of Nazi persecution of the Jews.

Films, books, and records had appeared through the media about the murder of millions of Jews in concentration camps. Irmgard had been convinced that I was never coming back. She was so sure that I was a victim.

For a long time I blocked the tragic past out of my memory, but in 1981 I made contact with a minister friend, Reverend Wolfgang Bornebusch from Schermbeck. This was the beginning of a new life for me. I began to remember. I was able to express in words all that I had suppressed. But did I recall Irmgard and that moment we had to separate? Not until 1982. My return to Schermbeck was encouraged by the compassion of this young minister who saw the need to remind those village people that there had been a Jewish community that was a vital part of the success of the village for many years. My return was published in the local papers.

Irmgard read this article and saw my picture. Crying and in disbelief, she reached for paper and pen and began to write. "*Liebe Marga, Ich habe immer-noch dein kleines Nähkörbchen. . . .* I still have your little sewing basket. Would you like to have it returned to you? Now that I know you are alive and well, I am so very happy."

Tears running down my face, I wrote back to her. "Dear Irmgard, I can hardly find the words to express myself after all the years that have passed. Yes, I would love to have my sewing basket back, but please don't send it. I will return next year, we will have a reunion. You will be able to hand me my sewing basket. Thank you, dear friend, for giving me back some faith in humanity and your friendship."

Since our first reunion, and the indescribable moment when she handed me this precious piece of my past, we have met eight times. Each time we look at each other in disbelief.

My sewing basket will be part of my legacy to my grandchildren, in loving memory of friendship.

Children from the Camps Going to England

George Lauer
b. Hamburg, Germany, 1907

My wife Edith and I were inmates of the concentration camp Terezin (Theresienstadt), located in the heart of Bohemia (today's Czech Republic). On May 5, 1945, we were liberated by the Russian Army. Because of a typhus epidemic and because of the transportation difficulties at the time, it took several months to liquidate the camp. Edith and I were asked by the Czechoslovak government to stay on and help.

Edith was a social worker specializing in child care, and she was employed as such from the beginning at Terezin. On liberation she was responsible for children, mostly orphans, who were not taken to their respective countries. By the middle of June there were at least a thousand children left at Terezin.

About that time a group of people from the United Nations Relief Agency appeared at the camp. They told Edith that the British government, together with Jewish agencies, wanted to take one thousand children who had no relatives to be brought up in England; they wanted three hundred of the Terezin orphans to be the first contingent.

They assumed that children who had been through events such as these kids had would be difficult to handle. They asked Edith to come with the children and stay with them for some time. Edith agreed, provided that they would take me too.

In mid-August, we received word that a group of planes was coming to Prague to pick us up. Edith assembled the children. We walked to the train station, a walk of perhaps half an hour. Two extra cars were added to the train for us. On its frequent stops, many children ran out, and Edith had a hard time getting them back in. No wonder. This was the first time in years that these kids had been outside a camp. We actually lost two little boys who were left behind; rail workers caught them and sent them on the next train to Prague, where Edith was waiting.

The children slept those first two nights in an empty school, waiting for transportation to London. The planes were delayed by bad weather. The kids roamed the streets of Prague, much admired by many locals, who bought them sweets, toys, and other treats.

Finally, we got word that the planes had arrived. In the early morning everybody was bused to the Prague airport. At the airport, we were greeted by the

British military attaché. While three hundred kids milled around us, we were told that there were only nine planes, not ten, as we had expected. This meant that Edith, who had made lists of how the children would be distributed, had to rearrange everything. She did this in some fashion while we all walked across the field.

The planes were four-engine bombers with no seats. The facilities were two buckets behind some old blankets. We distributed the kids somehow into eight planes, keeping the youngest ones for the ninth plane, in which we would ride. Eight planes took off one after the other with a great roar. In the remaining plane, Edith tried to settle the little ones down by sitting them on the floor in small groups. I was standing with a crewman at the steps, ready to crawl in, when two Czech customs agents ran toward us. They had heard we were taking children out of the country and that this was not allowed. One of them said, "We don't even know who is leaving!" This gave me my cue. I told the crewman, "Let's get the hell out of here!" He phoned the captain, while I told the agents that I had a complete list (!) of every person and handed it to them. We slipped up the steps and pulled them up as the pilot started all engines and the poor customs agents had to run away from the propeller wash.

On the flight, Edith had her hands full quieting the kids down. Most of them were sick. One little girl had to go to the toilet every ten minutes, she was so excited. All planes made a refueling stop in Holland. Everybody sat on the grass in beautiful sunshine. The crew took out their food, big loaves of white bread and chunks of cheese. When they realized that we had no food, they shared with us. Then we took off again to fly to Windermere, England. During the flight the captain called me to the cockpit where they all listened to the radio to hear Japan's surrender. It was August 15, 1945, and the end of the war!

Landing in Windermere, everybody was loaded into buses and taken to a former war workers' camp which had been prepared for the children. On the way we drove through some smaller towns where people lined the streets and cheered. At the camp we were greeted by a group of social workers, most of them previously trained by Anna Freud. I left after a few days, having been hired by my former professor to work in a chemical factory in Chesterfield. Edith stayed with the children, first in Windermere, later with the younger kids in a children's home in the south of England.

Edith had become very close to the children. The closest was a little girl, age six, named Zdenka, who had attached herself to Edith on the plane, considering her to be her mother (her real mother had been lost at Auschwitz). Zdenka was a lovely girl with dark, curly hair. She did well in school and learned English quickly. She was heartbroken when after fifteen months we left for the United States as originally planned. We were later told that Zdenka ran away from school to catch up with us!

When we settled down in New York we tried to adopt her, but it proved to be too difficult, in part because of the committee's reluctance to have any of the kids adopted except by relatives. However, we kept in touch with Zdenka over all the years, writing back and forth, exchanging photos so that we could observe her growing up. She lives in London and came several times to visit us in Pittsburgh. When Edith passed away in early 1993, she called me, and we write to each other frequently. Zdenka has visited me twice since then, to mourn with me.

The Chief of the Gestapo

Robert R. Mendler
b. Nowy-Targ, Poland, 1925

When the German army occupied Nowy-Targ, Poland in 1939, I was thirteen. I was assigned to work as a house boy for the Chief of the Gestapo.

I did all kinds of work for him, to the best of my ability. But no matter how hard I tried, every day when he came home from his office, he would punish me for no reason. His beatings and screaming were unbearable.

After work I went home and cried to my mother. "Why is he punishing me?" I asked. "I do my best but he's never satisfied."

My mother tried to encourage me. "The war will be over soon, and times will be better."

But in truth, I grew more and more bitter at this cruel and unjust man. And during the succeeding years of the war when I was sent to several concentration camps, I could never forget him. He had put a mark on me. All through the years I prayed—even when I lost my faith—that I would find him some day.

On April 25, 1949, I left Germany for the United States. The journey from Bremerhaven took ten days on a transport ship, the steamship *Marine Jumper*. There were three thousand displaced persons on the ship.

Three days before reaching our destination in Boston, as I was going downstairs for lunch, I saw him. It was the man I had dreamed and prayed to God to let me find some day. He was on his way up the stairs, but I couldn't reach him because there were many people between us, coming up the stairs with their food. The kitchen was below and we had to go down to get our food and carry it up to the dining facility.

The only thing I could do was scream—"A Nazi!"—and point my finger at him.

Suddenly the ship became riotous, a jungle. Everyone behind him was trying to put their hands on him, to kill a Nazi. People beat him, pulled him by the hair, pummelled him anywhere they could lay hands on him. After all, how many times did one get a chance to see and capture a Chief of the Gestapo—and on top of that, one who was escaping with us to the land of the free?

The ship's police immediately came to his rescue, or he surely would have been killed. They put him in quarantine, under guard. But we still weren't satisfied; we wanted to dump him in the ocean. The captain and crew couldn't control the crowd and their noise.

The next day, May 2nd—which was, fittingly, the anniversary of my liberation from concentration camp—a U.S. Coast Guard cutter pulled up to our ship and picked him and me up, taking us to Boston.

Here, however, the emigration office didn't know what to do with us. I suggested that they send a radio photo of him to my hometown in Poland—I was so sure that I had the right man.

A few days later the reply came: we want him for war crimes in Poland against the Jewish people and humanity. The emigration office sent him back to Poland to stand trial. I learned later that he had a short trial and was hanged.

After this—from this miracle that happened to me—I began to believe that there is a God.

Herr Schluemper

Arnold Blum
b. Nuremberg, Germany, 1922

After emigrating from Germany to the United States, I joined the army. Through my work as a liaison with the Germans in Blumenthal, a small town between Vegesack and Bremerhaven, I got to know a German Social Democrat. It was he who first told me about a local Nazi, Herr Schluemper, who had bragged about his participation in the events of the Kristallnacht.

My sources in Blumenthal told me that Schluemper had been cleared after a perfunctory denazification trial by the British, to whom had been assigned the Bremen enclave for postwar administration.

This aroused my interest and I made some discreet inquiries about town as to Schluemper's reputation. Everyone who knew him confirmed that he had been a bad actor, an active Nazi who had bragged about beating up Jews and plundering their property during Kristallnacht.

I decided that Schluemper would have to be tended to, and that I would do it.

Personal interventions of this sort were frowned upon by the United States Army. I had to be very careful to avoid being discovered. I borrowed a field jacket without insignia of rank or unit identification patches from a friend, and found a cap without branch of service piping. I strapped on a German P-38 pistol in a shoulder holster and put on the field jacket over it. I also put on army gloves to protect my hands, since I did not want to rip my skin if I hit the man in the mouth. The pistol was only intended as a precaution in case he should prove to be more than I could manage with my hands alone.

I took the duty driver into my confidence and asked him to take me to Schluemper's neighborhood, which I had reconnoitered before. I asked the driver to leave the engine running until I got back.

We arrived about two hours after dark. I got out of the command car and walked back to Schluemper's house. The entrance was on the side. I entered the garden gate by the sidewalk and walked back till I found the door and rang the bell.

After a short while, a light went on inside and a teenage girl opened the door.

"Good evening, miss. I am looking for Herr Schluemper's house. Am I in the right place?"

"Yes, you are, sir."

"Could I speak to him, please?"

"May I know in what connection?"

"It is a personal matter I wish to discuss with him."

She called "Vati!" and after a short time, a middle-aged man of medium height and stocky build appeared in the light of the hallway. He wore slippers, an old-fashioned undershirt and trousers held up by suspenders.

"Are you Herr Schluemper?" I asked.

"Yes."

Meanwhile the girl went back into one of the rooms, leaving us alone.

In a business-like voice I said, "Herr Schluemper, it has come to my notice that you were an active Nazi. Is that right?"

He seemed taken aback and said, "What do you want from me? I have already been cleared by the British."

"This is of no interest to me at all," I answered.

He continued, "Sure, I was a member, like so many. I paid my dues, but never was very active."

"That's not my understanding," I said. "I've made extensive inquiries about you with people who know you well. They tell me you've been very active, and I can be quite specific. You participated in the beating of Jews and the destruction of their property in Bremen during the night of Wednesday, the 9th, to Thursday, the 10th of November, 1938, and you even bragged about it."

"I had nothing to do with that."

"Herr Schluemper, you are not only a liar, but a *gottverfluchter Schweinehund!*"

With these words I let fly a tremendous haymaker which landed on his nose. He raised his arms to defend himself, but I caught him under the chin with a left uppercut which straightened him. Then I hit him again, even harder than the first time, and caught him on his left temple, knocking him down. His head hit the concrete floor with a thud and he lay at my feet motionless. I was tempted to kick his head, but did not.

The girl, who had heard the commotion, came running out of her room and screamed for help. I took another look at the prostrate figure at my feet, repeating *"gottverfluchter Schweinehund!"* and walked out the door.

The girl kept screaming for help. I was tempted to run, but resisted the urge. When I arrived at the command car I climbed in next to the driver and he took off immediately.

"What did you do to the s.o.b., kill him?"

"I don't know, and I don't give a ——!"

We returned to headquarters without incident. I returned the field jacket to my friend's locker, put away the hat, the pistol and the gloves. I washed up and got dressed to go to the enlisted men's club, the Schnucky-Putzi Bar.

The Miracle

Malka Baran
b. Warsaw, Poland, 1927

I lived in Poland with my younger brother, mother and father. I attended school, played with friends, celebrated birthdays and holidays, lived the life of a child.

When I was twelve my country, Poland—my city, Chestochowa—lost their independence after only one day of resistance. The German army entered and life began to change. Decrees were issued, pamphlets were distributed, hate posters and pictures appeared on buildings, billboards, and store fronts . . . all proclaiming "hate the Jew, the Jew is evil." Jewish children were no longer allowed to attend schools. My friend and I continued our studies in secret, in our teachers' homes. Then our teachers disappeared—"sent away to work," was the rumor. Soon my family's doctor was no longer available. He too disappeared. Next my father's printing shop was closed by the Nazis and the machines removed for the German army. We were given rations for a while.

Incidents of violence against the Jews occurred more and more often. A rabbi was brutally beaten on the street by German soldiers, his beard cut in a grotesque way. My brother and I, as well as our friends, were no longer allowed to play outside.

Then came the decree: Jews are no longer permitted to live in all the areas of the city. They must move to the ghetto within two days. No one is allowed to leave the ghetto; those who dare will be shot on the spot.

And then, early one winter morning, before dawn, you are awakened by your parents, who are fully dressed. Whispering, they tell you to quickly get ready to leave. You run to the window and see the street lined with German SS troops, machine guns in their hands. From all the apartments and houses your neighbors and friends, young and old, are being driven out into the middle of the street.

And then the knock on the door—not a polite, gentle knock—but a bang! The door flies open and you are pushed out. You see your parents, white as chalk, being screamed at: "Out! Out!" You run down the stairs, the SS man's gun almost in your back, and you join the others in the middle of the street, arranged in rows, row by row, "Order! Order!"

This is how my world began to crumble. I was fifteen.

The rest you study in history books; but there are things history books do not tell.

They don't tell how you die little by little—how your heart breaks when your mother is taken away that morning, and your father is beaten by a soldier because he dares to try to go with her, and is thrown back to the line. We didn't know it then, but my mother, only thirty-five, was sent in one of those cattle trains to Treblinka—to the gas chambers, to be murdered.

And you don't have time to mourn because one cruel event follows another. Without a home, without a bed, a prisoner, shouted at, driven from one place to another, you exist. Your father and brother are with you. You huddle together, shocked and helpless.

Then you die again when your father and brother are taken away "to work," they say . . . and they never return . . . shot on the railroad track . . . my brother, thirteen, my father, thirty-seven.

And then you don't care anymore. You have stopped living. And you are taken to a concentration camp and become a useful prisoner in a labor camp.

For almost three years you merely exist, wearing the same skirt, blouse, and coat in which you left your home on that morning, eating the piece of dry bread in the morning and water with potato peels in the evening, sleeping on a long board, sixteen women in a row, fully clothed—no linen, no pillows or blankets, two additional boards above you—being counted like cattle each morning and evening.

Days follow days, months follow months. You are hungry, cold, sick. You want to die but you don't die.

And then you are liberated! The cruel German overseers are suddenly gone and you are alone. The Jewish prisoners—alone, their spirits broken, their bodies—skeletons.

You don't know what is happening. No newspapers, no radios, no communication. You hear someone shouting: "Come, come! You are free! The Russians are here!"

You are being pushed and you follow the crowd.

You approach the gates and are being pushed through them.

You continue on to the city, the city that was once your home.

You see jeeps and tanks with Russian soldiers, some wounded.

You hear shooting. You run into a building and hide in the cellar.

You crumble into a corner and you cry. For the first time, you cry.

My new life slowly unfolded. Like a newborn baby, or a person after a long and horrible sickness, I took step after step toward an emotional and physical recovery.

I am now a wife, a mother, and a grandmother.

I am a teacher and love my profession.

And I believe in miracles.

If I can love, laugh, create new lives, feel joy as well as pain—isn't that a miracle?

And if I still believe in human kindness—and I do—isn't that a miracle too?

To Bear Witness about the Holocaust

Alexander Zwillich
b. Boryslaw, Poland, 1925

The Germans herded the Jews of Boryslaw, my native town, from the ghetto into the forced labor camps—the next step in the degradation of the Jews. I was put into a small camp in Truskawiec, a town near Boryslaw.

We were a small group of people who worked in the nearby rotary oil rigs. I worked as a roughneck—a job that under normal conditions requires a robust grownup man, not an undernourished teenager. This type of work was then, and still is today, difficult, dirty, and often dangerous.

One afternoon, while in the Boryslaw camp for treatment of an injury I sustained at work, I decided to look for Mr. Carl Unter. He was the former director of the Jewish Orphanage in Drohobycz, where I had lived from 1936 until the outbreak of war. All my family having been "deported," I did not have anyone living in the Boryslaw camp, and to see Director Unter seemed somehow appropriate. This may have been because while I lived in the orphanage he was to me and some others of us, I guess, a father figure.

I found Mr. Unter sitting on a crude bunk in the communal quarters in what used to be a machine shop. The anticipated pleasure of seeing him, however, turned to sadness, for I found him a much changed person from the one I knew before the war. Though we both lived in much diminished circumstances, the life style of Director Unter was proportionally much more reduced than mine. His life style before the war had appeared to me, an orphan from a poor household, splendid. Therefore, his descent into the hell of the labor camp looked to be much deeper than mine.

Mr. Unter recognized me, greeted me warmly, invited me to sit on the bunk opposite his, and we began to talk. Initially, I felt awkward sitting across from the director and talking to him as if we were equals. After some time, I no longer remembered that before the war, when I lived in the orphanage, the few conversations between us were short and one sided: he talked and I listened.

Now, however, he treated me as if I were a grownup while I continued to show him the same measure of respect I always did. To me he was the director; the Nazis could not diminish his stature in my eyes. Though not physically imposing, his demeanor was that of a gentleman. His blue eyes still had the keen look I well remembered, and he was as neatly dressed as possible under the circumstances. There remained in his look traces of the former officer of the Austrian Army, a man to be respected.

Our conversation began with current topics—the individual and common tragedies we had experienced. Soon, however, Mr. Unter brought the conversation to a personal level. At one point he said to me, "I strongly doubt that I will survive the war." I politely attempted to disagree, but he went on: "You are young and in good health and have a chance to live through the catastrophe that has befallen us. It is for you to try to survive and be a witness of what is happening to us Jews. Someone must live to tell of the terror."

The seriousness of the moment strongly affected me, and I promised solemnly to try to fulfill the mission with which he charged me. I did this partly because of the impact the moment had on me, and partly out of respect for Mr. Unter. We did not say much else after that, and I left.

Though our talk strongly impressed me, its effect did not last long. Life was precarious, and the uncertain future did not allow thoughts other than those concerning minute-by-minute survival. The idea of a mission sank into my memory.

Some months after my visit with Director Unter, the Nazis deported the Jews of Boryslaw, me among them, to concentration camps located further west. I never saw the director again.

The war ended, and I had the good fortune of fulfilling the first part of the mission given to me by Carl Unter—I survived the Holocaust.

Looking back now, I wonder how much his charge to survive influenced me in a conscious way. I do not know. I'm willing to ascribe to it a modicum of importance.

In any case, it was only after my liberation from the concentration camps that I fully recognized the importance of that conversation with Mr. Unter.

Then, my seemingly forgotten mission emerged from the recesses of memory, demanding fulfillment. I did not resist; on the contrary, I willingly began, and still do bear witness of the Holocaust, but only to listeners who I think should hear it. To those, I tell my story as I remember it.

Mr. Unter, wherever your spirit may be, I've kept my promise!

It Shall Not Be Forgotten Nor Forgiven!

Rubin Udler*
  b. Braila, Romania, 1925

Shortly after the outbreak of the war in 1941, all my mother's relatives from the small town of Artsyz, in Southern Bessarabia, ran away before the advancing Romanian and German armies. My mother's parents, sister and brothers and their families, altogether sixteen people, were only able to get as far as Odessa before it was surrounded by the enemy. In October 1941, the fascists occupied the city and immediately began to persecute the Jews. Endless humiliation and privation were visited on them. Local marauders and the Romanian soldiers robbed them of items of value. Other valuables were bartered for bread or soup, or used as bribes to extend the stay in Odessa rather than be given over to torture by the Romanian gendarmes or German SS.

The governor of Transnistria, G. Alexianu, issued many orders aimed chiefly at the annihilation of the Jewish population of Odessa and environs. After January 1942, none of our relatives remained in Odessa.

Here is what happened to them.

Nooham Gleizer, my uncle, whom I remember as a modest man, was driven to suicide. He had been forcibly separated from his wife Chayka, a calm and dutiful woman, and from his twelve-year-old son Uzya, a very obedient boy. My uncle was beaten and sneered at to the point where he must have lost all hope. Early one day, he said part of the morning prayer: "O look down from heaven, and see how we are become a mockery and derision among the nations; and accounted as sheep led to the slaughter, to be slain and destroyed; to be buffeted and disgraced. And yet, for all this, we have not forgotten Your name . . . " Then he hanged himself with his pants belt. One can hardly imagine the depth of despair to which he was driven by the Romanian monsters. I still find it hard to believe that a mature Jew would take his own life, in defiance of his religion.

My mother's elder brother, Uncle Etsik, was married to Chona Kooza, a native of Shtefaneshti, a shtetl near the Romanian town of Botoshani. They had two children: Misha, same age as I, and Rita, two years younger. They were fine, gifted, and excellent students. Chona, an intelligent woman, astute and resolute, persuaded her husband that they should voluntarily appear before the

---

*Translated from Russian by Alexander Zwillich.

Romanian police in Odessa. She was going to explain in Romanian to the commissioner of the police who they were and where they were from. The Romanians, among whom she had lived before marriage, and whom she considered good people and God-fearing, were going to let them go home to Artsyz.

After the four of them went to the police, they disappeared without a trace. Chona, it appears, made a fatal error. Those Romanians were not the ones she knew, but legionaries, imbued with the spirit of nationalism and wild anti-Semitism.

My mother's younger brother, Mottya, with his wife Dora and their two children, Unah, six years old, and Fira, one year old, attempted desperately to gain time before the deportation to the ghetto. With Mottya were my grandmother Udel and grandfather Wolf, and their youngest daughter Sonya, who took care of them, her husband Velvel, and son, Ezya.

Mottya was strong, clever, bold, and full of energy. He spoke Romanian and German well, and was often successful in buying his way out of the clutches of the executioners. But his luck eventually ran out. During one roundup all of them, from the babe-in-arms to the seventy-six-year-old man, were deported.

After the war, when we obtained permission from the Soviet government to travel from Belgorod-Dnestrovsky to Beltsi, that is, from the Ukraine to Moldova, with a special pass, my Uncle Mottya told my mother the following story.

The Jews from Odessa, caught in the roundups, either walked in convoys or rode in open freight wagons to Slobodka, a deportation ghetto. After they arrived in Slobodka, my relatives spent several days and nights in an unheated hut. They were frightened, hungry, and cold. Children and oldsters sat or lay on a dirt floor in a corner, where they tried to help each other keep warm.

Mottya and his sister's husband, Velvel, used to leave the hut covertly to try to get something to eat and to find out what was going on. One time, however, Velvel did not return. His disappearance made our relatives even more fearful, and they cried endlessly. What happened we do not know. He may have been caught and sent away to do heavy labor some place from which he did not return. He could have been shot by some gendarme who did not like his looks.

In the selection actions, families were separated. The Jews were segregated into categories: old people, unattached children, the sick, et cetera. The segregated groups were transported from the ghetto, no one knew where to. In one such selection my grandparents, Aunt Sonya and her son Ezya were separated from the rest of the family. By a miracle, Uncle Mottya, his wife Dora, and their children found themselves on the same train.

They were sent to a ghetto in the village of Suchaya Balka in the district of Berezovka, where for two and a half years they went through indescribable suffering. Death was their constant companion throughout the terrible and seemingly endless time.

In the spring of 1944, my Uncle Mottya came out of the ghetto looking almost like a skeleton. His wife and children were even more wasted than he.

After Uncle Mottya told us the story, my mother and he cried for a long time, shedding bitter tears over their lost relatives: father and mother, brothers and sisters-in-law, sister and brother-in-law, nieces and nephews.

Uncle Mottya said *Kaddish* in the plundered local synagogue, my mother and Aunt Dora cried without limit, and we—Unah, little Fira, and I—with heavy hearts remembered our dear relatives.

At the destroyed and desecrated Jewish cemetery in Beltsi we placed flowers on the mass grave of the victims shot by the Romanian legionaries or Iron Guards (Romanian fascists), German fascists, and local monsters.

To remember our perished twelve relatives, we had their names engraved on the granite headstone of my Uncle Mottya following his death in 1975.

The world still does not comprehend, it seems, what happened to these people! Contrary to what some current politicians say, the Romanian fascists were no more "humane" than the German fascists. From June 22, 1941, until May 1942, the Romanians tried methodically, without mercy, day after day, in every village, in every city of Bessarabia, Bukovina, and Transnistria, to annihilate the Jews. Without any compassion even for infants, pregnant women, or weak oldsters, the Jews were either killed or deported to the death camps and ghettos in Transnistria, where most of them died a horrible death. The few who survived were sent to slave-labor camps where they continued to live under very difficult conditions until March 1944.

The deaths of the Jews took many forms: they died from cold, hunger, sickness, executions by hanging and bullets, burning and drowning. How many died under what condition no one knows, because the executioners did not leave documentation of their savagery.

After the war, when the demographic data of the war years, the war-crime trial testimonies of witnesses and the accused, the pertinent accounts of the gendarmerie, principal reports and other documents were analyzed, it was established (the numbers differ among investigators) that in Bessarabia, Bukovina, and Transnistria about 400,000 people were murdered for being Jews.

Can we possibly and should we possibly forget these horrible deeds and forgive the killers? No! We cannot, and what is more important, we shall not! The spilled blood demands it.

Addendum
Seen with My Own Eyes:
Stories by American Liberators

An American soldier, in a letter from Germany in April 1945, writes: "It was so horrible that had I not seen it, I wouldn't have believed it." Another soldier, upon viewing all the death and destruction, says, "That day we knew why we were fighting this war." And a nurse at Gusen, upon hearing of Holocaust deniers, concludes, "I knew I finally had to speak." These words summarize the shocked reactions of all liberators who saw the forced marches, the concentration and forced labor camps at the end of the war.

The stories in this section visualize telling, somehow typical events. Heart-rending scenes are drawn for us: a dead prisoner lying at the side of a road, clutching a photograph of his family; a U.S. tank column halted by rows of "twisted, disfigured, starved, naked, charred, dead male bodies" sprawled across a road; haggard and filthy women freed from a slave labor camp, sobbing and clinging to their liberators. Detailed accounts of liberators' arrivals at two concentration camps are contained in "A Letter from Dachau" and "I Saw Buchenwald." At Dachau, we are shown not just dead bodies but barracks, crematory, and gallows, instruments of mass murder "more gruesome than any fiction writer could imagine." The writer at Buchenwald takes us along with him on "an eerie Tour of Horror." His tour, conducted by a camp internee, relates details of the prisoners' lives and shows us the physical plant: torture weapons, crematorium and other death houses, barracks, the laboratory where human beings were used for medical experiments, the sports arena where prisoners "played" games with SS troops who were armed with clubs.

These stories don't merely put the lie to those who would deny the facts or the importance of the Holocaust. They reaffirm and deepen the pathos of the stories written by survivors throughout this book. In fact, the liberators if anything describe the horrors in more awful, more graphic terms than our writers were able to bring themselves to use. The details that come out force readers to accept, even while we cannot imagine, the immensity of Nazi crimes in World War II.

The final story in this section was written by a man who left Germany after being released from Dachau concentration camp, then returned as an American soldier. "Re-Entry" thus speaks for both survivors and liberating American soldiers. The story concludes with the writer's feeling of mixed hope and sadness at all men's potential for good and evil. "Re-Entry" becomes an eloquent and fitting statement with which to conclude and sum up the meaning of this book.

A. B.

The Photograph

Lee Kessler*

Technical Sergeant, 8th Air Force Division, 306th Bomb Group, 368th Bomb Squadron

As the Russians advanced through Hungary and approached the Danube River in late March of '45, the Germans evacuated our prisoner of war camp and marched us toward the west. We marched past a place called Mauthausen. A group of prisoners from the concentration camp was coming down the road. They were Hungarian Jews, guarded by the SS. We were halted at the side of the road for these walking skeletons to pass, but when they came even with us their guards stopped them. One of our guys threw a cigarette toward them. They mobbed toward it, like a pack of hungry dogs. The SS beat them back.

A spectacle was made for our benefit of one who was too weak to get up. As we moved on we heard pistol shots, and we knew what they were for. All those who fell from exhaustion and could not get up were shot. Two prisoners followed in a wagon and loaded the bodies.

As I came upon one of the bodies at the side of the road, I noticed a crinkled photograph near his hand. He lay with one arm stretched out, as if reaching for the picture. He had been shot in the head. I moved off the road to get a better look at the photograph and was about to pick it up when a guard hollered for me to get back.

The picture was of a woman and two children. As I looked back, a butterfly landed on the man.

During the rest of the march, I thought about this man, dead by the side of the road. Probably the last thing he looked at was this picture of his family—all he had left. And where were they? Dead or in some other camp, I guessed.

Some time in the fifties I started my drawing, but finally put it away because I felt no one would understand what I was trying to portray. It lay in a drawer until two years ago. Then at a prisoner of war convention, I heard another POW being interviewed. He told a story about how he saw a man, who was lying on the ground, pull a picture from his pocket. As the man kissed the photograph, the guard shot him.

---

*Sgt. Kessler was shot down over Germany and was a POW for two years.

Drawing by Lee Kessler

Germany, 1945: View from a Tank

Henry L. Marinelli
Captain, 493rd Armored Field Artillery, 12th Armored Division, 7th Army

Death Scene at Landsberg, Germany

Our 12th Armored Division had just crossed the Rhine river, on a flimsy pontoon bridge, moving into Worms, Germany. We had the German military army on the run, averaging fifteen miles a day.

In March of 1945, warm spring air had finally arrived. Our tanks motored along the beautiful countryside, past the farmers plowing fields, the trees and rolling terrain deceitfully picturesque. Ox-drawn carts with large oblong wooden tanks sprayed cow urine on the ground, causing a noxious stench.

In the distance, smoke came from inside the dense forest. Ordinarily, this scene is not unusual in day-to-day combat. But Captain Meuser, in the lead vehicle, felt something was curious about it. Motoring at a faster pace, we approached a dirt road. The column turned left through an open wire gate, into a large fenced-in enclosure. Several feet inside, our vehicles came to an abrupt halt. A panoramic view could be seen from the top of my tank.

Row after row of twisted, disfigured, starved, naked, charred, dead male bodies lay sprawled across the road, blocking our advance. Clouds of dark smoke rose above the camp, which reeked of burning tar and flesh. Flames burst out on all sides of the barracks, which were built halfway below the ground to prevent escape. No doubt, before our arrival the Germans must have poured gasoline on the roofs of the barracks with the internees inside.

A mix of emotions—disbelief, rage—overwhelmed us; tears blinded our eyes.

After recovering from the shock, our first reaction amid the confusion and excitement was to aid any possible survivors. Scanning the thin disfigured bodies, I noticed a skeleton-like man doubled up in agony, unable to make a sound. His arm was outstretched, motioning for help. Lifting up his head, I tried to make him eat a piece of K ration, but he could not ingest the food. Just then, one of our medics shouted out, "Don't give them any food, the Red Cross is coming and will administer any care they will need."

Suddenly three survivors appeared in front of me. They tried to communicate with me in German, but to no avail. Their faces were incredibly sad. All three were too emaciated to draw tears. The one clothed in a green and white striped uniform, with little energy left, gave me a weak but grateful smile. Through gestures I asked them to pose in front of the half-buried barracks, and to pull up their pants legs. My comrades and I took group photos standing among the burning dead. I wanted these pictures as a testimony, to record these atrocities for posterity, so that this should never occur again.

As our thoughts turned to seeking those responsible for these acts, we heard gunfire. Two German guards and a woman had fled into a nearby woods. We chased them, shooting until all three surrendered with upstretched arms, trembling with fear. We had enough hate in our hearts to shoot in retaliation for the victims inside the death camp.

Captain Meuser, who had fled Germany with his parents when Hitler took power, shouted questions at the prisoners in fluent German. He was raging mad. I had never seen this side of him. Hardly ever did he display any emotion back in training.

The captain ordered his driver to fetch the *Bürgermeister* from Landsberg. The jeep spun off with great speed. The driver returned quickly. Captain Meuser always carried a whip. Slapping his boots, he started lashing out in German. After five minutes of his raging, the *Bürgermeister*, trembling, with a shaky voice, began giving excuses and denials. He said he knew nothing about the atrocities. The captain ordered him to bring civilians to clean up the compound.

That day, we knew why we were fighting this war.

The Slave Labor Camp

To expect trouble on this beautiful spring day in April was remote from our minds.

Our column was spearheading now toward Munich, Germany. We had just accepted a new member into the U.S. Army. A scrawny, shaggy, mixed-breed dog from the death camps had decided to jump into an army half-track named Lovie. He was undernourished and dirty; we fed him K rations. Elliot, the driver of Lovie, named him *Kaputt*, which means "all is finished" in German.

Looking out over the landscape, we noticed wooden towers. Pillars of huge, sinister-looking lumber stretched upward twenty feet above the ground. On top of each was a platform for sentry guards to keep watch over what we soon saw were slave laborers.

The column came upon a small, picturesque country village. In the middle of town we were confronted with six or seven German officials waiting to surrender. Two were dressed in German uniforms. An elderly male civilian with a huge belly was waving a white flag. He appeared to be the town *Bürgermeister*.

When he saw them, Captain Meuser vehemently slapped his right boot with his whip, denouncing the mayor for enslaving humans against their will. The mayor responded meekly, his head hung low. Then the mayor got into the captain's jeep and they sped to the other end of town. The rest of us followed quickly.

We came upon a dilapidated building enclosure with a large swinging gate. A group of mostly women hung on the wire fence screaming and weeping with joy, knowing they would soon be set free. As the mayor opened the gate, cheers rang out. The women all looked haggard, bewildered. Their clothes were worn out, dirty and torn from overwork. A few had men's working pants under their dresses, with working shoes on. Odors of uncleanness came from their bodies.

Inside the barracks, about fifty people shared living quarters, with no running water. Each family or group had a fifteen-gallon galvanized bucket for a toilet. The stench was overwhelming. There were few openings for the sun to penetrate, so that a dim, dismal atmosphere hung over the room.

A few women became hysterical and lunged with their fists at the mayor's face and body. Some knelt near our feet and with their arms clutched our legs, sobbing. Some women hugged us. About a dozen women ran toward the houses, jabbering in Polish, looking for the German civilians who had mistreated them for so many years. The Polish women told us about how the German soldiers had raped them and the farmers had beaten them to produce more work in the fields.

At the same time the dog, Kaputt, started barking furiously while grabbing the mayor's pants leg and shaking it back and forth. He sensed that these were the enemies who had mistreated him at the death camp.

It took only minutes for the liberated people to vanish from this hideous village. Gathering their few possessions, they scattered toward the road of freedom.

Gusen: A Nurse's Tale

Marjorie Butterfield
First Lieutenant, 59th Field Hospital, 3rd Army

We arrived at Gusen Concentration Camp in Austria about two weeks after the camp had been liberated. I was an army nurse, assigned to the 59th Field Hospital.

The camp was surrounded by a high wall, the terrain barren, the buildings drab. Over a thousand men with shaved heads either sat dejectedly on the ground or aimlessly milled about. They were all so emaciated, they looked as if they could hardly stay alive.

Actually many of them didn't. Every morning, a truck picked up the dead bodies and took a full load to the cemetery nearby.

The patients in the hospital were suffering from tuberculosis, typhus, infections, anemia, and diseases caused by severe vitamin deficiency. When taking care of our wounded soldiers in the Field Hospital we had plenty of antibiotics, whole blood, plasma, and intravenous feedings. Here, there was a tremendous shortage of all these necessities. We felt helpless.

If ever patients needed to be comforted, needed tender loving care, these unfortunate souls did, but it was difficult because of the language barrier. All of us—doctors, nurses, and corpsmen—were given the opportunity to take German lessons. But progress was slow, and I hoped that I could convey by a tender touch or the look on my face that I cared.

Although we had enough food for ourselves, there was not enough for the patients. One day on my way to our mess hall I saw two men boiling chicken feet that had been thrown in the garbage, to make soup. I couldn't eat my lunch that day.

On the Women's Ward, there were only about sixty-five patients, and they were in better physical shape than the men. Many were well-educated and could speak English. They were of various nationalities and religions. They told me about the hardships, indignities, and cruelties they had endured. None of them knew what had happened to their families, except for those who had seen them killed or led to the gas chamber.

One day there was great excitement among the women. One of them had started her menstrual period! Stress and malnutrition had caused all of them to cease having periods. Since one of them became a "normal woman" they all felt it would soon happen to them too.

All the nurses longed to see the women smile, and we found how little gifts brought out those bright looks. Since we couldn't shop in a store, we searched our belongings to give them makeup, underwear, pens, pencils, toothpaste, toothbrushes, and combs.

Our patients were courageously determined to make new lives for themselves as they began to have hope now that the war was over. Their first goal was to find out about their families, and our Red Cross workers began to search for information for them. But perhaps that hope was in vain as, after two months, the camp was put in the Russian zone of the Army of Occupation, and our hospital was sent to Czechoslovakia.

I tried to suppress all the memories of that camp, and refused to talk about it when I returned. But one evening forty years later, I heard a man on television saying that the Holocaust never happened and that it was false propaganda to turn people against the Germans. Then I knew I finally had to speak.

A Letter from Dachau

Arthur Peternel
Captain, 48th Engineer Combat Battalion,
1108th Combat Engineers, 5th Army

APRIL 29, 1945

Dear Collie,

Yesterday I witnessed one of the most horrible sights that anyone can imagine. It was so horrible that had I not seen it, I wouldn't have believed it. Even now, I wonder if what I saw could possibly be true in this civilized world.

I visited the German concentration camp at Dachau. You've probably read about it in the newspapers, but I want to put here in writing what I actually saw, so that you will know that the horror of what was described in the paper is not propaganda.

It was one of those cold, blustery, spring days, with rain, snow and sleet mixed with short periods of sunshine. The fruit trees were in blossom, patches of flowers seemed to shimmer in the chill air.

As I approached the far edge of town the road ran parallel to the railroad track. A train had been left standing on the tracks. Through the open doors of the box cars, I saw them—bodies. Cars full of them! They apparently had died of starvation, for the bodies were thin and emaciated, just skin and bones. A full-grown man, and his thighs were no bigger around than my arm.

The enclosure covered several acres. Inside were prisoners of all nationalities, numbering, I was told, some forty-five thousand. They were housed in filthy wooden barracks, surrounded by a high barbed-wire fence, electrically charged, so that they could not escape. All were garbed in striped uniforms, and as an added precaution to prevent their escape, giant dogs had been trained to attack any man in the striped uniform. I was told that from thirty to forty died per day, from lack of food or wounds that had been inflicted by the guards. These dead were unceremoniously dumped on a pile and later carted off.

But the most horrible sight of all was the crematory. There was carried on the most systematic mass murder program that a fiendish brain could conjure. The men were brought to this place and forced to remove all their clothing, take a hot shower, and then forced into a gas chamber and asphyxiated. Later the bodies were cremated, and the ashes supposedly placed in earthenware jars and sold to the surviving relatives of the deceased.

Our troops entered this place, apparently, during an operation. In one room were about a hundred nude bodies, stacked like plucked chickens in a butcher's showcase. These bodies apparently had just been removed from the gas chamber and were awaiting cremation. In another room were several hundred more bodies, in a jumbled heap. These were probably the ones who had died in the enclosure and were awaiting their turn to be cremated.

I learned from one of the prisoners that the trainload outside were coming from another concentration camp, but the guards, upon hearing the approach of our troops, stopped the train and beat to death all the ones who were still alive. From the looks of the bodies, few were alive, and those who were, were too weakened from starvation to resist. In the crematory all the bodies were of men, and on the train, only two were women. These bodies, like the others, were strewn haphazardly in the boxcars, as though they had gone through the same rough treatment as the men. All these very likely were Jews, for near one of the cars, my sergeant found a Jewish Bible.

Near the crematory was also a gallows where some of the prisoners were hanged. Behind was a concrete wall, where many had faced the firing squad. The whole place was cloaked with the most horrible stench that you can imagine, so bad that several times I almost retched.

This camp had been in operation for twelve years, all the dirty work being done by the prisoners. I asked a French prisoner who was showing us around how they could do such work. He said that in their starved condition, they'd do anything in order to get food.

I had witnessed death by violence many times before, but this was different. It wasn't just death, it was murder, conducted on a mass basis. I realize now that many of the privations I have endured have not been in vain, if it will enable us to stamp out this Nazi regime.

One incident brought this thing closer to home. One of our men had been imprisoned in this camp, and today he went there and found his records still there. He also found his cousin, a man of twenty-seven, who looked sixty. The cousin did not know this man from our outfit; in fact he remembered practically nothing. His brain was so warped, he remembered very little of anything prior to his entry into the prison camp.

Later we entered a town several miles from there, and I interrogated some civilians. One girl, a comely lass about twenty, spoke excellent English. She said that she knew the prison camp was there, but she was entirely ignorant of what went on. She claimed she was so glad to see us, because that meant the end of Nazi domination. It is so strange, none of these people claim to be Nazis; they were just forced to obey the rules of the Nazis who were in power. I noticed this girl was wearing a wedding ring, so I asked her where her husband was. She replied that she wasn't married, but would like to get married. I asked her who she planned on marrying and she said, "Perhaps an American soldier, who will take me to America." I told her that the American soldiers wouldn't even talk to her sociably, let alone marry her. She couldn't understand why; she wasn't responsible for the deeds of the Nazis. But it was just people like that who permitted the Nazis to gain power, so they are all to blame.

I haven't written this very well; the papers probably do a much better and dramatic job. But they cannot express it strongly enough to give the people back there the full horror of it all; it is more gruesome than any fiction writer could imagine. The people who are responsible for this thing cannot be called human. They are beasts, and I shudder to think what this world would be like were it Nazi-dominated.

Just got a flash that Hitler is dead. Mussolini was hanged. Things are coming to a dramatic climax. Surely the end is in sight. Perhaps it will be over, ere you get this. Let us hope so.

Till again,

Art

I Saw Buchenwald

Jack LaPietra
Captain, United States Army Air Corps, 9th Air Force,
XIXth Tactical Air Command, 312th Fighter Control Squadron

APRIL 12, 1945
WEIMAR, GERMANY

The moon hangs low over Buchenwald tonight; the sky is starry; the air is warm. There is a ring around the moon—a very deep orange-colored ring which could easily pass for red. To those of us who toured *Konzentrationslager* Buchenwald this afternoon, it is definitely red—as red as the blood which flowed from the human veins of its miserable internees. God knows enough blood has gushed down its large concrete trough—to be blotted up by the dry earth within the electrically-charged barbed wire confines of this diabolical camp.

Somewhat vaguely, I recall the barbarous cruelties and atrocities related in the volumes of ancient history. How far removed they seemed—deeds of centuries ago; deeds of uncivilizedness; small unpleasantries which inevitably accompany the transformation of a world! Could such a thing take place today? Impossible! Except maybe on some undiscovered cannibal-infested island. Even then death would be more or less a speedy procedure—a head whacked off suddenly or a quick plunge into boiling oil.

Until today, thus ran my thought. But I toured Buchenwald, the day after our unit liberated it. It was still "in the raw." Go with me now on the same eerie Tour of Horror.

Weimar, Germany, is a fair-sized city 130 miles southwest of Berlin. A good highway leads out of Weimar to the concentration camp, and our jeep made the four or five miles in a few minutes. A huge factory, completely bombed, flitted by and the wire enclosure of Buchenwald loomed ahead. As we stepped inside the main gate and scanned the square mile of camp area, wondering which way to turn, one of the internees approached and asked in amazingly good English whether we wanted a guide. Of course, we welcomed his offer.

Our guide's name was Reinhold Schienhelm. He was a native of Lorraine, France; age thirty-eight; *Konzentrationslager* Number 42588; reason for internment—espionage and pro-Ally sentiments (actually, he was a telegraph operator who refused to work for the Nazis); civilian occupation—seaman; traveled widely—spent some time in the United States; date of internment—September 1942. He spoke freely about what he knew, readily answering all my questions. When he mentioned things which seemed incredible, I cross-examined him to see whether he would contradict himself, but he always had a logical explanation or "on-the-spot" proof. Never was he offended; he seemed to expect us to doubt him. No less than four times during the afternoon he pleaded, almost tearfully, "You must believe all this; it was much worse than what you see now!"

As we tramped from place to place the story of *Konzentrationslager* Buchenwald unfolded.

Most of the inmates were political prisoners—Poles, Czechs, Russians, French, Romanians, Hungarians, Italians, Belgians, and a few Germans (the majority of these prisoners were Jewish). It appeared that all were male. It is impossible to state how many had been "handled" by the camp during its four years of operation, but the total dead was over 83,000. Of these, 51,000 were killed "officially," using such methods of execution as hanging, beating, shooting, and electrocution. The remaining 32,000 died a "natural" death of starvation or poisoning. All bodies were disposed of by cremation. A quota of prisoners to be eliminated was established for each day—the number depending on the influx of new prisoners. Needless to say, the six-oven crematorium never had much time to cool. Many of the inmates were children, from three years of age up. There were over 1,200 children in the camp.

The daily food ration was the same for all—one loaf of bread for six men, served at 4:00 A.M., and one liter of soup for each person, served at 6:00 P.M. Three times a week a slice of cheese or smoked meat was added to the ration. Deviation from this menu occurred now and then—an indication to seasoned internees that international representatives on their routine inspections of camps were expected that day.

The camp was manned by SS Officers (*Schutzstaffel*—Storm Troopers) and troops; they in turn were assisted by habitual criminals who did the menial work. The SS personnel lived with their families in fine buildings adjacent to the camp grounds, enjoying modern conveniences and comforts.

The first torture weapon we saw was the "beating block." Punishment for any misdemeanor, regardless of its insignificance, took place here. The victim was laced to this pillory in a prone position and beaten with a leather strap or a wooden club—the latter being used on days when the killing quota was high. A few feet away was a platform with a pole attachment; this they termed "hanging on the tree." After the beating ordeal, dazed victims were suspended here by their hands—and the excruciating pain increased as they recovered from unconsciousness, only to lapse back into it.

The crematorium, a one-story building, featured six ovens, all of which contained charred remains of human bodies. In one of the ovens a complete skeleton rested; in another there was a half-melted skull plus a few chalk-like ribs with bits of unburned flesh still clinging on. High above the ovens hung a plaque on which was inscribed in German: "Allow not disgusting worms to eat my body . . . give me the clean bright flame." Each furnace operated at full capacity—fifteen bodies per cremation, 450 per day. Victims of the various murder weapons were taken to the crematorium in small carts and dumped down the basement chute. If they were already dead, they were loaded into a lift, raised to the furnace room, and stacked into the ovens. Those who were only unconscious were lifted up into one of the thirty-six nooses which hung conveniently along the white wall, where they were allowed to die before the "bright flame" did its work.

On those days when the quota was high, the crematorium had to serve as a murder house, also. Prisoners were marched to the basement under some pretense. Singly, each descended the steps, opened the door, and, as he entered, was clubbed by an SS guard. An attendant then lifted the limp body and slipped the head into one of the nooses on the wall. When the thirty-sixth body was suspended, the longest-hanging prisoner was lowered and piled onto the elevator and taken to the furnace room. This continued until all the victims were done away with. While all this murdering took place, a large machine in one corner of the basement ground out noises loud enough to drown the cries that accompanied the clubbing.

The camp itself was divided into two sections—the "Big Camp" and the "Little Camp." All internees had to spend a three-month test period in the "Little Camp," where conditions were absolutely deplorable. Those who survived the ordeal and showed a willingness to abide by the camp policies were "promoted" to the "Big Camp." Here, conditions were slightly better.

The 75-foot-long wooden barracks in which the internees lived were crudely constructed. In the "Big Camp," the prisoners had wooden bunk beds. About a hundred men were assigned to a building. In the "Little Camp," there were no beds—just shelves, four layers of shelves about three feet apart vertically and six feet deep, with the end nearest the wall slightly inclined so as to act as a pillow. These shelves lined both sides of the barracks and "accommodated" five hundred men. We walked through one of these barracks where approximately two dozen occupants were still billeted. If ever anyone saw living death, here it was—hueless skin stretched tightly over scissor-edged bones, dull eyes peeping through dark sockets, spindly legs and arms too weak to support the sixty or seventy pounds of emaciated torso. Here was grotesqueness in the highest order. Some of these "skeletons" hobbled up and down the aisle, using the shelved bunks for support; others, apparently dead or very close to it, rested on their wooden mattresses. Outside the door, three of them lay dead, recently evacuated by some of the stronger inmates. Their half-naked bodies were partly clad with the striped clothing all internees wore. Soon the cart, which made a systematic tour of the entire camp, would come along and take these bodies to the crematorium area where they would be stacked on an ever-increasing pile.

On my way out of the barrack, one of the men raised his thin arm to his lips in a gesture for a cigarette. I gave him what was left of my pack plus a few chocolate bars. Two or three others saw this and came crawling toward us. A near riot started. In pity and utter disgust, I left. The angry shouts and ravenous cries from within the building gradually subsided, but even now they are ringing in my ears. I don't know who finally ended up with the chocolate, but Reinhold, our guide, said that the victor wouldn't live much longer after he ate it, for the shock would be too much for his stomach.

The laboratory, our next stop, resembled the other barracks, but the interior was cozy and pleasant. Most of the rooms were now occupied by internees who had recently moved in because of the better living conditions they afforded. The laboratory had been staffed by maniacal SS doctors—men who no doubt had great medical skills, but insane minds. They used the cream of the prisoner crop as guinea pigs for medical research. All new internees were given a physical examination. The healthiest were selected and quartered in a special barrack known as Block 36. Here, living conditions and food were excellent, and for three weeks the selectees ate three good meals a day and lived a life of leisure. Then, unsuspecting, one by one, they were called to the laboratory and sacrificed to "science." All types of disease germs were injected into these healthy men, and results were observed daily until death overtook them. The bodies were then dissected, and all affected parts were preserved in large jars carefully labeled. An entire room was lined with shelves displaying every organ of the human body, and many skeletons. The most ghastly sight was a jar in which floated, almost life-like, a half head. When we turned the rectangular glass container, the head's profile with its agonized face and its half-open eye stared back at us as if to say, "Tell the world, so that it won't happen again." The other side of the cloven head, exposing the bone and matter of its construction, bore silent witness to the meaning of those words. Silently I said a short prayer for this man—and for those who still expect him to return. May they never learn of his plight.

Our guide was hardened to all this. His only comment was, "In America you use mice and rabbits; here they use human beings."

The commandant, a beast well-versed in methods of torture and murder, had a wife, Ilse Koch, who was even more brutal than he was. One of her hobbies was collecting tattoos. When the inclination moved her, she attended the physical examinations of newly arrived prisoners, inspected them for exceptional tattoos, noted the prison numbers of those possessing tattoos she desired, and turned in her list to the SS in charge. These men received a murder priority, and in a few days, the tattoos, plus a good sized section of skin, were going through a tanning process. Eventually, these same tattoos formed a pretty lampshade in the commandant's comfortable home. If the tattoo supply became too large, choice specimens were preserved in jars and put on display in the laboratory until they were needed.

Next, we passed some low buildings a bit removed from the barracks. They were storerooms for grain and potatoes. Two large barns housed some pigs—a few of the many which the SS could not take when they fled. Our guide told us about how a small pig was missing one day, and since an internee was suspected of stealing it, the entire camp had to go without food for five days as punishment.

At the eastern end of the camp were two large buildings. One was nicely constructed, high, with a beautifully paneled interior somewhat resembling a gymnasium. Along one end a balcony extended outward, overlooking the straw-covered floor below. This was the "Sports Arena." Emaciated prisoners "played" with SS troops, the latter armed with clubs. Wives of the SS troops were the spectators, yelling their approval each time a club descended on a shriveled, helpless form.

The other building was of stone construction, one story, containing numerous stalls and three or four rooms. The rooms were thick-walled and soundproof—another murder house! On one occasion over four hundred Russian soldiers, prisoners of war, were exterminated the same day they arrived. Here is how it was done. All were marched outside to an area at one end of the building. They were told that this was a physical examination. One by one they entered the building, stripped, and were conducted by an SS trooper (dressed in the white clothes of a doctor) toward the soundproofed room at the other end. Another SS (also in white) met the victim, escorted him inside the room, closed the door tightly, walked over to a height-measuring device, and positioned him with his back to a blanket-covered wall. Behind the blanket still another SS trooper stood with a pistol in position, and, on a short signal, a bullet went racing through the prisoner's skull, embedding itself in the padded wall of the room. As the body slumped forward, the "doctor" caught it and dragged it out of the room. He handed it over to another white figure who then carried it outdoors, dropping it on a large concrete pavement which was slanted toward the center so that the blood would drain and run toward a trough which emptied into the dry earth. As more bodies piled up, the blood ran faster and faster. When the pile could accommodate no more, the drained bodies were loaded into carts and taken to the crematorium. The carts made many trips that day.

As we crossed the large parade ground, six or seven inmates were building a wooden, pyramid-shaped monument. It was near completion. On the front were three large letters, "K.L.B." (*Konzentrationslager* Buchenwald). Underneath the letters was the figure "51,000," commemorating those murdered officially.

Soldiers were still pouring in and out of the camp. I paused and took one last look at this inhuman place—at the gate, through which all prisoners entered, and at the long smoke stack of the crematorium, through which 83,000 had departed.

A shudder ran through me; an unexplainable feeling tugged at my stomach. Quickly I did an about-face. We headed straight for our jeep.

How the German people ever permitted this to exist—along with other camps such as Auschwitz, Lublin, Erla, Nordhausen, Dachau—is beyond my comprehension. Most Germans claimed they knew nothing of the atrocities—but they did; it couldn't be otherwise!

I have written this down because the world must remember. Elie Wiesel said it best. He said, "We must remember, not only because of the dead; it is too late for them. Not only because of the survivors; it may be even too late for them. Our remembering is an act of generosity aimed at saving men and women from apathy to evil, if not from evil itself."

Re-Entry

Arnold Blum
> b. Nuremberg, Germany, 1922
> Private First Class, G2 (Intelligence), 104th Infantry Division,
> 7th Corps, 1st U.S. Army

Late one afternoon a truck convoy picked us up in Malmedy to take us to Aachen. It was October 1944, and we were U.S. Infantry replacements destined to fill the gaps in the ranks of units depleted in the battles around Aachen.

We dozed while riding on the hard truck benches, our rifles held vertically between our legs, but woke to the distant rumble of guns. The rumble got louder as we got closer to our destination. The canvas truck roof precluded our seeing upward or to the sides, but we caught glimpses of gun flashes through the rear window of the truck cab.

It was completely dark when we stopped in the clearing of a woods inside the German border, where we were ordered to get off. After my eyes had adjusted to the dark I noticed, ghost-like, a tent camp where we would spend the night. The trees around us were arrayed in neat ranks and files, composing in turn large rectangular groves.

The next morning we boarded the trucks again, which took us to a large complex of buildings, a former German army camp outside Aachen.

I felt very strange being back in the land of my birth and that of generations of my family, the land for which my late father and his brothers had fought in World War I. The five and a half years of my absence had totally estranged me.

There were many facets to my estrangement. The architecture of the camp buildings was heavy and stolid. The walls were thick, the windows small, the roofs large and steep-sided. It all looked like the administration building in Concentration Camp Dachau, from which I had been released six years earlier. I felt unclean, as though I had touched something filthy and vile.

Germany had become an abomination in my mind, a somber, dank dungeon. The very orderliness and rectilinearity of the woods, where we had spent the previous night, and the camp, where we now found ourselves, combined to recreate in my mind an overwhelming feeling of oppressiveness from which I had been subliminally freed in America.

The camp itself represented to me a site of institutionalized aggression. From it, its former occupants had set out to overpower and suppress its neighbors, to metastasize the Hitlerian cancer of hate, a symptom of accumulated darkness in the German national essence.

I did not realize as I do today that this darkness is endemic to all peoples, that it is characteristic of the human psyche when it falls victim to self-veneration and becomes oblivious to aspirations of oneness with God and the world.

Today as I relive these memories, I perceive, both hopefully and sadly, that people everywhere are far more the same than they are different. Within them all, they harbor the potential for good and evil. I am similarly persuaded that man has not changed since he first appeared in the universe. He has only improved his tools.

Biographies of Survivor-Authors

Photographs, except those on pages 334 and 335, by Joy Berenfield

MALKA BARAN was born on January 30, 1927, in Warsaw, Poland, the daughter of Isak and Bella Klin. During the Holocaust she was in the Ghetto, then in H.A.S.A.G. labor camp, both in Czestochowa, Poland. Neither her parents nor her one brother, Heniek, survived the Holocaust. All but one of her large extended family—approximately seventy people—were slain; the one aunt who survived searched for her niece until 1960, when she finally found her. In the United States Mrs. Baran has been a student, wife, mother, and teacher. She is married to Moshe Baran; they have two children and six grandchildren. Mrs. Baran wrote the following stories in this book: *Snapshots, The Child, The Tiny Flame, The Barber,* and *The Miracle.*

MOSHE BARAN was born on December 1, 1920, in Horodok, Poland, the son of Joseph and Esther Weisbord Baran. During the Holocaust he was in Horodok Ghetto, Krasny Ghetto/forced labor camp in Bielorussia, and the forests and swamps near Wileyka-Ilia, Bielorussia. Mr. Baran had one brother and two sisters. His brother, Joshua, and one sister, Mina, survived the Holocaust; his mother was the only surviving mother from his hometown. His father and one sister perished. In the United States he has worked in real estate management. He is married to Malka Baran; they have two children and six grandchildren. His stories in this book are *A Shtetl's Life Is Ended* and *The Farmer Kowarski*.

SHULAMIT BASTACKY was born on August 25, 1941, in Vilna, Lithuania. During the Holocaust she was hidden in a basement in Vilna. Both her parents, Simon and Dora Bastacky, survived the Holocaust. She has one brother, Mark, who was born after the war. Ms. Bastacky earned a Master's degree in Social Work from the University of Pittsburgh. Her story in this book is *Beyond Memory*.

ARNOLD BLUM was born on April 2, 1922, in Nuremberg, Germany, the son of David and Melanie Stern Blum. His father died before World War II; his mother survived the Holocaust. Mr. Blum emigrated to the United States in 1939 and served in the U.S. Army from 1943 to 1946. He is a metallurgical engineer and has worked as an engineer and corporate manager in the United States and Israel. He is married to Rita Strauss Blum. Mr. Blum wrote the following stories in this book: *An Action against the Jews, Dachau, Herr Schluemper*, and *Re-Entry*.

WALTER BERNARD BONINGER was born on June 21, 1928, in Hamburg, Germany, the son of Martin and Hermine Gaertner Boninger. Neither of his parents survived the Holocaust. At the beginning of the Holocaust he was in Antwerp, Belgium, and in several places in England. He came to the United States in 1940. In the United States he has been a social worker, part-time cantor, and since 1984 has been a rabbi. He is married to Lonnie Boninger; they have three children and five grandchildren. Rabbi Boninger's story in this book is *A Definition of Survival.*

LEON SOLOMON BRETT (with grandchildren Jacob and Sonja Brett) was born on September 6, 1922, in Skudvil, Lithuania, the son of Shmuel Elyeh and Shifra Leiserowitz Brett. During the Holocaust he was in Lithuania, first in a jail in Shavel, then in Shavel Ghetto, and finally with a partisan detachment near Shavel. After liberation he became a watchmaker. He is married to Sarah Luel Brett, who was in Lodz Ghetto, Auschwitz and Mauthausen; they have three children and six grandchildren. Mr. Brett had three brothers and one sister. Only his brothers, who emigrated to South Africa before the war, survived the Holocaust; his parents and sister perished. He wrote the following stories in this book: *War Arrives in Lithuania, What Ever Happened to the Jews of Skudvil?, The Law in Lithuania,* and *Lithuanian Friends.*

RUTH LIEBERMAN DRESCHER was born on January 23, 1934, in Stuttgart, Germany, the daughter of Eduard and Gerty Alexander Lieberman. She left Germany with her parents and one sister in August 1939. An older brother and sister had left in 1936 and 1938 respectively, as teenagers. Mrs. Drescher earned a Bachelor's Degree at City College of New York and a Master's Degree at the University of Pittsburgh; she is a social worker and artist. She is married to Professor Seymour Drescher; they have three children and two grandchildren. Mrs. Drescher's story in this book is *A Life-Defining Impression.*

STEVEN J. FENVES was born on June 6, 1931, in Subotica, Yugoslavia, the son of Lajos (Louis) and Claire Geréb Fenyves. In 1944 he and his family were deported from his hometown, which had previously been taken over by Hungary, to Auschwitz-Birkenau. He was later sent to Nieder Orschel, a satellite camp of Buchenwald, and then sent on a death march to Buchenwald, where he was liberated. After the war he returned to Yugoslavia, left for France in 1947, and came to the United States in 1950. He served in the U.S. Army Corps of Engineers during 1952–53, and then studied at the University of Illinois, where he earned his Ph.D. and joined the faculty. He is presently University Professor of Civil Engineering at Carnegie Mellon University. He is married to Norma Horwitz; they have four children and four grandchildren. Professor Fenves had one sister, Esczti F. Votaw, who survived the Holocaust. His mother perished in Auschwitz and his father died in 1946. Professor Fenves's story in this book is *Resist in Everything!*

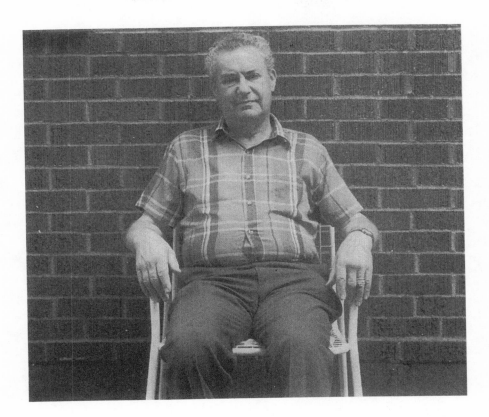

SIMON GELERNTER was born on August 26, 1926, in Lodz, Poland, the son of Henoch and Hessa Miller Gelernter. During the Holocaust he was in Lodz Ghetto and in concentration camps at Birkenau-Auschwitz, Poland; Falkenberg and Wolfsburg, Germany; and Ebensee, Austria. After liberation he worked in the ORT school. He is married to Francine L. Gelernter; they have two children and four grandchildren. Mr. Gelernter had two brothers; none of his family survived the Holocaust. He died in 1997, on a ski trip. His story in this book is *A Family Gone, One By One.*

CYNA GLATSTEIN was born on March 16, 1928, in Sochachev, Poland, the daughter of Rabbi Yehuda Leib Wolman and Hanna Ehrenkrantz Wolman. During the Holocaust she was in Sochachev Ghetto and Warsaw Ghetto, and later hid, by using false papers and passing as a Christian, in several villages and towns in Poland and Germany. She is married to Rabbi Mordecai Glatstein; they have three children and five grandchildren. She has continued to study Hebrew and secular subjects throughout her life. Mrs. Glatstein had three sisters and two brothers; only one sister, Rachel Wolman Jacobowitz, survived the Holocaust. The rest of her immediate and extended family, including her parents, perished. She wrote the following stories in this book: *Betrayal, The Harbinger of What?, In Constant Terror, The Killing Hunger, Unsung Heroes,* and *The Golden Chain of Judaism.*

SAM GOTTESMAN was born on October 20, 1923, in Irsava-Ilosva, Czechoslovakia, the son of Isak and Iseni-Sheindel Berger Gottesman. During the Holocaust he was in Ilosva-Munkacs Ghetto and in Auschwitz, Wüstegiersdorf, Bergen-Belsen, Hildesheim, and Hanover concentration camps. He and his wife, Lea Lebovits Gottesman, have one child and one grandchild. Mr. Gottesman is a picture framer and salesperson. He had four sisters and two brothers. Only one sister and his father survived the Holocaust; his mother, two brothers, and three sisters perished. Mr. Gottesman's story in this book is *A Son in Deed*.

ESTHER HAAS was born on May 8, 1919, in The Hague, Netherlands, the daughter of Michel and Anna Eyl Blok. During the Holocaust she was in Westerbork Transit Camp and in Auschwitz. After the war she was a housewife and worked in a store owned by her husband, Joseph Haas, who is deceased. Mrs. Haas's parents and two sisters did not survive the Holocaust; only one sister, Klara, survived. She wrote the following stories in this book: *The Tenth Woman on Block Ten, My Sister Rieke,* and *The Kindness of Strangers.*

DORA ZUER IWLER (with photograph of her grandmother) was born on July 1, 1923, in Chodoròw, Poland, the daughter of Juda and Sima Austein Zuer. During the Holocaust she was alternately in hiding and imprisoned in Jonowski camp; toward the end of the war she was sent on a forced march, escaped and again went into hiding. She had two brothers, Moshe Lazer and Yitzchak, and one sister, Miriam; none of her family survived the Holocaust. Mrs. Iwler and her husband, Israel, have two children and three grandchildren. She wrote the following stories in this book: *Parting*, *The Wagon*, and *Posing as a Christian*.

VLADIMIR LANG was born on January 2, 1925, in Osijek, Yugoslavia (now Croatia), the son of Alexander and Rosa Lang. During the Holocaust he and his parents were hidden in a town near Bologna, Italy, then in Milan; they finally escaped to Switzerland. He and his wife, Agnes, have two children and three grandchildren. Mr. Lang's only sister, Maja, perished at age 10. His story in this book is *Among the Righteous*.

GEORGE GUSTAV LAUER was born on August 23, 1907, in Hamburg, Germany, the son of Paul and Mathilde Wiener Lauer. After attending college in Germany he lived in Prague, Czechoslovakia—under Nazi rule—from 1938 to 1943. He and his wife, Edith, were deported to Theresienstadt, where he headed the Sanitation Department. They remained there after the war to assist in the liquidation of the camp and the dispersion of the children. Subsequently he earned a Ph.D., spent a short time in England as a research chemist and then emigrated to the United States, where he was a research supervisor. Dr. and Mrs. Lauer had two children and four grandchildren. Dr. Lauer died in 1996. His stories in this book are *Theresienstadt* and *Children from the Camps Going to England.*

RAFAEL LEVIN was born on March 19, 1905, in Vilna, Lithuania, the son of Leiba and Faiga Segal Levin. During the Holocaust he was in Kovno Ghetto and Kovno Concentration Camp; on the way to Dachau Concentration Camp from Kovno, he jumped out of the train and escaped. Mr. Levin was a principal in a Jewish school in Kovno and after the war was a teacher, then school principal in the United States. He had three brothers and two sisters. Only two of his brothers and one sister, who emigrated from Lithuania before the war, survived the Holocaust; his parents, one brother and one sister perished. His wife, Rachel Abromovitz Levin, and their daughter, Eta Levin Hecht, also survived the war. His story in this book is *Miracles*.

ETA LEVIN HECHT was born on October 7, 1938, in Kovno, Lithuania, the daughter of Rafael and Rachel Abramovitz Levin, both of whom survived the Holocaust. During the Holocaust she was in Kovno Ghetto and later was hidden with a Christian family in Alexotas, a suburb of Kovno. She is married to Warren Hecht; they have three children and two grandchildren. Her story in this book is merged into her father's story, *Miracles*.

EDITH RECHTER LEVY was born on February 21, 1930, in Vienna, Austria, the daughter of Joseph David and Yite Beila Kipel Rechter. After Kristallnacht, the family fled from Vienna to Antwerp, Belgium. In 1941 they were deported by the German occupying forces to Waterschei, in Limburg, Belgium. She, her mother, and two brothers survived in hiding in Brussels, Belgium; her father perished in Auschwitz. Dr. Levy, who has an M.A. degree in German and French and a Ph.D. in Education, is a published author and university teacher of Holocaust educators. She and her husband, Mark, have two sons, one daughter, and six grandchildren. She wrote the following stories in this book: *A Mother's Courage, A Narrow Escape,* and *The Aftermath.*

ERNEST LIGHT was born on July 9, 1920, in Uzhorod, Czechoslovakia, the son of Herman and Serena Polak Light. During the Holocaust he was at first in various forced labor camps in Hungary and Transylvania. In 1944 he was discharged from a hospital in the labor camp in Bor, Yugoslavia and returned home to Horlyo, Hungary. Later that year he was taken to Auschwitz and from there to Warsaw, Dachau Concentration Camp, and Muhldorf Concentration Camp. Mr. Light had five brothers and four sisters. Only three brothers and one sister survived the Holocaust. His parents, two brothers, and three sisters perished. He and his wife, Sara, have two children and three grandchildren. He wrote the following stories in this book: *In the Dark, How Many Made It?*, *An Unforgettable Passover Seder*, *A Surprise Package*, and *An Ending and a Beginning*.

JOLENE MALLINGER (left, with sister, Belle Weinberg) was born on March 16, 1923, in Hrabovo, Czechoslovakia, the daughter of Herman and Lea Herschkowitz Gottesman. During the Holocaust she was in Auschwitz, Christianstad, and Bergen-Belsen concentration camps. She had nine sisters and four brothers. Three sisters, Belle, Esther, and Faige, and four brothers, survived; her parents and six sisters perished. She and her husband, Abraham Mallinger, have two sons and two grandchildren. Mrs. Mallinger's story in this book is *Auschwitz, 1944*.

HERMINE KATZ MARKOVITZ was born on March 15, 1926, in Volovice, Czechoslova-kia, the daughter of Samuel and Regina Kahan Katz. During the Holocaust she was in Antwerp, Belgium, and later was hidden in Marseilles, France. She had three brothers and three sisters. Only one sister, Devorah, survived the Holocaust; the rest of her immediate family, including her parents, perished. Mrs. Markovitz and her husband, Benjamin, have two children and three grandchildren. Her story in this book is *The Convent in Marseilles.*

ROBERT R. MENDLER (before the war, Roman Reibeisen) was born on July 6, 1925, in Nowy-Targ, Poland, the son of Mendel Wolf Reibeisen and Hermina Mendler Reibeisen. During the Holocaust he was at first in Nowy-Targ Ghetto and several forced labor camps in Poland. Later he was in the following concentration camps: Zakopane, Czarny-Dunajec (where he worked for Hobak Werker Lumber Yard), Krakow-Plaszów, Ostrowiec, Auschwitz-Birkenau, and Auschwitz-Buna Monowice in Poland; and Sachsenhausen, Oranienburg, Flossenbürg, and Pocking in Germany. He had one brother and one sister. All of his immediate and extended family—seventy-two people—perished. After the war he owned a shoe business. On May 13, 1995, he received an honorary Doctor of Humane Letters Degree from Seton Hill College. He and his wife, Joan Pretter Mendler, have two children and three grandchildren. His story in this book is *The Chief of the Gestapo.*

RAY NAAR was born on October 15, 1927, in Salonika, Greece, the son of Isaac and Lily Sides Naar. During the Holocaust he was in Salonika and Athens, Greece, and then in Bergen-Belsen. All of his family—his parents and one brother, Jacques—survived the Holocaust. Dr. Naar is a clinical psychologist. He and his wife, Claudine Simone Naar, have one son and two grandchildren. His stories in this book are *Mazel* and *Kaleidoscope: Salonika, Greece, 1945.*

GERTRUDE S. NEWMAN was born on June 2, 1928, in Munich, Germany, the daughter of Leo and Emmy Landauer Leiter. With her parents, she emigrated to the United States in 1939. She was married to Ernest Newman. Her story in this book is *Leaving Germany, Leaving Home.*

FRITZ OTTENHEIMER was born on March 18, 1925, in Constance, Germany, the son of Ludwig and Klara Metzger Ottenheimer. He emigrated to the United States in 1939 with his parents and sister, Ilse, and served in the U.S. Army in Germany as a liberator in 1945 and 1946. After the war he worked with the U.S. military in the de-Nazification process in Germany. He attended college in the United States and worked as an engineer. He and his wife, Goldie, have two children and four grandchildren. Mr. Ottenheimer's stories in this book are *Herr B.* and *German Roulette*. These stories are extracted from his memoir, *Escape and Return* (Pittsburgh, Pa.: Cathedral Publishing, 1999), which has been translated and published in Germany as *Wie hat das geschehen können?* (Hartung-Gorre Verlag, Konstanz).

MARGA L. RANDALL was born on March 20, 1930, in Lemförde, Germany, the daughter of Louis and Johanna Adelsheimer Silbermann. After leaving her home in Lemförde, she lived with her grandparents and aunt in Schermbeck until Kristallnacht in 1938. Following this, she was in semi-hiding with family members in Berlin. She had two brothers, Herbert and Manfred, and one sister, Hilda, all of whom, in addition to her mother, survived the Holocaust. She emigrated to the United States with her mother and sister in 1941. Mrs. Randall has two daughters, one son, and three grandchildren; she was married to Jordan Randall, who is deceased. Her stories in this book are *A German Family* and *The Sewing Basket*. They have been selected from her autobiography, *How Beautiful We Once Were* (Pittsburgh, Pa.: printed by Reed and Witting Company, 1999).

SARA REICHMAN was born on July 1, 1942, in Yanova Dolina, Ukraine, the daughter of Shmuel and Miriam Gorodetser. During the Holocaust she was "adopted"—that is, hidden—by a Polish family. Her father, Shmuel, survived the war. Mrs. Reichman and her husband, Milton, have two children. Her story in this book is *Lost Families.*

JACK SITTSAMER was born on December 30, 1924, in Mielec, Poland, the son of Moses Ithamer and Perla Sima Montag Sittsamer. During the Holocaust he was in concentration camps in Mielec and Wieliczka, Poland; Flossenbürg, Germany; Leitmeritz, Czechoslovakia; and Mauthausen and Gussyn II, Austria. Mr. Sittsamer had two brothers and two sisters; none of his family survived the Holocaust. He and his wife, Maxine, have two children and four grandchildren. His stories in this book are *The Abandonment of Mielec* and *The Long Road after Liberation*.

LIBBY TENENHAUS STERN was born on August 23, 1926, in Suceava, Romania, the daughter of Motke and Tema Tenenhaus. During the Holocaust she was deported to Camp Kazmaza in Ukraine, where her parents perished. She escaped, went into hiding, and found her way to the Shargorod Ghetto. Mrs. Stern, who is a bookkeeper, and her husband, Mark, have two sons and four grandchildren. She wrote the following stories in this book: *I Choose Life, The Promise,* and *The Last Hiding Place.*

RUBIN YAKOVLEVITCH UDLER (with son, Arthur Udler, and grandson, Ilya Udler) was born on September 27, 1925, in Braila, Romania, the son of Yakov Aronovitch and Dina Vladimirovna Gleizer-Udler. During the Holocaust he was in Odessa, Ukraine, while it was under Romanian occupation; in a ghetto in Odessa; and in forced labor camp–ghettos in Transnistria. After the war he earned his Doctorate at the Institute of Linguistics, U.S.S.R. Academy of Sciences in Leningrad. In 1989, Professor Udler was elected Corresponding Member of the Academy of Sciences of Moldova. He has held distinguished positions as professor, department chair and researcher, Chief of the Dialectology and History of Language Department of the Language and Literature Institute, and Deputy of the Academic-Secretary of the Social Studies Department of the Academy of Sciences of Moldova in Kishinev. He is presently a Center Associate in the University Center for International Studies at the University of Pittsburgh. His parents and one sister, Ester, survived the Holocaust. Professor Udler and his wife, Mira Ilinitchna Alexenberg-Udler, have two children and three grandchildren. They came to the United States in 1992. He wrote the following stories in this book: *Horrors of War, The Skull with the Golden Braid, A Saintly Person, Flight to Freedom,* and *It Shall Not Be Forgotten Nor Forgiven!*

VIOLET WEINBERGER (left) was born on September 10, 1928, in Uzhorod, Czechoslovakia, the daughter of Martin and Ida Roth Weinberger. During the Holocaust she was deported to Auschwitz, then transferred to Krotingen and Stutthof, and finally sent on a death march. She had five sisters and one brother. Only three of her sisters, Irene, Rose, and Ela, survived the Holocaust; her parents, two sisters, and her brother perished. She and her husband, Eugene Weinberger, have two children and four grandchildren. She wrote the following stories in this book: *Nazi Murderers, The Psychologist,* and *Captain Zimmer.*

IRENE BERKOWITZ (right) was born on June 19, 1923, in Uzhorod, Czechoslovakia, the daughter of Martin and Ida Roth Weinberger. During the Holocaust she was deported to Auschwitz, then transferred to Krotingen and Stutthof, and finally sent on a death march. She had five sisters and one brother. Only three of her sisters, Rose, Ela, and Violet, survived the Holocaust; her parents, two sisters, and her brother perished. She was married to Max Berkowitz, who is deceased, and has two daughters and six grandchildren. Mrs. Berkowitz wrote the following stories in this book: *The Girl with Wooden Shoes, The Volunteer Group,* and *One Day War, the Next Day Not.*

SAM WEINREB was born on April 5, 1928, in Bratislava, Czechoslovakia, the son of David and Freda Jakubovitz Weinreb. During the Holocaust he was in prison in Budapest and Irsava, Hungary, and then was sent to Auschwitz. He had two brothers and one sister; none of his family survived the Holocaust. Mr. Weinreb is a jeweler and watchmaker. He and his wife, Goldie, have two children and one granddaughter. His story in this book is *Bar Mitzvah Boy.*

ILONA WEISS was born on December 19, 1923, in Kosino, Czechoslovakia (later Hungary), the daughter of Joseph and Judith Weiss. During the Holocaust she was in a transit camp before being sent to Auschwitz, Kaufering, and Bergen-Belsen concentration camps. She had six brothers, four of whom perished along with her parents; her two sisters, Edith and Irene, and two brothers survived. Mrs. Weiss and her husband, Joseph, have four children and four grandchildren. She wrote the following stories in this book: *The Gypsies, The Concentration Camp Lottery, A Dream of Milk,* and *On the Way to Health.*

YOLANDA AVRAM WILLIS (with granddaughter, Julia Lynn Willis) was born on October 2, 1934, in Salonika, Greece, the daughter of Salvator and Karolla Avram. She, her parents and her brother, Moissis "Yiannis," all survived the Holocaust. The family lived in Larisa, Greece until the war started in 1940, then was hidden in Crete and in several places in Athens. After the war she attended the American College in Athens, then came to the United States to study. She earned an M.A. degree in Chemistry and a Ph.D. degree in Sociology. Dr. Willis worked in industry as a manager, educator and management consultant for 22 years. She is married to Elliott J. Goldstein, M.D., and has three children, two stepchildren, and three grandchildren. One granddaughter is named Julia—the name Dr. Willis used while in hiding. Her stories in this book are excerpted from her book by the same title, *A Hidden Child in Greece*.

JACOB WOLHENDLER was born on September 19, 1913, in Zawiercie, Poland, the son of Ephraim and Sarah Goldszer Wolhendler. During the Holocaust he was in Zawiercie until 1943, after which he was in various camps in Germany, where he was hidden under a fictitious Catholic name. He had one brother and three sisters; none of his family survived the Holocaust. In the United States, he has been in the furniture business. His story in this book is *The Beginning and the End.*

ALEXANDER ZWILLICH was born on October 22, 1925, in Boryslaw, Poland, the son of Samuel and Rozalia Schorr Zwillich. During the Holocaust he was in Boryslaw Ghetto and Truskawiec forced labor camp, and then in the following concentration camps: Plaszow, Wieliczka, Mauthausen, Melk, and Ebensee. After the war he completed his studies in engineering. He had three sisters; none of his family survived the Holocaust. Mr. Zwillich and his wife, Freda Bonn Zwillich, have one son and one grandson. His stories in this book are *In Praise of Manual Labor* and *To Bear Witness about the Holocaust.*

FREDERICK FORSCHER was born in Vienna, Austria, in 1918, the son of Moritz and Cornelia Berger Forscher. He emigrated to the United States in 1938. He had two brothers, Bruno and Walter. Both brothers survived the Holocaust, although his parents perished. In the United States, he earned a Ph.D. and worked in mechanical metallurgy; as an expert in energy matters, Dr. Forscher consulted for the U.S. government and worked for the Nuclear Regulatory Commission. He and his wife, Mia, have three children and eight grandchildren. Dr. Forscher died in 1996. His story in this book is *The Best-Laid Plans.*

DAVID KATZ was born in November 1919 in Sapinta, Romania, the son of Samuel and Frieda Katz. During the Holocaust he was captured by Russians and imprisoned in Siberia. He escaped but while trying to go home was captured by Germans in Ukraine. He was imprisoned and escaped once again, then fought with a partisan group in White Russia. After the war, he worked in the salt mines in Israel. In the United States he was employed as a tool and die-maker and taught Hebrew school in a synagogue. He had two brothers and three sisters. Only one brother and two sisters survived the Holocaust; his parents, one brother, and one sister perished. Mr. Katz died in 1979, leaving his written memoir to his remaining family. *Trying to Go Home* and *Friend or Enemy?* are excerpted from this memoir.

MARIANNE SILBERMAN was born on May 13, 1930, in Kassel, Germany, the daughter of Siegmund and Johanna Eichengruen Silberg. She emigrated from Germany with her parents and brother, Heinz, in 1939. Mrs. Silberman and her late husband, Herbert, have one son, Lenny. Her story in this book is *Escape to England.*

[These personal photographs are of authors who were not available to be photographed by Joy Berenfield.]

HERBERT SILBERMAN was born on October 23, 1920, in Lemförde, Germany, the son of Louis and Johanna Adelsheimer Silberman. During the Holocaust he was first in Dachau Concentration Camp. Upon being released and emigrating to England in 1939, he was interned as an enemy alien and sent to prison. Later he was sent to Australia, where he was released to serve in the Australian Army. Mr. Silberman had one brother and two sisters; all his family except his father survived the Holocaust. He and his wife, Marianne, have one son, Lenny. Mr. Silberman died in 2000. His story in this book is *A Kristallnacht Journey.*

RUTH WEITZ was born on May 5, 1929, in Podhoritzin, Poland, the daughter of Saul and Sarah Baum. During the Holocaust she was in Yachtrov Concentration Camp near Lvov, Poland. She escaped, went into hiding, and was apprehended and sent to Camp Pomyslany and then to Bittem in Germany. She had one brother and one sister; none of her family survived the Holocaust. Mrs. Weitz and her husband, Dave, have three children and three grandchildren. Her story in this book is *The Means to Survive.*

ARTHUR PETERNEL Captain, 48th Combat Battalion, 1108th Combat Engineers, 5th Army

PHOTOGRAPHS OF LIBERATOR-AUTHORS

MARJORIE BUTTERFIELD First Lieutenant, 59th Field Hospital, 3rd Army

JACK LAPIETRA Captain, U.S. Army Air Corps, 9th Air Force, XIXth Tactical Air Command, 312th Fighter Control Squadron

HENRY L. MARINELLI Captain, 493rd Armored Field Artillery, 12th Armored Division, 7th Army

ANITA BROSTOFF has taught, lectured, and written about writing and the teaching of writing for over 20 years. As an Assistant Professor at Carnegie-Mellon University, she taught business, technical, expository and short story writing and engaged in research into the writing process, working with University faculty and American Institutes for Research. She received a National Endowment for the Humanities grant in 1979 to create a secondary school writing curriculum. In this project she developed a textbook, *Thinking through Writing*, in conjunction with teachers. In addition to writing many articles in professional journals, she edited and coauthored *I Could Be Mute: The Life and Work of Gladys Schmitt*. Since 1981, Dr. Brostoff has been a consultant to business and industry, providing training in communication skills. As a consultant, she received several awards from the American Society for Training and Development for service as President of the Pittsburgh chapter and on regional and national levels. Recently, in addition to volunteering for the Survivors' Writing Project, she volunteers as a docent at the Carnegie Museum of Art. Dr. Brostoff lives in Pittsburgh with her husband, enjoying visits from her four children, their spouses, and seven grandchildren.